The Complete Handbook of
Personal Computer Communications

Alfred Glossbrenner

The Complete Handbook of

. . . .

PERSONAL COMPUTER

COMMUNICATIONS

. . . .

EVERYTHING YOU NEED TO
GO ONLINE WITH THE WORLD

. . . .

ST. MARTIN'S PRESS · NEW YORK

Design by Victoria Gomez

ISBN: 0-312-15718-5
Library of Congress Cataloging in Publication Number: 83-3232

First Edition
10 9 8 7 6 5 4 3 2 1

Contents

Introduction: 1
> *The Universe at Your Fingertips*
> *Any* computer can communicate • No programming required •
> How to use this book • Online in an instant: Hundreds of FREE
> phone numbers you can get right now

1 • Surveying the Electronic Universe: 7
> *An Overview*
> Information utilities • Encyclopedic databases • Free computer
> bulletin board systems • Electronic shopping, banking, and bar-
> ter • Computerized conferencing • The Electronic Yellow Pages
> • The phone numbers are *local*

2 • Accessing the Power: 17
> *What You Need, and Need to Know, to Go Online*
> Jet fighters and dripping faucets • Preventing cabling prob-
> lems • The numbers game: Bell 103, Bell 212A, RS-232, and
> IEEE-448 • ASCII • Commodore computers • How to choose a
> modem • Futuristic fantasies? • How to choose communications
> software • Transmitting VisiCalc™ files • Prestel, CEEFAX, and
> Antiope • The Electronic Universe Survival Kit

3 • The Source: 46
> *"America's Information Utility"*
> Electronic mail, bulletin boards, UPI news, and more • *Forbes,
> The Futurist, The Harvard Business Review,* and other publica-
> tions • Business information • Word processing • Jobfinders: The
> Online Career Network • Airline schedules • Hotel reserva-
> tions • Movie reviews • Online games • How to get a FREE
> Source subscription • Texas Instruments' TEXNET on The
> Source • How to move around on the system • Synergistic pos-
> sibilities • How to locate electronic lovers and pen pals • A three-
> session approach • For the experienced user . . . • RCV: The Se-
> cret Source Command

4 • CompuServe: 90
The Nighttime Utility
Electronic mail, CB Simulator, AP News, and more • *Popular Science, Better Homes and Gardens, Popular Electronics,* and other publications • Business information • The Microcomputer Advisor • FREE software • Megawar, Spacewar, and other games • The *World Book Encyclopedia* online • Menus, pages, and the command level • The National Bulletin Board • Using CompuServe CB • A three-session approach • For the experienced user . . .

5 • The Dow Jones News/Retrieval Service: 124
Money Matters, an Encyclopedia, and More
The *Wall Street Journal* online • Weather, sports, and movies • Current and historical market quotes • "Wall $treet Week" online • Free text search • *The Academic American Encyclopedia* • Getting to know the system • Dow Jones software

6 • DIALOG, BRS, and ORBIT: 143
The Encyclopedic Databases
The power and the potential • 55 *million* records • What's a bibliographic citation? • What's an abstract? • The Microcomputer Index™ • The International Software Directory • *Readers Guide to Periodical Literature* • Over 500 magazines and journals • The *Congressional Record* • Special deals for personal computer users

7 • The Information Bank® and NewsNet™: 165
News and Specialized Business Information
Full-text *New York Times* • *Advertising Age, Women's Wear Daily, Scientific American, Variety, Consumer Reports,* and more • Over $40,000 worth of newsletters • *Advanced Office Concepts, Fiber/Laser News, IRS Practices & Procedures, Real Estate Intelligence Report, Satellite News, Tax Notes Today, VideoGames Today,* and more

8 • Computer Bulletin Board Systems: 184
Free for the ASCII-ing
Hundreds of FREE CBBSs • A front seat at the Revolution • Over 2400 CP/M® programs—FREE • Bulletin board "families" • Special interest bulletin boards • Sex, SF, and Space Shuttles • The ham radio connection • How to start your own computer bulletin board

9 · Keyboard Commerce: 196
Electronic Shopping, Banking, and Barter
Save 40 percent on a Sony • Checking your checking account—online • Online barter: Offers you won't want to refuse • Actors/actresses/casting • Resorts/ski/vacations • Hardware/software/stereo equipment • And more

10 · Computerized Conferencing: 208
EIES and PARTICIPATE
The conferencing concept • Camaraderie and communication • Profiling "PARTI" • Adventure, science fiction, and UNIX • Toffler, CP/M® users group, phreaking, and the Eros Exchange (X-rated) • Handicapped PARTIers, four-by-fours, and the great outdoors • "Turnkey" conferencing software • Other systems

11 · Telecommuting: 228
Communicating to Work—The Home/Office Interface
"Cottage Keyers" • Benefits and drawbacks • How to become a telecommuter

12 · Getting Technical: 237
Bits, Bytes, and Other Telecommunications Basics
The ASCII code set • Control characters • Using translation tables • "Bit times"—the final component • Pieces of the frame • Parity, stop bits, and other arcana • How to connect two personal computers

Appendix A: *The "GIGO" Eliminator*   256
What to do when things go wrong . . . go wrong . . . go wrong . . . • The Troubleshooting Checklist

Appendix B: *Secrets of Using Telenet and Tymnet*   261
Free phone numbers • Tymnet's free online newsletter • Vital flow control commands • Special commands for error-free uploading

Appendix C: *Telex, TWX, FAX, Mail, Mailgrams™, and More*   270
How to send a Telex or TWX from your personal computer • Sending Mailgrams™ on The Source • Other electronic mail services • Personal computer software

Appendix D: *How to Turn Your Personal Computer into a Typesetter*   279
Control codes • Crossover cables • Translation tables • What you need to get started • Online typesetters

Appendix E: *Electronic Mail Directory*   287
Source and CompuServe electronic mail addresses • Consultants and communicators • Clubs and user groups • Educational institutions • Publications • Services • Software suppliers

Appendix F: *Database Directories and Publications*   295
Where to look for: Facts, figures, costs, and other information on over 1350 online databases accessible by personal computer

Appendix G: *The ASCII Code Set*   297

Appendix H: *Information Utility Quick Command Reference*   301
For quick reference when online • The most important commands for each of the three information utilities • Operating hours • Addresses • Toll-free customer support numbers

Glossary   309
Index   317

The Complete Handbook of
Personal Computer Communications

Introduction
The Universe at Your Fingertips

Ⅰf you're one of the four million people who own a personal computer—or one of the millions more who are thinking of buying
one—this book could change your life. You may not be aware of it,
but as a present or prospective personal computer owner, you are only a
few steps away from entering an expanding universe of incredible size
and power.

It is an *electronic* universe in which messages and information streak
across the continent or around the world at the speed of light. A place
where you can find a fact or find a job, play a game, publish a poem,
meet a friend, consult an encyclopedia, or do hundreds of other things
without ever leaving your office or home. It is a realm of myriad possibilities destined to forever change the way each of us lives, works, and
plays. But most important of all, it exists *today* and is open to anyone
with a personal computer. Indeed, accessing the electronic universe
may well be the best reason for buying such a machine in the first place.

This book will show you how to do it.

Any Computer Can Communicate

The computer you use can be as small as the Timex/Sinclair 1000
available at your local drug or department store for under $100, or as
powerful as a fully equipped IBM/PC complete with expansion interface
and $6000 hard-disk drive with 20 megabytes of storage. It can be an
Apple, Atari, Commodore, Texas Instruments, Radio Shack, or any
other machine—as long as it is a computer, it can be made to communicate. The same is true of dedicated word processors, those computer-
like machines made by Wang, IBM, DEC, Lanier, CPT, Xerox, and
many other companies.

The only additional hardware and software you will need for most
machines is a printed circuit/microchip board called a "serial card," a
telephone interface box called a "modem," and a telecommunications

software package. The total cost for all three items can be less than $300.

In some cases, you may be able to get the serial card, the modem, the software, *and the computer itself* for about the same amount of money. The Commodore VIC-20, to take but one example, is available at a discount for about $160. This machine includes a communications card as standard equipment. As long as you have a television set, your only additional expense will be $65 for the Commodore Datassette used to load and store programs and $100 for the Commodore VICMODEM ™, for a total cost of $325. (The Commodore modem comes with communications software on cassette and may include free subscriptions to CompuServe and Dow Jones, as well as a free hour on The Source.)

No Programming Required

Getting started in computer communications is not only relatively easy on the pocketbook, it is also easy to do. You do not need to be a computer programmer. You do not need to know any computer languages. As long as you can turn on your machine and get it to load a program, you will be able to enter and move about the electronic universe any time you like.

The only other piece of "peripheral equipment" you will need is some sort of guide to what is available and where, what it costs, how to access it, and how to use it to get the most out of your personal computer and its communications capabilities. That's what you'll find in this book. Designed to address a wide spectrum of interests and needs, it will tell you everything you need to know to go online with the world.

If you have yet to buy your first computer, you will not only discover the thousands of things you can do with such a machine when you connect it to a telephone, you'll also find a number of considerations that may help you in selecting your system. If you are familiar with computer programming, you're probably aware that telecommunications is a different thing altogether. This book will help you build upon what you already know and suggest ways to use your skills even more effectively. Finally, if you are already online with one or more databases, you may be interested in some of the other things you can do with your communicating computer or word processor.

How to Use this Book

Chapter 1 presents a quick survey of all that is waiting for you just beyond your personal computer keyboard. It presents a broad overview of what is available and where you can find it. Chapter 2 explains what you need to get started and what features to look for when choosing your serial card, modem, and communications software.

Chapters 3 and 4 introduce you to The Source and CompuServe, the two major information utilities. These chapters are also designed to dovetail with the instruction manuals supplied by the two services. As manual supplements, they contain many tips, suggestions, and samples not published by CompuServe and The Source. Chapter 5 presents the wealth of information available on the Dow Jones News/Retrieval Service, including that organization's online encyclopedia.

Chapter 6 tells you about the treasure house of information available on DIALOG, BRS, and ORBIT, the three major encyclopedic databases. Chapter 7 introduces you to the New York Times Information Service and NewsNet™, two databases providing news and specialized business information, and Chapter 8 shows you how to access over 450 *free* computer bulletin boards in North America. Chapter 9 explains how to save from 10 to 40 percent on tens of thousands of brandname items by shopping from your computer keyboard; it also introduces you to the rapidly growing phenomenon of electronic banking.

Chapter 10 explains how you can join and take part in dozens of ongoing, online conferences with individuals all over the continent, and how to save time and travel expenses by setting up a private, online conference limited to members of your organization. Chapter 11 explores the phenomenon of "telecommuting," or working at home with the help of your communicating personal computer.

Finally, Chapter 12 presents the technical side of data communications for those who want or need to know more about parity, stop bits, translation tables, crossover cables, and the other arcana of the field.

In the appendices you will find the GIGO eliminator, a troubleshooting guide for use when you get "garbage" on your screen; a section showing you how to access the free information provided by Telenet and Tymnet and how to use these networks most effectively; a description of how to send Telexes, TWXs, and other messages; and a section on how to turn your personal computer into a typesetter. The appendices also contain a directory of the online addresses you need to contact many publications, companies, and professionals via electronic mail; a list of communications-related publications and database directories; the ASCII code set, something you will learn about later; and a quick reference command summary for each of the three information utilities, which will be particularly useful to those who subscribe to more than one service.

Special Points to Remember

• The book assumes that you are familiar with your own equipment. It probably goes without saying, but different computers accomplish the same things in different ways. Fortunately, telecommunications is a reasonably standardized area, and all communicating computers can generate the same basic signals. But the actual keystrokes required by each machine may differ. Since it would be impossible to note all the variations, you may have to consult your manuals to find out how your particular system and software do things.

• With the possible exception of the Atari and its "firmware" cartridges, all computers require some form of programming/storage device. This is usually either a cassette tape recorder or a floppy disk drive. Generally speaking, the two are equivalent in terms of purpose and function. The tape simply takes a lot longer to feed in a program or to record information. Unless otherwise specified, when disk drives are referred to in the text, you can assume that the same information applies if you are using a cassette.

• Printers are also mentioned, but they are a convenience feature. Whether you have a printer or not has no bearing on your ability to enter the electronic universe.

• As with any book about computers, typography can be a challenge. Here are the rules that have been followed:

  An item bracketed by less-than and greater-than symbols refers to a single key on most computer keyboards. Thus when you see <ENTER> you will know that this refers to the key labeled "ENTER." <CTRL> refers to the "CONTROL" key *or its equivalent* on your machine.

  Commands set off in square brackets refer to simultaneous keystrokes in which all of the keys are pressed at the same time. For example, [<SHIFT><DOWN ARROW> <C>] is the sequence used to generate a "Control-C" on a TRS-80 Model III. All three keys must be held down together.

  The word "Enter" alone, as in "Enter your password," implies that you first type the required information and then press your <ENTER> key to send what you typed over the phone lines or into your own computer's memory. As with computers in general, you can type, backspace, and retype as much as you want when you are online. Nothing happens until you press <ENTER> or the word processor equivalent, <RETURN>. Note: a carriage return or C/R on some machines is the same as <ENTER>.

Some online systems understand only capital letters and some personal computers generate only these. Consequently, all commands are printed in capital letters. But this does not necessarily mean that you must always use uppercase when issuing commands from your keyboard.

Finally, throughout the text, you will find numerous "Online Tips" set off in boxes. These contain suggestions, ideas, and other information that is relevant, but not necessarily vital, to the issue at hand. Some are also addressed to the more experienced user and thus make no attempt to explain everything in detail. If you are new to this field, some of the information may not make much sense the first time you read it. Don't let that slow you down. Whenever you find an "Online Tip" that you do not understand, simply skip it and go back later after you have a little more experience.

Online Tip: If your personal computer is already equipped for communications, and you have a modem and communications software—you probably cannot wait to go online. As long as you have a general idea of how to operate your equipment, you can do it right now and obtain the phone numbers of *several hundred* free computer bulletin board systems (CBBSs) across the United States and Canada.

Set your system to the parameters listed below. Make sure you have also set your system to "download" or capture incoming information. Then dial the following number:

(213) 881-6880

Be sure to hit your <ENTER> key twice to tell the system that you're there. When the message LOGON PLEASE appears on your screen, type CAT. This is a system maintained by Novation, Inc., of Tarzana, California, manufacturers of Cat Modems. It is available 24 hours a day and offers not only an extensive list of CBBSs classified by area code but also more than a dozen other features including games, free programs, and (of course) online descriptions of the firm's products.

Online Tip continued

Set your system to the following communications parameters:
Full-duplex
Baud: 300
Word (character) length: 7 bits
Parity: even
Stop bit: 1
Echo: on or "enabled"
Modem setting: originate

...1...

Surveying the Electronic Universe
An Overview

The electronic universe consists of computers of all shapes, sorts, and sizes: mainframes, minis, and micros or "personal computers." It exists for the simple reason that all of these machines can "talk" to each other over the telephone lines. Thus someone with a little IXO Telecomputer—a unit that costs about $500 and fits in the palm of your hand—can tap the power of a multimillion dollar mainframe by merely plugging it into a telephone jack, switching it on, and dialing a number. And, of course, the same is true for you sitting at home or in your office with your Apple, Atari, Commodore, IBM/PC, or other microcomputer.

This is the fundamental fact upon which the electronic universe is based. But the endless variations on this theme are what make things so interesting. Today there are more than 1350 different computerized "databases," containing almost inconceivable amounts of information. There are more than 450 free, computerized bulletin board and message exchange systems. There are information utilities; computerized conferencing systems; and systems for sending and receiving electronic mail and Telex and TWX messages; as well as systems for electronic shopping, electronic banking, and more.

The important thing is that every one of these systems and services is available to you and your communicating personal computer. You have only to dial the phone and let your microcomputer talk to an organization's minicomputer or mainframe.

Where Did It All Come From?

Today's online information industry evolved from the remote data processing (RDP) services that began in the late 1950s as a low-cost alternative to buying or leasing a mainframe computer. In those pre-microchip years, few businesses could afford to have their own on-site mainframe computer. Yet they needed the power the computer could provide. RDP provided the answer. New companies sprang up with the sole purpose of acquiring and maintaining one or more large computers—and selling computer time to firms unable to afford machines of their own. This is called "time sharing," and it has nothing to do with Colorado ski lodges or Las Vegas condominiums.

The point is that for a mainframe in Columbus to service a customer in Cleveland, some form of electronic communication had to take place. Using a relatively inexpensive terminal, the customer had to be able to send his payroll, billing, accounts payable, and other information to the mainframe for processing, and there had to be a way to get the computer's output back to him.

This certainly was not the start of computer communications. But there can be no doubt that the needs of the RDP firms and their customers stimulated enormous growth and refinement in the techniques and technology of the field.

The result was a *delivery mechanism*—a well-developed system of computers, specialized software, standards and protocols, electronic packet-switching networks, and other components capable of reliably transmitting information from one computer to another.

Once the delivery mechanism was in place, it was only a matter of time before individuals and companies began to find ways to use it for something other than the transmission of the day's banking transactions to a remote mainframe computer. The only obstacle to further expansion was the cost of the equipment needed to use the delivery mechanism. The price simply precluded widespread usage.

The development of easily affordable microcomputers changed everything. The electronic information industry took off like a rocket and has been blasting ahead at full warp speed ever since.

A Handle on the Universe

In the process, an often bewildering array of systems and services has been developed and made available, and more are on the way. Some are offered by newly formed companies, and some represent additional or expanded offerings from established firms. The field is positively burgeoning with activity. This makes it fascinating and fun to watch, but it also makes it difficult to neatly classify everything in a unified system.

For example, you would not expect to find features on wine and living the good life nestled among electronic versions of *Cellular Radio News, Video Week, Tax Notes Today,* and other professional newsletters. But you will—on a database called NewsNet™. Nor would you expect to find movie reviews on a largely financial database like the Dow Jones News/Retrieval Service (DJNS). Yet, whether it's a hot stock or a hot new movie, DJNS can give you a quote on both.

Nevertheless, some form of classification, however imperfect, is essential. And here is the one we will use:
- Information utilities
- Encyclopedic databases
- News and specialized business information databases
- Free computer bulletin board systems (CBBSs)
- Electronic shopping, banking, and barter
- Computerized conferencing
- Telecommuting

To give you an idea of how these components fit together, we will briefly explain each of them in this chapter. For more detailed examples and an explanation of how you can take advantage of particular components, you will naturally want to consult the appropriate chapters elsewhere in the book.

Online Tip: The terminology of the electronic universe is still evolving. The word "database," for example, can refer to a specific collection of information like the Media General database available on DJNS. Or it can refer to the Dow Jones News/Retrieval Service itself, and similar organizations that offer many different databases.

Computer bulletin board systems may be referred to as CBBSs or as BBSs. "Computerized" and "services" are also used in place of "computer" and "systems."

The terms "log in," "sign on," and "log on" all refer to the process of entering the password and account number that will give you access to a particular database or service. The same is true of "log off" and "sign off." (For some reason no one ever logs *out* of a database.)

Information Utilities

"Information utility" is a term coined by The Source, one of three databases that currently fit that description. The other two are CompuServe and the Dow Jones News/Retrieval Service. The Source is sometimes referred to as STC for Source Telecomputing Corporation. CompuServe is frequently called CIS for CompuServe Information Service. And the Dow Jones News/Retrieval Service is usually abbreviated as DJNS.

Online Tip: Although it will be some time before it rivals the other three information utilities in membership or features, one firm that definitely rates "up and comer" status is General Videotex Corporation of Cambridge, Massachusetts. The firm's DELPHI system already offers an online encyclopedia and online banking services, and more features are planned for the future. For additional information, phone (617) 491-3393.

Online Tip: For free online information about Ontario, you might want to look into Infomart, a joint venture of Torstar Corporation and Southam, Inc. Infomart's main offering is its "Teleguide to Ontario," a service containing information on entertainment, accommodations, local attractions, and travel services in and around Ontario. The government of Ontario, the Canadian federal government, Bell Canada, and Infomart have committed a total of $16 million to the service, which contains some 6,000 online pages of information. Contact:

Infomart
164 Merton Street
Toronto, Ontario M4S 3A8
Canada
(416) 489-6640

The main thing that distinguishes an information utility from other organizations is that it offers *both* information and services. Designed to be used by the average person rather than by the professional researcher, each utility contains a variety of information on a wide range of subjects. But each also offers services, such as electronic mail, banking, and shopping; real-time communication and game-playing with other users; and the opportunity to write and run programs on mainframe computers.

The Encyclopedic Databases

Encyclopedic databases offer you access to information *in depth*. The major organizations in this area are DIALOG, BRS, and ORBIT. Each can be thought of as a convenient delivery system or gateway service that enables you to search as many as 175 individual databases covering everything from chemical formulas to patent law to all of the major magazines dealing with personal computers.

The various databases are supplied by independent companies or "information providers" (IPs). The encyclopedics repackage the information according to the needs of their particular system and offer it to the public. DIALOG, BRS, and ORBIT handle all of the billing and customer service, and each pays royalties to the information providers.

In the past, the three encyclopedics have been used primarily by scientists, engineers, librarians, and professional researchers. But all three have begun to respond to the personal computer phenomenon. The "Electronic Yellow Pages" files now available on DIALOG are just one example of a general trend to offer databases that will appeal to a broader public (see Figure 1.1).

News and Specialized Business Information Databases

This is a category created specifically to accommodate The New York Times Information Service (NYTIS) and NewsNet™. NYTIS offers, among other things, the full text of the *New York Times*. This is unusual, because most databases offer only brief abstracts or bibliographic citations. Often that is more than enough. But when you find that "these times demand the *Times*" on your personal computer terminal, it is nice to know that the complete text is available. NYTIS also offers you access to abstracts from many other newspapers, magazines, and other publications—many of them not available online elsewhere.

NewsNet, based in Bryn Mawr, Pennsylvania, offers electronic versions of nearly 150 different industry and professional newsletters. The database includes publications like *Hazardous Waste News, Computer Market Observer, Real Estate Intelligence Report*, and *Tax Notes Today*. There is even a publication called the *Newsletter on Newsletters*.

——————— **Figure 1.1. The Electronic Yellow Pages.** ———————

Prepared by Market Data Retrieval, Inc., of Westport, Connecticut, and available on DIALOG, the Electronic Yellow Pages can quickly answer the question: "How many banks are there with 'Boston' in their names and what are their phone numbers?" By refining your search further, you could also find out how many banks there are named "Boston" on Bayou Street in Boca Raton.

```
? ss bank? and Boston
        19     46814 BANK?
        20     86 BOSTON
        21     61  19 AND 20

? t 21/3/1-3
21/3/1
0040670
BANK OF BOSTON INTL
```

Figure 1.1 continued

P O BOX 71467
LOS ANGELES, CA 90017
PHONE: 213-680-1784
COUNTY: LOS ANGELES
CHIEF EXECUTIVE OFFICER: WM D HARTMAN

SIC: 6020A .(COMMERCIAL BANK)
ASSETS: A .(BANK: 100 MIL & OVER)
CITY POPULATION: 9 .(500,000 AND OVER)

THIS IS A HEADQUARTERS LOCATION

21/3/3
0015000
SOUTH BOSTON BANK & TRUST
HUPPS MILL PLZ
SOUTH BOSTON, VA 24592
PHONE: 804-575-7951
COUNTY: SOUTH BOSTON

SIC: 6020A .(COMMERCIAL BANK)
ASSETS: G .(BANK: SAVINGS-NO ASSET INFO)
CITY POPULATION: 3 .(5,000-9,999)

THIS IS A BRANCH LOCATION

Online Tip: The instant delivery of information made possible by an online database is obviously an important feature. But even more important is the fact that the information in a computerized database can be electronically *searched* for "keywords." To over-simplify slightly, when you conduct a keyword search you begin by typing in the word you have selected (anything from "applesauce" to "zirconium"). The computer then searches through the items in its database and tells you whenever it finds a "match."

This is obviously a tremendously powerful feature, and virtually every database offers it in some form.

Free Computer Bulletin Board Systems (CBBSs)

Each of the hundreds of CBBSs online today is in some respect a labor of love. Virtually every one of them consists of a personal computer that some individual has equipped to act for all the world like an information utility. CBBSs were originally designed as the computer equivalent of a real cork-and-thumbtack bulletin board (see Figure 1.2). But as we will see, many of them now offer a variety of other features as well.

――――――――――――――― **Figure 1.2. CBBS Messages.** ―――――――――――

All CBBSs enable you to scan the subject lines of the messages they hold. When you find one that interests you, you tell the system to stop and display the complete text.

Nr. 1221 = 15 lines, dated 0/00/00 From: JUDITH 0000
To: ALL Re: COOKIES

Nr. 1225 = 5 lines, dated 0/00/00 From: JERRY 00000
To: ALL Re: IBM PC OWNERS

Nr. 1228 = 9 lines, dated 0/00/00 From: DAVE 000000
To: ALL Re: ATARI BBS

Nr. 1307 = 16 lines, dated 0/00/00 From: JOE 0000000
To: ALL Re: S-100 SYSTEM FOR SALE.

  MSG: 261 <C> ( ) < 56 >
 DATE: 00/00 - 16:35
 FROM: DAVE 000000
    TO: ANYONE
 SUBJ: HELP!

I have a TRS MOD III with an auto-originate modem. I would like to use them to access The New York Times Information Bank each day. The Information Bank People were unable to assist in locating software that will provide a totally automated and . . .

  MSG: 326 <M> ( ) < 24 >
 DATE: 07/08 - 18:16
 FROM: DYLAN 000000
    TO: ALL
 SUBJ: HELLO!

H E L L O from TORONTO!
To try a good BBS in our area, dial (416)-624-5431, non-business hours, 24 hrs on weekends. I think you'll like it. Be seeing you soon. . . . . Dylan 000000

  MSG: 306 <M> ( ) < 39 >
 DATE: 06/21 - 11:28
 FROM: SITH LORD
    TO: ALL
 SUBJ: SCIENCE FICTION

COMING SOMEWHERE IN THE FIRST 2 WEEKS IN JULY . . .
A NEW BBS/SIG DEVOTED TO ALL ASPECTS OF SF MEDIA WILL
GO ONLINE. INITIAL HRS 6PM TO MIDNIGHT EST.
(EXPANDED LATER) CALL (617) 876-4885
COMING TO A COMPUTER NEAR YOU THIS JULY.

For example, you can read feature articles written and contributed by other users of the "board." (Often a particular bulletin board will be devoted to a specific topic, like science fiction, coin collecting, old movies, sports trivia, and so on.) You can read instructional information and expert tips on using various hardware and software packages. Some boards will actually transmit software programs to you over the phone, though normally you must first contribute some programming of your own to the collection. Many offer lists containing hundreds of phone numbers for *other* bulletin boards across the continent.

Electronic Shopping, Banking, and Barter

Thanks to Comp-U-Card of America, Inc., you can browse through descriptions and prices of over 50,000 items: everything from color televisions to clothing by Izod to Cross pen sets. Items are offered at discounts ranging from 10 to 40 percent, and you can enter your order from your keyboard. You can access Comp-U-Card directly, or you can use the versions of the service available on The Source, CompuServe, or DJNS.

Other services available principally through the information utilities enable you to search for and buy books, records, audio tapes, and software. If you are interested in *trading* your goods or services for something, you can use the system to arrange a barter deal. Both information utilities also allow you to place classified ads on their main bulletin boards at no charge.

Computerized Conferencing

The best way to understand computerized conferencing is to first think of a real conference in which Peter flies in from Pittsburgh, Beth arrives from Barstow, and George, who is always on the road, comes in from wherever he has been. You all sit down at the big table in the conference room to discuss whether the firm should buy a widget or a wumpus. Feasibility studies have been done; various financial analyses have been prepared; and there are a number of reports to present. Everyone contributes their best thinking on the subject—everyone but George, who has a major client to meet and has to leave early. You yourself have an appointment at four, but by 3:45 the issue is still not settled; and Beth and Peter both have to leave tomorrow.

Now picture a computerized conference designed to accomplish the same thing. All of the reports and studies are sent over the telephone to a central computer. Once there, they can be called up, read, and commented upon by Peter and Beth sitting at home or in their home offices.

With a portable computer, George can do the same from whatever hotel room he happens to be in at the time. Information, ideas, suggestions, comments, and comments on comments can all be exchanged at the convenience of the participants. A decision can be reached and confirmed by voice telephone. And nobody has to fly anywhere. Except George, who's *always* on the road.

This buttoned-down business application is only one of hundreds of other possibilities offered by the Electronic Information Exchange System (EIES) and PARTICIPATE, two of the most highly developed computerized conferencing systems. PARTICIPATE is available on The Source. EIES is accessed directly through Telenet.

Telecommuting

Telecommuting, or "communicating to work," is the rapidly growing phenomenon of company employees performing their jobs at home with the aid of a communicating personal computer. Telecommuting is based on the fact that in many cases the physical location of employees has no bearing on their ability to do their jobs. For example, the largest portion of an executive's job involves the manipulation of information. If the executive can obtain the information from the firm's central computer and communicate results and decisions to that same machine, there is no reason why that portion of the job cannot be performed at home or at poolside. The same is true of jobs that involve data entry. If information must be "keyboarded" (typed at a computer terminal), it does not matter where the terminal is. And as long as a certain number of items are entered and communicated to a central computer each day, it does not matter when the actual work is performed.

Telenet, Tymnet, DataPac, Uninet, and Others

In the individual chapters that follow we will look at each of these subjects in greater detail. But before we do, there is one final point you should be aware of, and that concerns how you access all of these different services and databases.

DIALOG's computers are in California. CompuServe's are in Columbus, Ohio. The Source Computer Center is in Virginia just outside of Washington, D.C. DJNS is in Princeton, New Jersey. There are databases and computers scattered all over the United States, and if you had to pay regular long-distance telephone charges each time you accessed them, the electronic universe would quickly lose much of its appeal.

Fortunately, most people can access the majority of the electronic universe by making a *local* telephone call. The technology that makes this possible is called "packet switching" and the firms that provide it are called "packet-switching networks."

Neither of these subjects will be addressed in great detail in this book, because all you need to know is that the networks exist and that they are the primary means of accessing the available databases and services. They are not free. The cost for using them may be built into charges of the database, or it may be broken out and listed as a separate charge. Yet in virtually every instance, the cost will be less than a long-distance phone call of the same duration.

The only situation in which you will not be able to make a local call is if you live some distance from a major metropolitan area. If that's the case, you will probably have to make a toll call to the nearest city.

The two largest networks are GTE's Telenet and Tymshare's Tymnet and DataPac (the Canadian system). Uninet, a service of Uninet, Inc. of Roseland, New Jersey (201) 228-8900, is a recent arrival and may offer less expensive rates, but it may not be available for all databases.

Each network has a slightly different sign-on procedure, but these are always explained in the instruction manuals you receive as a subscriber to a particular database or service.

The materials you receive from a database will also contain a complete listing of Telenet, Tymnet, and any other network numbers. But if you don't know what number to dial, you can either call the Customer Service "800" number for the particular database, or follow the instructions in Appendix B, "Secrets of Using Telenet and Tymnet."

In the chapters that follow, we will describe each of the major databases and services in much greater detail. But first, let's look at the gear you will need for life online.

...2...

Accessing the Power
What You Need, and
Need to Know, to Go Online

By themselves, computers are nothing more than elaborately arranged piles of purified sand. But as everyone knows, a computer can be an incredibly *versatile* sandpile to play in—if you bring along the right toys. In more dignified parlance, that means software (computer programming or instructions) and peripherals (add-on equipment). To accomplish any given task in the computer world, you have to have the right equipment and the right software to tell your machine how to use that equipment. And getting your machine to communicate is no exception.

To endow your personal computer with the equivalents of speech and hearing, you need five items:

- A plug-in communications card
- A device called a "modem" *(m*odulator/*dem*odulator)
- A cable to connect the two
- A communications software package
- A telephone!

As anyone who has spent as little as five minutes in a computer store knows, hardware and software designed to accomplish the same basic microcomputer functions are available in a bewildering variety of configurations with an equally bewildering number of standard and optional features. Consequently, as you might expect, the total cost of these components can be as low as about $300 or as high as $1200 or more. It all depends on your preferences . . . and your pocketbook.

Indeed, the diversity of both new and established products on the market today is so great that it would be impossible to describe the various configurations of features (or lack of same) that each offers. Then too, each computer manufacturer does things a little bit differently. Modems can be used with any communicating computer, but communications cards and software are "machine specific"—you can use only cards and software designed for your particular machine.

However, since each component is designed to accomplish the same thing, regardless of the brand of computer, it is definitely possible to present a set of guidelines for selecting your equipment and software. You will find these guidelines in the "What to look for" sections of this chapter. Since you don't need any technical knowledge beyond a familiarity with your own machine, you may want to turn to these sections now.

You might find it helpful, though, to have a general overview of these components and a basic understanding of what each does. That is what we will present in the next section. You will find more detailed information in Chapter 12, but be sure to read this chapter first, since Chapter 12 picks up where the following sections leave off.

What Is Going On—and Off—Here?

Just Among Ourselves

Computers are great conversationalists. When under a full head of steam, a computer's keyboard is constantly talking to its "brain" or central processing unit (CPU). For its part, the CPU is constantly talking to the video monitor, ordering the disk drives around and accepting their backtalk, telling the printer to "make it march, fella!" and addressing memory locations on a wide variety of subjects. The same is true of word processors, those computer cousins that have chosen a life dedicated to the service of writers, secretaries, and enlightened executives.

All of which is to say that a computer's components are constantly communicating with each other. The key point is *how* they communicate; and the answer is "eights bits at a time." You can think of bits as on/off pulses, voltage differences, or 1s and 0s. But for the moment, think of them as particles of information. Like a single letter of the alphabet, a single bit is virtually meaningless in and of itself. However, when you put a number of letters together, you have a *word* that means something.

The same is true with microcomputers. One bit alone doesn't mean a thing. But eight bits . . . well, now we're talking. Most microcomputers—even many of the newer 16-bit machines—carry on conversations with their components in 8-bit words. In fact, an 8-bit unit or "byte" is even called a "word" in computerese.

Now for the confusing part. Unfortunately, what microcomputers think of as a "word," you and I think of as a single letter. As far as a microcomputer is concerned, the English word "The" actually contains *three* "words" or bytes. When you hit the letter "T" your keyboard sends the CPU the following combination of bits *all at once:* 01010100. When you hit "h" it sends 01101000. And when you hit "e" it sends 01100101.

Imagine, if you will, the 1s and 0s in a byte streaking through your system like a formation of jet fighters flying eight abreast. If you picture the white contrails such a formation would leave in the sky, you will have a pretty good idea of why this type of computer communication is referred to as "parallel." In parallel communications, all eight bits travel together in parallel formation, and all arrive at their destination at the same time. This is a computer's natural way of talking, and not surprisingly, it takes eight wires to bring it off. Thus it is logical to assume that if you could run an eight-wire cable from your personal computer to McLean, Virginia, or to Columbus, Ohio, your machine could talk directly to the computers at The Source and CompuServe.

The problem is that the only practical way to connect your computer to theirs is by telephone line. And telephone lines don't contain nearly enough wires. In fact, with a telephone line, you can only send and receive *one bit at a time.*

A Dripping Faucet

What to do? The only solution is to somehow change things so that your computer will talk to the outside world one-bit-at-a-time, instead of eight-bits-all-at-once. Instead of a fighter formation, what you really want is more on the order of a dripping faucet, with each individual droplet representing a bit.

That is the job of the communications card that you buy and plug into a slot inside your machine. The card itself is a printed circuit board containing a number of microchips and a plug receptacle or "port." It fits into one of the slots on the computer's main circuit board, or "bus," and among other things, it is responsible for converting the computer's internal parallel communications into serial output in which the bits are doled out one at a time, in a series. For this reason, it is also called a "serial card." (The microchip that sits at the heart of the serial card is often called a "UART," for universal asynchronous receiver/transmitter. Though it is not accurate to do so, you may hear the card referred to by this name as well.)

Online Tip: Among the best-selling machines on the market, only one brand uses a different kind of card. Commodore computers use an IEEE-448 interface. This is the parallel equivalent of the serial interface, and it requires a special Commodore modem. An

Online Tip continued

> IEEE-448 interface card is standard equipment with Commodore machines. You do not have to buy and install a separate card. Commodore also sells a kit for converting the IEEE-448 parallel output into serial output, enabling you to use non-Commodore modems.
>
> For more information, you might want to purchase the following book:
>
> *PET® and the IEEE-448 Bus*
> by E. Fisher and C. W. Jensen
> McGraw-Hill, $15.99

The port at the rear of the card is called an RS-232-C interface. This sounds complicated, but it is not. RS-232 (the "C" is often dropped) refers to an electrical standard that says, in effect, "Mr. Computer Manufacturer, we don't care what goes on *inside* your machine, as long as it always comes *out* the same way." If you count them, you will notice that there are either 25 holes or 25 pins in the RS-232 plug on the communications card. Without getting into why there are 25 and not just 8 holes or pins, suffice it to say that each pin or hole can be used to transmit or receive a particular signal. The RS-232 standard dictates what pin or hole will be used for each specific signal. This is one of the few reasonably standardized components in the whole world of microcomputers. *And it is the reason why you can buy virtually any brand of modem and connect it to your computer.*

> **Online Tip:** If you own a serial—as opposed to a parallel—printer, you already have a serial card in your machine. With the proper software, you may be able to unplug your printer and plug in a modem in its place. Ask your dealer or technical representative for more details on this money-saving possibility.

A Sound Approach

At this point, your communications card is installed and your bits are marching out into the world single file. Everything is fine until they run smack into the phone line. The problem is that phone lines are designed to carry sound, not digital information. Here's the difference.

Bits are actually voltage levels, and, computers being what they are, there can be only two such levels—one level to symbolize the 1 or "off" state, and one for the 0 or "on" state. A bit is either one or the other—

there is no in-between. Sound, on the other hand, varies all over the place, rising and falling from one tone to another.

To understand this more clearly, think just in terms of sound for a moment. If you could hear digital information, you would hear a series of sharp clicks and clacks, or clock-like ticks and tocks. And that is *all* you would hear. If you saw this series on an oscilloscope, it would look like this:

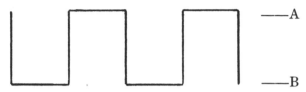

Notice that the transition from level B up to level A is sharp. There is no gentle curve indicating a gradual buildup. It's click-clack-click-clack, and no excuses!

Sound, on the other hand, is nothing but curves. Think of the way an old fashioned air-raid siren begins with a low sound and gradually works its way up to a piercing tone. Then the sound gradually falls and the process begins again. On an oscilloscope, that sound looks rather like this:

Here you can see the gradual transition from level B up to level A and back down again, like the "gently rolling hills" of a real-estate ad. This is the kind of signal telephone lines were built to carry. And there's no arguing with them. They will *not* carry any of this click-clack digital stuff.

It is for this reason that modems were invented. A modem is a device that *mod*ulates and *dem*odulates your computer's digital signals. Or to put it another way, a modem converts the bits coming out of your computer into *sound* and then sends the sound out over the phone lines. That's the modulation part. The demodulation process is the exact opposite. The modem takes the sound coming in from your correspondent's modem, converts it into digital pulses, and sends the pulses to your machine.

We Will Receive! You Will Kick Off!

A modem converts the 1 bits coming from your computer into one specific sound frequency, and it converts the 0 bits into another specific frequency. That's fine for outgoing bits, but what about the incoming ones? How can a modem tell the difference between a 1 bit from your computer and a 1 bit coming in from your correspondent's machine? The answer is that modems use *two pairs* of frequencies for a total of four in all. One pair is used to represent outgoing 1s and 0s and the other pair is used for the incoming 1s and 0s.

Think of each pair as two pieces of galvanized pipe, arranged like a double-barreled shotgun. Now mentally, put one pair on top of the other so that you are looking down four barrels at once. If you are a modem and you want to communicate with another modem, the biggest question to be answered is which set of pipes you should use to send out data and which set you should watch for incoming data.

Both you and the other modem are capable of either sending or receiving data through either the top set of pipes or the bottom set. But obviously you cannot *both* use the top set to send and the bottom set to receive, or vice versa. One of you will have to be set to send information out through the bottom pair of pipes and receive through the top pair, while the other will have to be set to send through the top and receive through the bottom.

These two settings are called the "originate" mode and the "answer" mode. But these two terms can be slightly misleading. It really does not matter which modem is set to which mode. What matters is that one modem be set to originate and the other be set to answer. Since the modems used by all dial-up databases and computer bulletin board systems are, by convention, set to answer, you will have to set your modem to originate whenever you call them. However, if you want to communicate with a computer-owning friend, you will have to decide between yourselves who is going to be "originate" and who is going to be "answer."

Online Tip: You will often hear 300-baud modems described as being "Bell System 103–compatible." The term "Bell 103" simply refers to a widely accepted standard (like RS-232) governing which specific tone frequencies will be used for 1s and 0s in the originate mode, and which will be used for 1s and 0s in the answer mode. In the originate mode, a 1 bit is represented by a tone of 2225 cycles per second (hertz or Hz), and a 0 bit by a tone of 2025 Hz. In the answer mode, 1 bits are tones of 1270 Hz, and 0 bits are 1070 Hz. (A Bell 113 is an originate-only system and should be avoided.)

Standards called "Bell 202," "Bell 212A," or "Racal-Vadic" apply to the phase shift keying (the *phase* of the signals is shifted instead of the frequency) used in 1200-baud modems. The main difference between the Bell and Racal-Vadic standards is the specific frequencies they use, but since most databases will accept either, this need not concern you.

Far more important is the difference between Bell 202 and Bell 212A 1200-baud modems. A Bell 202 modem can only communicate at 1200 baud and only in *half-duplex*, something you want to avoid since most databases require full-duplex communications. A modem that is Bell 212A–compatible, however, can communicate at both 300 and 1200 baud and in either full- or half-duplex. *If you buy a 1200-baud modem be certain that it is Bell 212A–compatible.*

Telling the CPU What to Do

Like your communications card, your modem will also have an RS-232 port. You link the two by simply plugging a flat 25-wire "ribbon cable" into each port.

Online Tip: Your dealer should cover this for you, but it's worth checking all the same. Most communications cards and modems have female RS-232 receptacles and thus require a ribbon cable with male plugs on either end. But some communications cards have male ports and thus require a cable with one female plug for the card and a male plug for the modem. Be sure your dealer sells you a cable with the right "sexes" for your equipment. The plugs are called DB25 connectors.

Online Tip: In addition to male-female compatibility, there is another distinction that is vital to be aware of when buying a cable to connect your computer to your modem. All modems are set up to receive information from a computer on pin 2 and to send information to the computer on pin 3. In technical jargon, modems are wired as Data Communications Equipment (DCE).

Most computer serial cards, in contrast, are wired to send information to the modem on pin 2 and to receive information from it on pin 3. This is called Data Terminal Equipment (DTE) wiring.

If your computer card is wired this way, you'll have nothing to worry about, since the two forms of wiring match perfectly. How-

Online Tip continued

> ever, the cards in some computers, like the one used in the Os-
> borne 1, are wired like modems (DCE) instead of like computers
> (DTE). Directly connecting two DCE-wired devices won't work
> since both expect to send and receive information on the *same*
> pins. Consequently, if you have a DCE-wired serial card, you must
> use a crossover cable that will connect pin 2 of one device to pin 3
> of the other and vice versa.
>
> The cross-over is made by re-wiring the pins on one plug of a
> standard cable. Your computer store will either have such cables
> prepared or be able to make one up for you. The important thing is
> to find out whether your computer's serial card is wired DTE or
> DCE *before* you bring your equipment home. Since the salesperson
> may not know the difference, you may have to take the initiative.

The final component you need is communications software—the prepared computer programming that tells your machine how to use all the
hardware you've assembled. If you have an Atari, your software resides
in a plug-in "firmware" cartridge. But for most other computers, communications packages are available on floppy disk or cassette tape, at
prices ranging from about $25 up to $150 or more. The price differences
reflect additional features and increasing ease of use, which we will consider later. For now it's enough to say that communications software is
responsible for telling your computer to send the characters you type
out via the serial port on the communications card; for establishing and
maintaining the connection between your system and another; for making sure that the incoming information gets displayed on the screen; and
for performing all the other little chores that make communications
possible.

The Fogglesworth Connection

To use a little computerese, communications software makes your
computer "act like a terminal." Picture a large university computer
housed in air-conditioned splendor in the recently donated Fogglesworth Hall at the center of the campus. The Fogglesworth computer
has all the "brains," all the processing capability, and all the information
files. But in the Engineering quad, in the Psychology wing, even in the
English department, you will find terminals connected to the main
computer.

On the outside, these terminals look very much like your personal
computer. They have a keyboard, a CRT (television-like) display, and a
number of wires sticking out of them. But appearances can be deceiv-
ing, for in fact, that is about *all* they have. Designed solely as a way of

accessing the Fogglesworth computer, they enable you to establish a connection, enter commands, and read whatever the computer sends you. But once the information scrolls up and disappears at the top of your display screen, it's gone. The machines have no memory, no storage capacity, no computer "intelligence" at all. For this reason, they are called "dumb terminals."

This is what your PC must be made to resemble as far as CompuServe, The Source, DJNS, or any other database is concerned. Or, to put it another way, the database computers have got to think that they are talking to a dumb terminal. A communications software program is responsible for creating the illusion.

Online Tip: Some computer manufacturers may supply you with a communications program as part of your DOS (disk operating system) package. The IBM/PC DOS diskette, for example, contains a program called "COMM.BAS" that will allow your computer to emulate a dumb terminal.

Talking ASCII

Finally, a communications program also tells your computer to talk to the outside world in ASCII (pronounced "as-key"). This is the American Standard Code for Information Interchange, and as its name implies, it is another standard that nearly everyone uses. ASCII is not difficult to understand. It's really a very practical solution to a very important problem. The problem is that computers can communicate only in numbers. So how do you get them to send and receive letters?

Easy; you just assign each letter a number and send the number. Software on both ends of the connection makes the necessary conversion.

The ASCII code set runs from 0 to 127, and it contains a discrete number for each capital letter, each lowercase letter, each digit from 0 to 9, and a clutch of punctuation marks. Thus, when a communicating computer or word processor anywhere in the country sees an 84, followed by a 104, followed by a 101, coming in the RS-232 port on its communications card, it knows it should display the letters "T," "h," and "e" on its screen. (See Appendix G for the complete ASCII code set.)

The letters, numbers, and punctuation marks do not exhaust the available ASCII code numbers. And that's a good thing, because you must also have numbers to symbolize and communicate things like the action of the <ENTER>key, the <RETURN> or carriage return key, the <BACKSPACE> key, and other non-character information. There must even be a code number for a blank space.

Most of the time you won't have to give ASCII a second thought. Your hardware and software will take care of things for you. However, there is one more point about ASCII that it would be helpful to understand, and that is the whole matter of "control characters."

Control characters are not really characters at all. They are just ASCII numbers. They get their name from the fact that they are used to control various communications functions. On many machines you generate them or "send them out the door" by holding down a key marked <CTRL> and striking one of the letters from A to Z. (There is no <CTRL> key on the TRS-80 Model III. Instead you must press the <Down Arrow> and the *left* <Shift> key and then hit the desired letter.)

The ASCII code numbers generated this way range from 1 to 26, with Control-A being an ASCII 1 and Control-Z being an ASCII 26. It is a neat and tidy system, but in the end, who cares? Well, the databases care. For example, suppose you wanted to freeze the display on your screen so that you could take more time to read the information. Or suppose you wanted to say, "Hey, wait a minute. I don't want to read a report on the Norse Vikings, I want the ones who play football in Minnesota. Get me out of this!"

In both cases, you would probably send the database a control character. Sending a Control-S (an ASCII 19) to The Source, for example, will stop the display from scrolling. Sending a Control-Q (ASCII 17) will restart it. And, if you do not have a <BREAK> key on your keyboard, you can send a Control-P (ASCII 16) to stop whatever is appearing on your screen at the moment. When you think about it, what else *could* you send that would have a special meaning? By themselves, your letter keys generate letters. It is just not possible—or practical—for any one letter to have two meanings. And that is why you need the <CTRL> key and control characters.

Online Tip: The term "asynchronous" is often used to describe the kind of communications we have been discussing. This is as opposed to "synchronous" communications. In synchronous communications, data flows in an uninterrupted stream from one computer to another. The only way the two computers can tell where one letter of a message ends and the next character begins is through very precise timing. Thus, in synchronous communications, there can be no pauses between letters. In asynchronous communications, however, the spots where a letter or character begin and end are marked with special bits. You can thus send characters in irregular bursts—the way you do from a keyboard—and no one gets upset. Because of those special bits, the timing of the two computers does not have to be synchronized.

What to Look For: How to Choose Your Hardware

Communications Cards

The main circuit board of a microcomputer contains all of the connections needed to tie all of the machine's components together. Usually this board will also contain a number of empty sockets, or "expansion slots," to allow you to plug smaller printed-circuit boards or "cards" into the main circuit. Each card, of course, endows your computer with a particular feature or capability, and it goes without saying that it must be designed specifically for your particular machine.

The communications card you need will be available either from your manufacturer or from an independent company. A card typically runs about $150, and there are really no features to distinguish one from another. In some cases, you may even find that your machine comes with a communications card built in. This is true with the Osborne portable and with the Apple III, for example, and it may eventually become a standard practice.

Saving Your Slots

A communications card, per se, may have no distinguishing features, but there *is* something else worth considering, and that is how you decide to use your expansion slots if your particular system has them. For example, suppose that your system offers a total of five expansion slots, and you want to equip your machine to run a printer, accept the paddles and joysticks used for playing games, display color graphics, and communicate. Since each of these four functions can require a separate card, you will have only one empty slot left. If you decide that you need more memory, a fifth card and your last slot will be required.

If at some point in the future you find that you need even more memory or you want to add some other card-carried function, you will face a number of inconvenient and possibly expensive alternatives. It is for this reason that many computer manufacturers and independent companies have begun to offer single cards that combine two or more functions but still occupy only one slot.

Fortunately, communications circuitry and an RS-232 port are frequently one of the functions included on such cards. For example, both Quadram Corporation of Norcross, Georgia, and Seattle Computer Company in Washington offer memory expansion cards for the IBM Personal Computer. The cards offer a minimum of 64K (kilobytes) of additional memory and several columns of empty sockets. More memory can be added when you want it by purchasing additional chips to plug into those sockets. Indeed, each board can provide a total of 256K when all of its sockets are filled.

In addition, Quadram's Quadboard includes a parallel printer port and a battery-driven clock/calendar, while the Seattle product comes with special software that will allow your machine to treat a portion of the board's memory as if it were an additional disk drive.

Most significant of all, each board also provides an RS-232 port and communications circuitry, eliminating the need to buy a separate board for that purpose. The only hurdle is the price. With 64K of memory installed (the minimum available configuration), these products and similar boards for other computers list for around $600, though that may change as memory prices fall.

Modems

There are two major types of modems: "acoustic couplers" and "direct-connect" modems. The difference is the way each makes its connection with your telephone line. An acoustic modem uses a pair of rubber cups designed to accept a telephone handset. The handset is placed into the cups, and the modem sends and receives its tones through the mouth- and earpieces.

A direct-connect or "hard-wired" modem plugs directly into a modular telephone jack. This is usually a jack on the wall, though some modems plug into the handset jack on the telephone itself and require you to plug the handset into *them*.

Acoustic modems used to be significantly cheaper than the direct-connect variety, but this is no longer true. Today about the only advantage to an acoustic modem is that you can use it with any telephone, whether or not a modular jack is available. If you are in a hotel room or office where you cannot unplug one of the phones and plug in your modem, perhaps an acoustic modem still makes sense. But if your home phones do not use modular connections, you have only to buy an adapter plug to make the conversion. Radio Shack and other stores sell these adapters for about $5.00.

> **Online Tip:** If you want to connect your telephone and modem to the *same* wall jack, you may need an adapter with one modular male plug and two female modular receptacles. Cost: about $7.00.

Direct-Connect or Acoustic?

The main problem with acoustic modems is outside noise. If the handset is not securely mounted in the modem's cups, or if for one reason or another the modem picks up some outside sound, that noise will interfere with your communications. In addition, any time you are dealing with actual sound, there is always the possibility that the sound will cause something else to vibrate and give off a harmonic tone. And finally, after about an hour or so of being used to send nothing but high-pitched tones, the carbon in the mouthpiece microphone can become compacted, a condition that considerably reduces its accuracy. (The solution is to rap the telephone handset gently on a table or to install a special high-performance microphone sold by some acoustic modem manufacturers.)

All of the above conditions can cause transmission and reception problems. And all of them are eliminated with a direct-connect modem. Because a direct-connect modem sends its frequencies directly into the phone lines, there is far less chance of interference.

Online Tip: Another alternative open to owners of Apple IIs, IBM/PCs, and any S-100-bus computer is a modem-on-a-card. These are communications cards with built-in modems that allow you to plug your telephone directly into your computer. Examples include the Micromodem II™ and Micromodem 100™ card from Hayes Microcomputer Products, the Apple-Cat II™ from Novation, Microperipheral's PConnection™, and PMMI's MM-103™. Prices are in the $350 to $400 range.

Online Tip: Direct-connect modems *can* be used even if no modular jack is available. You can buy a telephone extension cord with a modular plug at one end and four colored wires at the other. If you attach alligator clips to the wires, you can unscrew the mouth- and earpieces of many telephone handsets and connect the clips to the appropriate contact points. (Just follow the color scheme.) Plug the other end of the cord into the modular receptacle on your modem, and you're in business.

It's not pretty. But it works.

Speed of Transmission: 300 Baud or 1200 Baud?

The other major distinction among modems is the transmission speeds each is capable of. Transmission speed is measured in "bauds" and referred to as "baud rate." The term comes from J. M. E. Baudot, the inventor of the Baudot telegraph code, and it was originally designed to describe the transmission capabilities of a telegraph facility. Both the term and its technical definition are leftovers from those days. Technically, the baud rate is the number of signal events (the signal for a 1 bit and the signal for a 0 bit are both "events") that take place on a communications line each second.

It may not always be precisely accurate to say so, but most of the time the baud rate is equal to the number of bits transmitted per second—abbreviated, of course, as *bps*.

Online Tip: For technical reasons, each character transmitted consits of 10, not 8, bits when transmitted. Thus a rate of 300 baud divided by 10 equals 30 characters per second.

Most people could not care less. What is most important about baud rates is that there are two of them (300 baud and 1200 baud) used in most microcomputer communications, and one of them is four times faster than the other.

Some modems can send and receive at just 300 baud, others can do 0 to 300, and some can handle any rate from 0 to 1200 baud. Naturally, you pay extra for the high-speed capability. The 300-baud Hayes Smartmodem (direct connect), for example, lists for around $280, while its 1200-baud counterpart sells for close to $700. (At a *discount*, the same units may be available for about $220 and $525, respectively.) You will also be charged extra to send and receive information at 1200 baud on The Source, DJNS, or other databases.

Is 1200 Baud Worth It?

Ultimately only you can decide. But here are a few points to consider. Ideally, you should try to arrange a demonstration of *both* speeds. Seeing both speeds in action is the only way to get a real feeling for how they compare. Second, you should give some thought to how you plan to use your communications capabilities. It is very difficult to read text when it is scrolling up your screen at 1200 baud. And you will not be able to type fast enough to take advantage of the extra speed when sending from your keyboard. So if you feel that you will be communicating primarily to send and receive short electronic messages, to chat with others who are online with The Source or CompuServe, or to get news and other information, 1200 baud may not be worth the extra expense.

However, if you think you will be downloading or capturing substantial quantities of information, as might be the case when using DJNS to collect a variety of indicators on each stock in your portfolio, then 1200 baud has definite advantages. Although database charges for a 1200-baud connection are typically *twice* what they are for a 300 baud one, you obtain your information *four* times faster. A 1200-baud capability can also be very important if you will be doing a lot of uploading or sending of previously typed information directly from your disk drives. Be sure to check, though, to make sure that your disk drives can read and write at 1200 baud. Otherwise you will want to load information into a buffer and send it from there.

Clearly, if you can afford it, a 1200-baud modem can be very nice to have. But it is by no means essential. And if you elect to stay with 300 baud, you'll be in good company, since that's what the majority of people choose.

Online Tip: Many computer dealers who sell subscriptions to The Source can demonstrate that service to you. Since you are probably interested in both The Source and a modem, you might suggest to the dealer that a Source demo at both 300 baud and 1200 baud would help you with both decisions.

Originate/Answer and Full- and Half-Duplex

There are modems that will only operate in the originate mode, but there is no point in buying one. There just is not a significant price difference between "originate only" modems and "originate/answer" modems. In actual operation, you usually select the mode by throwing a switch on the modem. Most of the time you will use the originate mode to mate with the answer mode used by databases and bulletin board systems. But there will undoubtedly be times when you will need to be able to select either mode, as when sending information directly to a friend's or an associate's computer.

Full-duplex and half-duplex refer to whether or not a modem is capable of sending and receiving at the same time. Half-duplex communication is very similar to the way two people communicate on a walkie-talkie or CB radio. One person says, "This is the Great Fafad. Talk to me. *Over*." The other person says, "Oh, Great Fafad, this is Scrid. *Over*." And so on. Only one person can talk at the same time. The data communications equivalent of "Over" is a "line turnaround," and just as when talking on a radio, it causes delays.

Full-duplex communication, on the other hand, is like talking on the telephone. Both parties can send and receive simultaneously. In full-duplex communications, for example, the database computer is constantly asking your machine, "Are you ready?" and your machine is constantly responding, "Yes, I am ready." Without full-duplex, there would be a line turnaround delay between each question and answer.

Some databases can handle half-duplex communication, but all recommend full-duplex. Unless you own a Radio Shack TRS-80 Model I and want to communicate without buying an expansion interface, it is difficult to imagine a situation in which you will ever need half-duplex. Since there is virtually no difference in price, you should definitely buy a modem with full-duplex capability.

You should also make sure that the direct-connect modem you buy is approved by the Federal Communications Commission (FCC). This means that the unit is certified to meet government standards regarding the frequency and purity of the tones it generates. Certification is necessary to make sure that modems do not produce stray signals that can confuse phone-company equipment.

Online Tip: Modems all require some kind of power source. Since telephone lines operate on direct current, most modems come with an AC/DC converter that plugs into a standard electrical outlet. This is something to keep in mind when designing your "computer corner." However, at least one manufacturer (Universal Data Systems, or UDS) offers units that draw their power from the phone line. This is a nice feature, but if possible you should try such a unit before agreeing to purchase it since it might affect ordinary telephone reception in your particular area.

The modem you buy should thus offer each of the following *basic* features and capabilities:

- Direct connection to the phone line
- 300-baud communication speed (Bell 103–compatible; Bell 212A– or Racal-Vadic–compatible for 1200-baud modems)
- Originate/answer modes
- Full-duplex capability
- FCC approved

A basic modem meeting all of these qualifications will cost around $100. The battery-powered Signalman MK1 RS-232 modem by Anchor ($100) is one example, as is the DataSpeak O/A-300 ($130), manufactured by the Kesa Company of Sunnyvale, California.

Whistles and Bells

The normal procedure for using a modem is to set it to originate mode, dial the local number of the network that will connect you with the database, and wait until you hear a high-pitched tone. Then you just flip on your modem, listen for it to generate *its* tone, and hang up the phone. The word CONNECT will appear on your screen, and you'll be all set to communicate.

As with any other product, however, additional features are available at additional cost. One of the most useful of these "whistles and bells" is a collection of monitor lights. All modems provide an LED (light-emitting diode) to indicate that they are on. But many also have LEDs to indicate other things as well. Perhaps the most important of these is the one that tells you that the modem is detecting a "carrier." This means that the modem is receiving signals from a network or database and that the connection still exists—even if nothing new is appearing on your screen at the moment.

Occasionally, for example, you may type in a command to the database and have to wait for a response. If for one reason or another your connection should happen to be broken while you are waiting, you would have no way of knowing it from the screen. But if your modem has a carrier detect light, you can easily see whether you still have a connection.

Two other LEDs are particularly helpful. These are the ones that blink whenever data is being sent or received. If you ever have problems communicating, they can help you identify the cause. For example, if nothing is appearing on your screen, but the transmit data light flickers the way it should when you type, you will know that your data is getting out the door and can assume that the problem lies with the database or your correspondent.

And speaking of diagnostics and problem solving, another feature many more expensive modems offer is a self-testing capability. This feature enables the modem to "listen to itself" to make sure that everything is working as it should. It can be useful when trying out new hardware or software, but other than that you probably won't use it much. The indicator lights mentioned above will usually be enough to tell you whether the modem is operating properly.

Finally, a number of the top-of-the-line direct-connect modems in both the 300-baud and 1200-baud classifications offer an auto-answer/ auto-dial feature. "Auto-answer" means that the modem is capable of picking up the phone and generating a tone that will allow a caller to access your computer whether you are present at the time or not. "Auto-dial" means that the modem will accept commands from your computer to automatically dial the telephone.

Futuristic Fantasies?

If that in itself doesn't exactly make your mouth dry with excitement, consider just one of the possibilities. You, your computer, and your automatic modem are all in Los Angeles. You've got an associate in New

York who has a report to send you from a computer there. But you also have a date for dinner at eight. Before you go out, you switch on your computer, load in the appropriate software, and turn on your auto-answer modem.

At 11:01 PM Eastern Standard Time, when New York long-distance rates drop by 60 percent, the phone in your California pleasure dome rings. As your modem picks up the phone line, you are miles away picking up your glass of Beaujolais Jadot. Your New York associate talks to your computer and sends it the report. The report is captured and recorded on your machine's floppy disk. Then your modem hangs up the phone. After a late night frolic in your hot tub, you return to your machine, and there is the report ready and waiting.

Now suppose that your associate in New York *also* has an auto-answer/auto-dial modem, and suppose he has it connected to a digital clock. In that case, he too could turn on his equipment and go out for a night on the town. The results would be the same. The only difference would be that at 11:01, his clock-controlled *modem* would dial your number. Your two computers would then hold a deep and meaningful conversation between themselves, during which the report would be transmitted. Both machines would then hang up the phone.

This is not the stuff of futuristic fantasies. It can be done right now with a total hardware investment of about $500 per computer, using the Hayes Stack™ 300-baud Smartmodem ($280) and its companion Chronograph ($250). The Chronograph has a built-in calendar to the year 2100, making it possible for you to set your equipment to automatically dial the phone and deliver material several days or several weeks from now.

Of course none of this can take place without the proper software, and at present a completely automated process probably has little application for most people. But virtually everyone can benefit from an auto-dial feature when accessing databases and CBBSs. In its simplest form an auto-dial modem will enable you to enter telephone numbers from your keyboard, hit <ENTER>, and have the modem dial the number for you. But more elaborate alternatives are available. Software authors have been quick to take advantage of this modem feature, and many programs now exist that require only a single keystroke to both dial and sign on to a database.

What to Look For: How to Choose Your Software

The one thing all communications software or "comm programs" have in common is the ability to turn your computer or word processor into a terminal. They will make sure that your system talks ASCII and that it sends and receives information through the RS-232 port. And all of them will let you set communications parameters like baud rate, parity sense, word length, number of stop bits, and so on. You do not have to have any idea at all what these things mean to communicate effectively. All you have to do is to find out what parameters or "protocols" the database uses and set your system accordingly.

Since most online services and bulletin boards use the same parameters, you may have to set your parameters only once. Or you may have to set them every time you go online. It all depends upon the power of your communication software. Once you move beyond the basic terminal program, you enter a realm of differing features and prices. The number of features included in a comm program is limited only by the programmer's imagination, skill, and financial resources. And oddly, full-featured programs are not always more expensive than less capable ones.

If you are just entering the electronic universe, you could do far worse than to buy a program with the basic features you really need and then upgrade if necessary at a later date. The cost for such a basic program will be between $25 and $50 in most cases.

Online Tip: Andrew Fluegelman of *The Headlands Press* has a truly unique offer for IBM/PC owners. Send him a blank, formatted disk, and he will put a program called "PC-Talk" on it and return it to you. The program supports the Hayes Smartmodem and has built-in access programs for The Source and CompuServe, as well as a number of other features. You are even encouraged to copy the diskette and pass the program around. "PC-Talk" is completely free. But you and anyone using a copy of it are asked to make a small donation. If you take advantage of this offer, do your part to make this noble experiment a success and send the donation. The address is: Freeware, *The Headlands Press*, P.O. Box 862, Tiburon, CA 94920. CompuServe ID: 71435,1235.

The Most Important Features

There are three major capabilities to look at when considering a communications program. They are upload/download capability; the ease with which you can set, change, and use communications parameters; and the extras. "Upload" refers to whether or not you can say to your computer, "You have a file stored on disk called XYZ.TXT. Now, I want you to send the whole thing out the communications port when I give the word." In effect, you are loading the file or document or whatever up out of your machine and into the communications stream, and you are doing it *directly* from your disk.

This can be an important feature because it will permit you to prepare a letter or other document "offline," that is, without being connected to any communications network or database. You can correct your mistakes with your word-processing or text-editing software and record the final copy on a disk. Then, when the time and telephone rate are right, you can dial up the database or electronic mail service, and tell your system to upload the whole letter or message.

Even more important is an ability to "download" or capture the information that comes streaming in from a database and onto your screen. Inexplicably, a number of comm programs are still offered without this most essential of capabilities, so be certain to check carefully before you buy. The details depend on the equipment and the program, but virtually all programs offering this feature use some kind of "buffer." A buffer is nothing more than a "holding tank" consisting of a lot of microchips in your machine. Usually the program will allow you to open and close the buffer using commands from your keyboard. This makes it possible for you to selectively capture incoming data instead of having to take it all. Obviously, the program should let you do this quickly and easily. If it does not, you should consider a different comm package.

When you are finished and have disconnected from the communications network, you can "write the buffer to disk." That is, you can tell your machine to take all the information in the buffer and record it on a floppy disk under whatever filename you please. At your convenience, you can then list the file to take another look at it, or you can use a word-processing program to put it into whatever format you like.

An ability to download incoming information is probably *the* most important feature to look for in a communications program. However, as a second-best alternative, make sure that the program you are considering will support a printer. This means that the program will give you the option of turning your printer on or off. When on, the printer will print out each line exactly as it appears on your screen, and at the same time that it appears. This will at least give you a "hard copy" (a printed record) of the information you have received.

Online Tip: Upload and download capability can save you a lot of money, depending upon how and how much you use online services. Preparing a letter offline and then uploading it to a database or electronic mail system obviously requires less time than typing it while you are online. Since you are charged by the amount of time you spend online, the savings are clear.

Download capabilities can be even more cost effective. Once you have some experience, for example, you can be in and out of a database very quickly without worrying about reading all of the information as it scrolls up your screen. You can simply download it and read it later at your leisure. Remember, if you can communicate at 1200 baud, you will usually be charged only twice the 300-baud rate but take in information four times as fast.

In addition, CompuServe, The Source, DIALOG, and other databases all allow you to store information on their systems. But of course you are charged for that service. If you can download the information you want (and upload it later), you can maintain your own files on your *own* diskettes and avoid storage costs.

The second main area of consideration concerns the setting and ease of use of communications parameters or protocols. Setting protocols is analagous to adjusting the color, brightness, contrast, and other dials or knobs on your television set. The key point to remember is that *your* protocol settings must match the setting of whomever you are communicating with.

For example, the literature you receive from The Source may specify "No parity." Your communications program will at some point ask you something on the order of "Parity: (Enter E for Even, O for Odd, N for None)." All you have to do is hit <N> for None, and that's that. The same procedure applies to all the other settings.

The question is: How easily can you get to that point in the program? Will you have to set your parity and other parameters *every* time you want to use a database, or can the program *record* your settings for The Source and CompuServe on disk after you have entered them the first time and use them automatically every time thereafter? Finally, how involved a procedure is it—can you change settings "on the fly" (while you are actually online), or must you disconnect first and call back later?

These are the kinds of points to look into when considering this portion of a communications program. One word of caution is appropriate here, however, and that concerns the *number* of parameters the software will allow you to set. You will have to set the baud rate, regardless of the system or software you are using. And you will probably also have to tell your system whether you want full- or half-duplex communications, the type of parity, the word or character length, the number of stop bits, and whether or not you want your keyboard characters echoed (displayed) to the screen. The actual selection will depend upon your system and software "default" values—the settings it uses automatically, in the absence of human intervention.

The trouble is, many of the more powerful programs ask you to determine a lot of other settings as well. This wide range of choice is part of their power, for in the hands of a technical expert such programs can accomplish amazing things. But for the average user, they serve only to confuse matters. And in many cases the manuals supplied with the software make things worse. If you don't already know how to set a loop-timing value, for example, you cannot necessarily count on the manual to tell you.

The ideal program feature when it comes to the setting of protocols, for most people, is one that will allow you to select just the basic parameters for communicating with a given database, and record them so you never have to worry about them again. Some programs even come with the protocols for CompuServe and The Source already recorded, allowing you to hit a single key that tells the machine which service you want to talk to.

What Else *Can We Add?*

Computer programmers at their best are true artists, with all the creativity and imagination that this implies. Sometimes their most notable achievements are visible only to other programmers as they parse the strange codes of their trade. But sometimes their inventiveness shows up quite clearly at the user end as an extra capability here or a unique feature there in the software they create.

This is exactly the case with communications programs. There are so many programs with so many extra features that it is almost as if every software house in the country had asked, "Yes, I know we already do this and that, but what *else* can we add?" Not that one should complain; more features ultimately mean more power and greater convenience. But their number can nevertheless make choosing the right program something of a challenge.

Of all the various extras you might look for in a comm program, an auto log-in feature is the one you will probably appreciate most. Usually it is combined with an auto-dial module for use with an auto-dial modem, if you have one. If not, the log-in feature can be used after you have manually dialed the phone.

Here is how it works. Whenever you log in or "sign on" to a database, there are a number of pieces of information you must supply. For example, when you dial your local GTE Telenet access number to access the Dow Jones News/Retrieval Service, here is what you will see:

```
CONNECT                         <----- Hit <ENTER> twice.

TELENET
609 17A
```

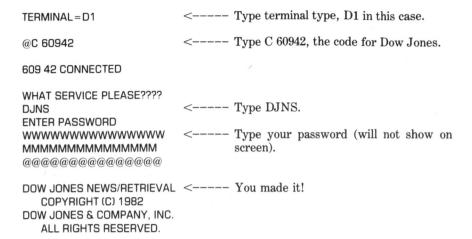

TERMINAL = D1   <----- Type terminal type, D1 in this case.

@C 60942   <----- Type C 60942, the code for Dow Jones.

609 42 CONNECTED

WHAT SERVICE PLEASE????
DJNS   <----- Type DJNS.
ENTER PASSWORD
WWWWWWWWWWWWWWW   <----- Type your password (will not show on
MMMMMMMMMMMMMMMM   screen).
@@@@@@@@@@@@@@@

DOW JONES NEWS/RETRIEVAL <----- You made it!
   COPYRIGHT (C) 1982
DOW JONES & COMPANY, INC.
   ALL RIGHTS RESERVED.

This looks complicated, and admittedly it is not the easiest thing in the world the first time through. Fortunately, Dow Jones and nearly everybody else in the industry is working to create simpler log-in procedures. But until these new procedures appear, it can be awfully nice to be able to let your computer handle the whole thing.

Typically you will "configure" the software once, using a special part of the program. You will enter all of the log-in information, including the phone number if you have an auto-dial modem. After you have checked it, your machine will record it on the program disk. From then on, your system will log you in to the database automatically whenever you tell it to. Most programs with this feature will allow you to record *several* log-in sequences, but if you plan to use a lot of databases, it is worth checking for the exact number the program will permit.

Online Tip: Very important. If you are interested in a program with an auto-dial feature *and* you plan to use MCI, ITT, or any of the other alternative long-distance telephone services, be sure that the program you are considering can accommodate the 24 or more digits you will have to dial when using these services.

The more feature-filled programs usually cost around $100 to $150. Here are just some of the capabilities they include:

• Optional line feed control. Tells you tell your printer to space up one line each time it receives an <ENTER> or <RETURN> from your correspondent. Often a standard feature.

- Buffer status report. Lets you check how much room is left in your "holding tank."

- Buffer auto-dump. Automatically pauses to write the contents of the buffer to disk when the buffer is full.

- Translation tables. Lets you convert one or more incoming characters so that they are displayed on your screen as something else. A second table will let you do the same thing to the characters you transmit.

- Programmable keys. Lets you send ASCII code numbers for characters that are not on your keyboard. Some keyboards, for example, have no keys for square brackets. With this feature, however, you can program a key or keys to transmit the ASCII codes that will cause "[" or "]" to appear on your correspondent's display.

- Ability to transmit command files. Command files are computer programming that cannot be sent without a feature like this.

- A simple computer bulletin board. Fully equipped bulletin board programs are sold separately (see Chapter 7). However, some comm programs offer a very basic bulletin board capability as an extra feature.

Online Tip: Some programs, available from several companies, are specifically designed to access the Dow Jones News/Retrieval Service. This type of program usually has two features. The first allows you to record a list of the stocks you want to follow and to specify certain indicators. Once the list is set up, the program will automatically dial and sign on to DJNS. It will then automatically enter the commands needed to retrieve the information you seek.

The second feature is designed to be used offline. It will use your computer's power to analyze the information you have retrieved and print out one or more reports reflecting this analysis. Dow Jones & Company itself markets this kind of software, as do IBM and other manufacturers.

Online Tip: If you use VisiCalc ™ or other spreadsheet programs, you may want to look for a communications program that will allow you to send and receive VisiCalc ™ files. You may also want to be able to send and receive graphs and charts.

Data Resources, Inc. (DRI), of Lexington, Massachusetts, (617) 861-0165, and Visicorp, Inc., (408) 946-9000, have developed a program (VisiLink) to directly download information into VisiCalc™ files. Microcom (1400A Providence Highway, Norwood, Massachusetts 02062, 617-762-9310) offers a general comm program called MICRO-Courier™ for Apples, the TRS-80 Model III, and the IBM/PC that will let you transfer such files. The program sells for $100 to $150, depending upon the computer. And SSM Microcomputer Products, Inc. (2190 Paragon Drive, San Jose, California 95134, 800-227-2400) offers its Transend™ program for Apples. The cost is $89 and it may include a free subscription to The Source.

These are just some of the extra features that are available. Whether any or all of them are likely to be valuable to you is something only you can decide.

Read the Reviews!

Finally, there are so many different products available from so many different sources that it will be impossible to see a demonstration of each one before you make your selection. Consequently, before you buy *any* hardware or software product, it always pays to check the reviews published in the various computer magazines. You will find a list of many major consumer-oriented computer publications in the Appendices. Since one review may highlight one product feature, while another review focuses on a different feature, you should try to read a number of them before making up your mind.

Online Tip: Computer magazines must of necessity focus on the latest in an unending stream of new products. Consequently, you may have to look at back issues to find information on the communications hardware and software you are considering. Check to see if your library has a copy of the *Microcomputer Index* published by Microcomputer Information Services in Santa Clara, California. This publication will help you locate any article published in over 21 microcomputer magazines from 1980 to the present. If it is not available, try the *Reader's Guide to Periodical Literature* or ask your librarian for help. Many magazines in the field regularly sell copies of back issues, so if the one you are looking for is not available at your library you might try the publisher. Or if there are computer clubs or computer user groups in your area, it is better than even money that one of the members will have a copy of the issue you want.

Other Useful Information

A number of unrelated points have not been given a section of their own in this book, but are nevertheless worth knowing or thinking about. And here they are.

Find an Expert. Your need for support—help, advice, information, and so on—will vary with your knowledge and experience. You will rarely encounter any really serious problems. But if you do, or even if you are just curious about a certain aspect of communications, it is great to have someone to call upon. This is a good reason to develop a good relationship with a *knowledgeable* computer dealer. Dealerships being what they are at present, this can take some doing. But talking to a store's technical people or in-house communications expert is an excellent way to start.

Telenet, Tymnet, and Other Packet-Switching Networks. We have not said much about the networks that provide you with access to the different databases and online services. All you really need to know is that they enable you to dial what is usually a local telephone number to access any database anywhere in the country. Each has a slightly different sign-on procedure involving a code for the type of computer equipment you are using and a code to tell the network which database you want to be connected to. Lists of these codes, and step-by-step presentations of the sign on procedure for each network, are provided by all databases.

Logging Off a Database. All databases have a procedure for signing off as well as signing on. When you are finished using The Source, for example, you simply type the word OFF. The DJNS equivalent is: DISC (for "disconnect"). Logging or signing off is important because it closes the book on your session with the database and, not incidentally, stops the meter from running on your connect-time charges.

But what happens if you are accidentally disconnected without officially logging off? Well, this is not a serious problem thanks to something called "polling." All database computers are constantly checking to see if their customers are online. But they can't do this all at once. Instead, the database computer periodically cycles through all current connections, checking or polling each for online activity. If the computer comes around to your connection and nothing is happening, *it* will log you off the system and stop the meter.

If there is no activity from a connection within two minutes on DJNS, the computer will disconnect. On CompuServe, the period is 15 minutes.

And on The Source, it is three minutes. Consequently, disconnecting without officially signing off will not have a major impact on your connect charges.

Computer-to-Computer Connections. Almost without exception, any two microcomputers that are equipped to go online can also be directly connected to one another. Because telephone lines are not involved, no modems are required. But you *will* need a crossover or "null-modem" cable to make the connection. This makes sure that each machine's output signals go into the other's input port. If the two computers are identical makes and models, a simple connection should do the trick. But if they are made by different manufacturers or are different models from the same manufacturer, you will also need to know the "pin out" of each computer. This tells you what signals it sends and receives on what plug pins.

This sounds complicated, but it can definitely be worth doing, particularly if you are one of the growing number of businesspeople who own a *portable* computer. Making a direct connection will allow you to transfer files from a communicating word processor or computer at your office into your own machine, enabling you to work with them at home, on an airplane, or anywhere else. In addition, since no telephone connections are involved, you may be able to transfer information at a speed as high as 9600 baud.

See Chapter 12 for an overview of how to accomplish this task. Then contact a technical support person for the specific details that apply to your machine.

Prestel and Video- or Telewhatever. Your biggest problem with connecting your microcomputer to Prestel and similar services may well be figuring out whether what you are seeing is "videotex" or "teletext." It is possible to read articles in reputable publications that define these terms in contradictory ways.

Prestel, CEEFAX, Antiope, and other services are European systems similar to the information utilities. There are lots of differences, of course, but basically, these services are designed to turn your home TV set into an information center. Delivered by cable, by telephone, or by broadcast waves, the services come into your home as signals that must be decoded and displayed. This is usually done by a device supplied by the service, but it can also be done by your microcomputer.

Prestel, the system developed by British Telecom, is designed to come in over the telephone lines. It is the first such system to be offered in the United States, but more are coming. For more information on Prestel, contact the firm's American representative: Logica, Inc., 666

Third Avenue, New York, New York 10017, (212) 599-0828.

Prestel software and adapters are already available for the Apple II ($85), the TRS-80 Model III ($50), and the IBM/PC. An IBM/PC must have at least 64K, two disk drives, and an RGB color monitor; a special circuit board ($600) is required as well. For more information on the IBM equipment, contact Wolfdata, Inc., P.O. Box 31, Ithaca, New York 14850.

It May Be Tax-deductible! Finally, if you will be using your system to obtain information or send electronic mail associated with your business, you may be able to depreciate your hardware and deduct your online charges. As in all tax matters, it is best to check with your accountant or tax advisor.

The Electronic Universe Survival Kit

In addition to your hardware and software, there are a few very common items that can make your life online even more productive and rewarding. The first is a pen and a pad of paper. There will be lots of things you will want to jot down while you're connected to a database, such as:

• The names and account numbers of people you meet while on The Source or CompuServe. These numbers are the addresses you will use to send them electronic mail (see Appendix E).

• Notes on points you want to be certain to mention in the letters you send. This can be important because it is more efficient to enter the CIS or Source electronic mail modules once, and send all of your letters at that time, than to go in and out of the system's mail module every time you think of someone you want to write.

• Ideas. Lots of ideas. Sometimes being online can be like going to an amusement park with a lot of rides and attractions you want to be sure to visit before you leave. This is particularly true with the information utilities. Then too, sometimes things are more business-like.

For example, suppose you are online with DJNS reading a *Wall Street Journal* story about the machine-tool industry. That is your primary interest at the time, but in the course of the story some company is mentioned that looks like an interesting investment possibility. You decide that you would like more information on the firm and the trading history of its stock. So you make a note to check it after you have finished. Being online is a stimulating experience. If you do not make notes like this you can easily be distracted by some new piece of information or idea.

• Search strategies and "To-do's." Before signing on to an encyclopedic database, you will definitely want to make some notes on the key words you plan to use as your search criteria. Preparing a list of the things you want to do during a particular online session is an excellent idea before signing on to any database.

The second thing you should have is a database notebook—or several notebooks, one for each database you regularly access. You will always be downloading material or printing out information as it comes in while you're online. Over time this printed material can mount up. A notebook is the best way to keep track of it. Separated by dividers, the sections might contain printouts of your online electronic correspondence, the online instructions and documentation you have downloaded for various features, and so on. Be sure to set your printer to allow extra space on the left side of the paper for the notebook holes.

A third item that you will find extremely useful is an online address book. You will be meeting a lot of new people on The Source and CompuServe, and each one of them will have an electronic mail address. Source addresses look like this: TCA123. CompuServe's look like this: 71234,567. You'll be able to find an alphabetically tabbed telephone/ address book at most stationery stores for about $5.00. Buy one and then use it exclusively for your online correspondents.

It may also be a good idea to use one or more floppy disks exclusively for your online work. If you subscribe to several services, you should have a separate disk for each. This will make it much easier for you to locate the information you have downloaded when you need it.

Finally, if you don't already have one, you might want to consider buying a word-processing software package some time in the future. This will make it easy for you to "massage" the textual material that you download by removing unwanted words, reformatting paragraphs, moving blocks of text around, and so on. Some of the newer communications software programs include a text-editing or word-processing capability, but most are still designed solely for communications. It's yet another point to look into.

But right now, let's take a look at each of the major databases that are available to you now that your computer can talk to the outside world. The next five chapters will give you a clearer view of each database, what it has to offer, and how to use it most effectively.

...3...

The Source
"America's Information Utility"

Athena, the ancient Greek goddess of wisdom, the mind, and self-realization, is said to have sprung from the head of Zeus like a fully formed thought, complete and majestic in full armor. Something of the same order might be said about The Source, the information utility now owned and operated by the *Reader's Digest* Association. For all intents and purposes, The Source just miraculously appeared one day: a powerful, completely developed, round-the-clock information utility with all the features and enhancements one might reasonably expect such an organization to offer by the mid- or late 1980s—but not before.

It did not really happen that quickly, of course. But there can be no denying that The Source has always been far ahead of its time, and even in the fast-moving world of microcomputers and information services, the industry is only now beginning to catch up with it.

Based just outside of Washington, D.C., in the high-tech town of McLean, Virginia, The Source began life in June 1979 as the Telecomputing Corporation of America. These origins are still reflected in the older Source account numbers, all of which begin with the letters TCA, but there have been many changes since then. After a turbulent 15 months of wrestling with all of the standard difficulties of starting a new business, plus the myriad challenges of creating a completely new concept, the founders sold their business to *Reader's Digest* in the fall of 1980.

The company was renamed Source Telecomputing Corporation (STC), and *Reader's Digest*—the world's leading information repackager and marketer—set about pouring millions of dollars and all of its considerable expertise into making the "information utility" concept an economically viable reality. New features and services were added. A distribution network was created. A manual that deserves some sort of an award for its clarity and completeness was designed and produced.

In short, by August 1981, less than a year after *Reader's Digest* acquired The Source, all the components of a complete, full-feature information utility were in place. What was *not* in place at that point, however, was a sufficient number of personal computer-owning subscribers to access the wonders it had to offer. In 1979, the year The Source was founded, personal computer sales totalled some 535,000 units, according to the International Data Corporation. By the end of 1981, an additional 800,000 units had been sold.

The Source and its parent company waited. Losses mounted, but additional features were added and more improvements were made. Then the personal computer phenomenon caught fire, and in 1982, with computer cover stories appearing in nearly all major magazines, and with nearly two million units sold in that year alone, things began to change.

By the end of 1982, The Source could point to over 25,000 subscribers and a growth rate of over 1000 new subscriptions per month. To accommodate both current and future subscribers, a new 6100-square-foot computer center was established in September 1982. The center houses nine Prime 750 computers running under an improved and unified operating system, and it gives The Source the capacity to handle up to a quarter of a million subscribers. More than 100 direct dial and WATS lines were added to supplement the Telenet and Tymnet networks used by most of its subscribers. And to speed the delivery of United Press International news from UPI headquarters in Dallas, a UPI Series 6100 satellite dish was installed.

Today computer owners everywhere are learning what a small band of pioneer subscribers have known all along: There is nothing like The Source anywhere else in the world. It is truly an information utility *sui generis*.

What's Available on the System?

The Source offers over 1200 features and programs designed to appeal to a broad spectrum of interests and needs. Subscribers can take advantage of at least six different communications options, including a sophisticated electronic mail system that will not only deliver your letters to you the moment you sign on (if you so choose), but also allow you to send mass mailings to 200 or more other subscribers with a few keystrokes. Investors will find a full range of current information on stocks, bonds, and commodities, including an option to have their portfolios automatically updated and presented at sign-on. Businesspeople will find a wealth of economic, political, and trade information, as well as an option to set up their own corporate database/messaging systems through The Source's Private Sector.

Computer owners and game players, soap opera fans and travelers, poets and writers, people who like to talk to mainframe computers and people who just like to talk—all will find something of interest and value on The Source. It would be impossible to cover all 1200 Source features and programs and still have room for additional chapters. Therefore, what follows is a survey of some of the most popular and outstanding offerings. At the end of this survey, we will show you how to sign up and what it will cost to put these features at your command.

Communications

• Electronic Mail ("SMAIL" or "SourceMail"). One of the most powerful electronic mail systems available anywhere. Each subscriber has an electronic "mailbox" addressed by account number. Read and send letters, of course. But also file in your online storage area. Scan by complete subject heading, scan by key word in subject heading, by account number, or by date. Send letters "express." Request notification of when letter was read by recipient. And more. Probably the most popular of all Source features. *Everybody* likes to get mail, and SourceMail makes it easy to send an immediate reply.

• User Directory. Called DISEARCH for "directory search." Lets you search for other users by account number, first name, state or Canadian province, or key "interest" word (for instance, VisiCalc, telecommunications, Commodore, and so on). Directory listings are purely voluntary. Add, delete, or edit your own listing with companion program DIRECTADD (directory add). Good way to find electronic pen pals. See "The Synergistic Possibilities" later in this chapter.

• Bulletin Board. Called POST. Over 80 categories ranging from aircraft to Zenith. Types of messages limited only by imagination and good taste. Can be help wanted or just plain HELP! with a particular computer or noncomputer problem. Offers to sell, buy, announcements, and so on. Bulletin board is keyword scannable. (See Figure 3.1 for a listing of Source bulletin board categories.)

• Suggestion Box. Called SUGBOX. Send your ideas, comments, or criticisms to The Source staff. Also possible to propose computer games and other services you might want to offer in association with The Source.

—— **Figure 3.1. Source Bulletin Board Categories (POST).** ——

AIRCRAFT	INFOX
ANTIQUES	LANIER
APARTMENTS-RENT	LIBRARY-FORUM
APPLE	MERCHANDISE
ART	MUSIC
ASTROLOGY	NEC
ATARI	NOVATION
AUTOMOBILES-DOMESTIC	OFFICE-EQUIPMENT
AUTOMOBILES-FOREIGN	OSBORNE
AVIATION	OSI
BASIC	OVERSEAS
BULLETIN-BOARD	PARTI
BUSINESSES	PASCAL
CADO	PERSONAL
CBM/PET-COMPUTERS	PETS
CHATTER	PHILIPS
CLUBS	PHOTOGRAPHY
COLLECTIBLES	POLITICS
COMMODORE	PROPERTY/HOUSES-RENT
CP/M	PROPERTY/HOUSES-SALE
CPT	PROPERTY/HOUSES-SWAP
DATING	PROPERTY/HOUSES-WANTED
DEC	PUBLIC-FILES
DOCUMENTATION	PUZZLES
ENGINEERING	RKO-FORUM
FAIRS-AND-FESTIVALS	SATELLITE/TV
FORTRAN	SAYINGS
GAMES	SERVICES
GRIPES	SOAP-OPERAS
HAM-RADIO	SOFTWARE-SALE
HARDWARE-RENT	SOFTWARE-WANTED
HARDWARE-SALE	SOURCE
HARDWARE-WANTED	SPORTS
HAYES	STEREO/TV
HEATH	STUDENTS-CORNER
HELP-WANTED	TI-99/4
HEWLETT-PACKARD	TRAVEL
HOBBIES-AND-CRAFTS	TRS-80
HUG	USER-PUBLISHING
IBM	VIDEO

Figure 3.1 continued

VISICALC	XEROX
WANG	ZENITH
WEEKEND-GETAWAY	

- Online Manual Ordering. Lets you order Source manuals for advanced computer programming and other specialized functions. Manuals may also be ordered by calling Customer Service toll-free.

- CHAT. You can get an on-screen listing of every account number currently online, then type in command like CHAT TCA123. System will notify TCA123 that you would like to chat. CHAT can be automatically or selectively refused. Or begun. Permits real-time conversations with others online, often for less than cost of phone call. Can also be used to contact and converse with online Customer Service monitor. (If you need online help, type CHAT TCA088. Or phone Customer Service at 800-336-3300.) Exciting. You never know who you'll meet. Most users simply pick a number from the list of those online.

- Voicegram. Call (703) 734-7500 in Virginia, (800) 336-3330 in other states and provinces. Give operator your account number and password and account number of subscriber you want to send message to. Then dictate your message. Electronic mail will be sent as if you were entering it at your own terminal.

- Mailgram™. Combined Western Union-Source service. Type in a letter at your computer terminal and send it via Western Union Mailgram™. If entered prior to 4:00 PM EST, next-day delivery is virtually guaranteed, even for Alaska and Hawaii. (See Appendix C for more information.)

- PARTI. For "PARTICIPATE." Sophisticated, full-featured, online computerized conferencing for both closed and open-to-all groups. (See Chapter 10 for more information.)

- Newsletters. Found in the PUBLIC FILES or User Publishing section of The Source. (Type PUBLIC at the Source command level.) Independently produced. No charge for reading, but producers receive a royalty from The Source for each user-minute spent reading their creations. Typical newsletter titles include *Apple City, Applesource, The IBM/PC Gazette, Product Reviews,* and *SAUG Maga-*

zine (SAUG is short for Source Apple Users Group). News and information on various brands of computer equipment also available on bulletin board (POST).

News and Information

- United Press International Newswire. News, weather, sports, and more. Stories available two and one-half minutes after being filed by reporter or columnist. Scan hundreds of stories, features, and syndicated columns by keyword(s). Read forward or backward in time (oldest to latest story, or vice versa). With a little practice, you can make this feature give you everything from your hometown high school football scores to plot summaries of the week's soap operas.

- Political Action Report (PAR). Articles, essays, and interviews with the movers and shakers of the world.

- Electronic Magazines. Abstracts from nearly 30 major magazines and journals from Management Contents, Ltd. (See next section.)

Business-related Information and Services

- Commodity News Service (CNS). Tracks news and price activity on all major commodity exchanges. News wire section includes news; bulletins; weather; agricultural, economic, and political reports; and prices of treasury bills, commercial paper, and other financial instruments. Available at regular Source hourly rates. Price wire also available at extra cost. Prices updated every ten minutes.

- Market Quotes. From the UPI Unistox service. Stocks, bonds, commodities, money markets, metals, government paper, and so on. Daily averages from 11:00 AM to closing from NYSE, AMEX, and OTC. No extra charge for quotes.

- STOCKVUE. An extra-cost service provided by Media General Financial Services. Retrieve historical and current information on over 4000 stocks. Order the system to automatically compare and rank them on the basis of performance in 58 categories (earnings per share, P/E ratios, betas up and down, and so on).

- Create Your Own Portfolios. Using your storage space on The Source, you can create a file or files containing the symbols of any number of stocks. Then when using Unistox or Stockvue you need only type in the name of your portfolio file to get an update. No need to type in each stock name each time. Also, you can use special Source files to tell the system to automatically update your portfolio the moment you sign on.

• Raylux Financial Commentary and Raylux Business Outlook. Commentaries from registered investment advisors. Business outlooks from economists and stock market strategists and reports of federal and private institutions.

• *U.S. News & World Report* Washington Letter. An electronic edition of the printed version, available online at 8:30 AM EST each Monday. Brief concentrated stories on investment opportunities, economic trends, government and regulatory activities, and other developments likely to affect business and investments.

• Management Contents, Ltd. Online abstracts from *Forbes*, the *Futurist*, *Medical Economics*, the *Harvard Business Review*, *Venture*, *Vital Speeches*, and 21 other publications. A subset of the complete Management Contents service (500 journals), this extra-cost database dates from January 1981. And it is keyword searchable. Updated weekly. Hard copy of complete articles mailed on request. Article can be sent to you via facsimile machine *immediately* if you want.

• Compudex. A series of programs designed to put computational power of The Source's Prime computers at the disposal of businesspeople. Based upon your input, will calculate income statements, present value of up to four cashflows, cost of equity capital, and the like. Output reports can be filed on the system and sent to others via SMAIL.

• Model 1. A "what-if?" spreadsheet program for use in analyzing actual or hypothetical business performance. Free Model 1 manual available. User-friendly, but some basic knowledge of programming required.

• INFOX. Online data file management system for use in preparing payroll, personnel records, accounts receivable, inventory control, expense reporting, income statements, and other traditional business functions. Manual package and pocket reference guide available for $26.95.

• Private Sector. Customized, closed user groups. For an additional fee, The Source will help you establish a mechanism for delivering electronic messages and newsletters to members of your group. Also, set up private database or online library, member directory, bulletin board, and so on. The Source can develop special software, if needed, or advise you on creating your own for use on the system.

Personal Computing Information and Services

- Information, tips, advice, and updates on hardware and software available through user-published magazines and newsletters in the PUBLIC section. In addition, there is a bulletin-board category for nearly every major computer and word processor manufacturer. No Source- or manufacturer-supported newsletters, however.

- Software—Free and For Sale. No formal, Source-sponsored software sales, but there is at least one user-published catalogue of software for sale, and Source subscribers regularly exchange software among themselves online.

- Personal Filing Cabinet. Each Source subscriber automatically receives 4K of online storage on the system. Equivalent to approximately eight double-spaced typed pages. As part of the "account maintenance minimum," users are billed $1.00 a month for this space. Additional storage is available in 2K blocks, billed on a sliding scale that ranges from 50¢ to 5¢ per block. Useful for filing mailing lists, letters, programs, your stock portfolio, and anything else that you will use frequently. Saves you the trouble of re-keyboarding information each time.

- Programming. The Source offers computer programmers the opportunity to use its Prime computers to write and execute programs in BASIC/VM, Fortran 66, and Pascal. Manuals for each language are available at $19.95 each. Order online or by mail.

- Standard Programs. The Source offers a large number of standard programs for investors, home owners, scientists, engineers, and statisticians. Examples include calculating the after-tax yield-to-maturity of a bond, balancing a checking account, and computing a geometric mean and standard deviation. In all cases the user merely enters the required information and figures as prompted, and the system does the rest.

- The Source Editor. A powerful online word processor that will allow you to create, edit, and format text. In addition, you may execute a "global search and replace" routine to remove one word or name and insert another wherever it occurs in the text, order the system to sort a list, and select a mode in which every line is numbered. At your request, the system will even check your spelling for you. Although the program is well-documented in The Source Manual, an additional guide for new users ($19.95) is recommended to get the most out of the program. It will take you a while to master it, but if you don't have a word-processing program, it will be worth the effort.

• Automatic Placement at Sign-On. Your activities on The Source can be automated to an astounding degree. By taking full advantage of the various specialized files at your disposal, you can arrange to have your mail, the latest news on a particular subject, the current value of the stocks in your portfolio, or anything else automatically appear as soon as you sign on. (See "For the Experienced User" later in this chapter.)

If you like, you can arrange to have each of these things done—automatically—in succession. Or you can set things up so that while you are reading your mail or doing something else, the system will automatically be updating your portfolio or searching for news stories and placing the output in one of your files for you to look at later.

Education and Careers

• Interactive Drills and Instruction. A wide variety of quizzes and drills developed by the *Reader's Digest* Educational Division. Subjects include foreign languages, mathematics, language arts, college-level geography, and special programs for children. The system asks you questions, and you answer. Then it tells you whether you are right or wrong and, if appropriate, provides the correct answer.

• Collegecash. A directory and index of available grants, loans, scholarships, and financial aid packages for college students.

• The Career Network. Offered through The Source by Computer Search International, this service has two sections: Jobs and Resumes. Both are divided into approximately 40 categories. And both can be keyword searched for salary requirements, geographic location, job title, professional certification, size of business, and the like. The Career Network itself consists of several hundred executive recruiting firms across the country, and all actual employer/applicant contact and fees are arranged through them. There is no charge for placing your resume on the system, although this too must be handled by one of the member firms.

Online Shopping

- Comp-U-Store Division of Comp-U-Card. Online access to description and prices of over 50,000 products offered at discounts from 10 to 40 percent. (See Chapter 9 for more information on electronic shopping.)

- Other Services. MusicSource offers a large number of records and cassette tapes at a discount. RadioSource offers classic radio programs on tape. The Source's Professional Book Center offers over 600,000 titles. Will notify you by mail if a book is out of print, in which case the order is canceled. No charge.

    And a firm called Barter Worldwide, Inc., offers its services via The Source to bring together individuals and companies with something to trade (see Chapter 9).

Computer Conferencing

- PARTI. For "PARTICIPATE." A powerful teleconferencing program provided by Participation Systems, Inc., of Boston. Topics under discussion may range from management information systems and executives online to science fiction and software. You automatically receive the most recent contributions to any conference you have joined each time you enter PARTI on The Source, a fact not lost on participants in "Laughs," the PARTI conference on the latest jokes. Laughs aside, PARTI is so much fun and so useful that, once more people hear about it, it is destined to become one of the most popular services offered by The Source. (For more information on PARTI and computer conferencing, please see Chapter 10.)

Fun and Games

- Airline Schedules. AIRSCHED-D will provide an up-to-date listing of all domestic flights between the American, Canadian, or Mexican cities you specify, including departure and arrival times, flight numbers, type of plane, meals, and any stops in between. AIRSCHED-I will do the same thing for international flights. And CITY CON (-D and -I) will do it for connecting flights between cities or towns with no direct flights. Quick and convenient. And unlike the airline-supplied services used by travel agents, there is no built-in bias.

- Restaurant Guides and Reviews. Mobil Restaurant Guide includes over 6000 listings in 1800 U.S. and Canadian cities and towns. Keyword searchable by city and state, type of food, type of entertainment, and so on. Printout provides review, driving directions, price range, credit card information, and phone number. Additional database: Washington Metro Restaurant Guide.

• New York City Guide. What to do, where to go, how to get there, what it costs. Keyword searchable. Restaurants, art galleries, museums, specialty stores, boutiques, theater, cultural events . . . even "The Swinging Scene." Name, address, phone, review, tips, advice. Great for get away-weekend planning.

• Reservations for hotels, airlines, car rental, and tours. Free service. Make reservations from your terminal. Charge them on your credit card. Can pick up tickets at airline terminal or have them mailed to you.

• Movie Reviews. From Cineman Syndicate. Updated weekly. Capsule (about 80 words) reviews. Keyword searchable (film title, director, actor, subject matter, and so on). Reviews are subjective, of course, but seem to be generally on target.

• Over 60 Online Games. From Star Trek to Stocks, from Hunt the Wumpus to the Civil War simulation. Adventure (in regular and advanced versions), Pits, Othello, and Mastermind. (See Figure 3.2 for a complete list.)

——————————— **Figure 3.2. Games on The Source.** ———————————

Name	*Description*
ADVENTURE	Adventure (Unique and addicting)
ADV550	Adventure (Advanced version, expanded to 550 pts.)
AUTOBRID	Autobridge (Teaches bridge according to Goren)
BACKGAMMON	Backgammon
BACKGAMN	Another backgammon game
BIORHYTHM	Make a Biorhythm chart
BLACKDRAGON	Intrigue beyond belief!
BLACKJACK	Casino-style 21
CHECKERS	Game of checkers against the computer
CIVILWAR	Civil War simulation against the computer
COIN	Coin flipping

CRAPS	Shoot craps
DATES	Statistics concerning a particular date
DIGITS	The computer tries to guess the next number in a sequence
DODGEM	Two sets of pieces race across a board
ESTIC	Tic-Tac-Toe in Spanish
FARMER	Get the farmer, fox, chicken, and grain safely across
FOOTBALL	Monday Night Football
FROGS	Reverse two sets of pieces
GOLF	Golf for one or more players
GRIDIRON	Play football against the computer
GUESS	Guess the computer's number
HANGMAN	Hangman word game
HMRABI	Govern ancient Sumeria
HORSE	Horse race game
ICHING	A source for divination and guidance
IQTEST	IQ game of skill
KING	Govern the island of Setats Detinu
LEARN 21	A variation of the game of Nim
LGOLF	Large game of golf
LIFE	Life (colony generation)
LUNAR	Lunar landing simulation
MARKET	Companies compete to sell a product
MAZE	A maze generator
MIND	Mastermind
NIM	Ancient game of Nim
NIM2	Another Nim
ONEARM	Care to try your luck on the slot machine?
ONE-QUEEN	Compete against the computer moving a chess queen
OTHELLO	Game of Othello against the computer
PICA	Pica-Centre (Number-guessing game)
PITS	A NEW fantasy and exploration game
POETRY	Random poetry
POKER	Poker against computer
POSTER	Create a poster of 5×7 characters
PRINTWIZ	An easy to use poster message system
QUBIC	Game of Tic-Tac-Toe on a $4 \times 4 \times 4$ cube
QUEST	A very limited game (Not much fun)
RESCUE	You command a rescue starship
ROMAN	Convert decimal number to Roman numerals

Figure 3.2 continued

Name	Description
RUMMY	Play 500-Rummy against the computer
SINNERS	Compete against satan with sinners
SKETCH	Etch-a-sketch for the Tektronix 4010
SLALOM	Simulates a slalom run with you as skier
SONNET	Random Shakespearean sonnets (Weird)
SPLGAM	Fill in the missing letters
STARTREK	Star Trek
STOCKS	Play the stock market
SUMER	Rule ancient Sumeria (A different one)
SUPERBJ	Blackjack at its finest!
TARGET	Command a gun crew to destroy a fixed target
TARGET-M	Command a gun crew to destroy a moving target
TARGT2	Target practice as weapons officer on the *Enterprise*
TICTACTOE	Tic-Tac-Toe
TORO	Simulates a bullfight with you as matador
VEGAS	A regular casino of games from Las Vegas
WATCHMAN	You are a watchman patrolling a village
WHEEL	Roulette for up to seven people
WUMPUS	Hunt the wumpus
YEARS	Print a calendar for any year after 1582

- PRINTWIZ. Generates posters with page-size letters. Any text you specify. A variety of formats. Can be downloaded to your own system, printed out as it comes over the phone, stored in your online file cabinet, or all three. Neat way to amaze your friends and bring confusion to your enemies!

Other Features and Services

- Information On Demand (IOD). Independent research service offered via The Source. "Is there a market for Christmas trees in Hawaii?" "Give me a list of all Ph.D. dissertations on bananas." "Where can we shoot a TV commercial in August on a location that looks like the snowy woods of New Hampshire?" If it's available anywhere, IOD's worldwide staff with its access to over 150 databases will find it.

Source users receive a 10 percent discount on IOD services. An impressive, well-run service.

• Typesetting. A growing number of electronic typesetting firms are using The Source as a central transfer point for their customers. Upload your typed text and send to the typesetter. The firm will download the text, pump it directly into their typesetting machines, add a few special codes, and mail you the stats. Potential savings of up to 40 percent over conventional typesetting methods. (See Appendix D.)

• TOLLFREE. Source service providing toll-free numbers for airlines, air cargo, car rentals, credit card companies, ski resorts, newspapers, and other organizations. Keyword searchable. Probably better (but more expensive) than printed toll-free directories, most of which consist largely of hotel and motel numbers.

What Does It Cost?

The Source charges an initial, one-time-only signup fee of $100. That may sound a bit steep, but it is important to realize all that you get for your money. The signup fee covers registration, account setup, and Source ID and password assignment, for example. But it also includes a 275-page two-color manual, and lifetime subscriptions to *Source Digest* and the monthly *Sourceworld* newsletter (see the "Documentation and Instructions" section later in this chapter).

The $100 fee can be charged on any major credit card accepted at your place of purchase. And The Source offers a 30-day money back, no-questions-asked guarantee.

There is a $1.00 per month charge for account maintenance that includes two blocks of storage space on the system. This is your personal filing cabinet, and it amounts to 4K (kilobytes). Additional storage space is available at an extra monthly charge, depending upon how much you use. The Source also charges a $9.00 per month "minimum usage" fee. That is, if you use less than $9.00 worth of connect time each month, you will still be charged $9.00. At the lowest Source hourly rates, that comes to about one and a half hours per month. There is also a connect charge of 25¢ each time you sign on to The Source.

The total minimum monthly cost, then, is about $10.00. Although it is possible to set up an account with The Source directly, an option many businesses prefer, individuals normally use their credit cards. The Source sends out monthly statements (not bills) detailing charges, but billing is usually handled through MasterCard or Visa.

As a dedicated online-information-and-service-is-our-business, our-only-business organization, The Source is available 24 hours a day, with

two one-hour shutdowns during the week for updating and maintenance. The shutdowns usually occur between 4:00 AM and 5:00 AM on
Wednesdays and Thursdays. The cost per hour of connect time varies
with the time of day and with the baud rate. Here are the hourly rates
for standard Source service:

Services		Weekdays 7 AM–6 PM	Evenings, Weekends, & Holidays	Midnight to 7 AM daily
THE SOURCE; 1200 information and	300-baud service	$20.75/hr	$ 7.75/hr	$ 5.75/hr
communication services	1200-baud service	25.75/hr	10.75/hr	8.75/hr

The Source also has a separate rate structure for what it calls
SOURCE*PLUS services. These include certain portions of Management Contents, Ltd., the Commodity News Service, and Media General. They range from about 40 to 90 percent more than the standard
rates, depending upon the time of day. SOURCE*PLUS rates apply
only to the time you spend using these services, and the system will
always notify you that these rates are applicable *before* you begin using
a SOURCE*PLUS service.

In addition to commanding the system to give you an online printout
of all rates and applicable charges, you can also check your current
usage totals and file storage and you can order an online breakdown by
month or by day. There is no charge for the time spent using this
feature.

The Source Manual is so complete that only those who wish to do
serious programming on Source computers or those who plan to make
extensive use of the Source word-processing feature need order additional documentation. It's also important to point out that there is
no extra charge for accessing The Source through either Telenet or
Tymnet.

Online Tip: You can also access The Source via a WATS line by
dialing (800) 368-3343. This number applies anywhere in the continental United States, and there is a 25¢ per minute surcharge for
using it. This feature is intended to make it easy for business travelers to use The Source with portable terminals when they don't
know the local Tymnet or Telenet number. To accommodate the
incoming traffic, The Source has installed 100 WATS "ports" in its
new computer center.

How Do You Sign Up?

Source subscriptions and manuals are available from most major computer stores, including ComputerLand, Byte Shops, Heath Kit Electronic Centers, Xerox Retail Stores, Computerware, CompuShops, and others. To sign up, you fill out a Subscriber Agreement (name, address, phone, and credit card), pay the dealer, and pick up your Source Manual.

Online Tip: For the name of the Source dealer nearest you, you may call Source Customer Support at:
(800) 336-3300
In Virginia and outside the U.S., call:
(703) 734-7540
(Canadian callers may call collect.)

In some cases you can be online in a little over an hour, though normally it takes a bit longer. To activate your subscription and obtain your password and account number, the dealer must phone Source headquarters to give the contracts and fulfillment department your name and billing information. If the call is made between the hours of 9:00 AM and 6:00 PM EST, an account number and password can often be issued immediately, possibly even while you wait. Otherwise, the dealer will place the call and notify you or ask you to call back the next day.

Online Tip: In every case, the dealer *must* call first. However, should your dealer be late in getting back to you, you can call The Source yourself to obtain the necessary information. Dial (800) 336-3366 and ask for the contracts department (9:00 AM–6:00 PM EST).

Promotional Offers, Customized Accounts, and Demonstrations

Most people buy their subscriptions through a dealer, and there are good reasons for doing so, not the least of which is the opportunity to walk out of the store with a manual in your hand. However, there are almost always a large number of promotional offers available, and you might want to look into them. At various times, for example, products like the Atari Telelink Cartridge, the Commodore VICMODEM, the Hayes Micromodem, the Texas Instruments Telephone Coupler (modem), and SSM Microcomputer Products' Transend software package for the Apple II have included free time or free subscriptions to The Source with purchase.

Promotional offers do change. But if you phone the communications marketing department at The Source at (800) 336-3366, you can obtain a list of the current offerings. Who knows? You might be lucky enough to get both the modem or software package you want and a free Source subscription.

Online Tip: If you own a Texas Instruments computer, you may be able to take advantage of a special section of The Source called TEXNET. This section contains TI news and information; lists of TI dealers, service centers, and Source users; and free TI software that you can download directly into your Texas Instruments computer. With TI equipment you can also receive special onscreen graphics while connected to The Source and you can use a TI voice synthesizer that will *verbally* read out everything that appears on the screen.

In addition to your TI computer, you will need the TI telephone coupler or other modem, the TI Terminal Emulator II command module, and the TI RC-232 Accessories Interface (or Peripheral Expansion Box and an RS-232 card). In the past Texas Instruments has offered a free subscription to TEXNET and The Source with the purchase of all three items. It may do so again, so it's worth checking before you buy. (The voice synthesizer is neat, but it's not essential.)

You will also need a special TI Source account number. The Source application includes a space for you to specify your equipment make and model. If you specify Texas Instruments equipment you should automatically receive a TI account number that will give you access to TEXNET.

For more information, call The Source at (800) 336-3366.

Source account numbers always consist of at least three letters followed by either letters or numbers, like STC123 or TCM456. Individual numbers are normally assigned on a random basis, like license plates. However, if you are buying several subscriptions for your business, you may be able to request a special series of numbers. There are account numbers on the system, for example, whose first three letters are: CPT, RKO, and IBM. Providing such vanity plate account numbers is not a formalized process at The Source, and it may or may not be possible. But it is certainly worth looking into.

Finally, you might want to ask your dealer if it would be possible to see a demonstration of The Source. Many dealers have accounts in their own name or in the name of their stores, and an automated demo program is available on The Source. The dealer may be charged for the connect time used, so your request may be greeted with varying degrees of enthusiasm.

The reason is sheer economics. The Source is not a very high-profit item for a dealer, particularly when compared with the computer hardware and software offered elsewhere in the store. Industry figures vary, but on average a total of five salesperson hours is required to sell a single personal computer system to a single customer. Quite understandably, a dealer would much rather spend time selling equipment than demonstrating The Source, especially if that demonstration is going to cost money.

But there *is* a solution—or rather, several solutions. First, find out if the dealer has a Source account. If he does, you might arrange to bring a group of friends along to watch a demonstration at a convenient time. It does not matter whether they own computers yet or not. If their interest in personal computers is great enough for them to attend a Source demo, they will be warmly received. Clearly, presenting a single demo to three or more potential customers will make more sense to the dealer than offering individual demonstrations.

If the dealer does not have a Source account, you're still not out of luck. As long as he has a communicating computer, modem, and communications software in the store—and if he doesn't, you should probably not be doing business with him—a demonstration can be arranged. Here is how:

1. Find out what local number to dial for Telenet or Tymnet. You can call Telenet toll-free at (800) 336-0437 or, in Virginia, (800) 572-0408, for this information. Tymnet's toll-free number is (800) 336-0149.

2. Ask the dealer to set the communication parameters of the equipment for 300 baud as described in The Source Manual, and then look at the description of Telenet and Tymnet sign-on procedures in the manual.

3. Dial the phone. If you are using Telenet, type in the following when you see the "at" sign (@) appear on the screen: C 30147. There is no space between the "at" sign and the "C," so the screen should look like this: @C 30147.

   If you use Tymnet, respond to the "Please Log In:" prompt by typing: SOURCE12;PRIM;. Notice that there are no spaces and that PRIM; will not appear on your screen as you type it. When the plus sign (+) appears, hit <ENTER>, as described in The Source Manual.

Whether you use Telenet or Tymnet, you will be asked for your ID and password. In both cases, type: ID STCDMO DEALER

(Note the spaces and that the character after "M" is a letter "O" rather than a zero.) Hit <ENTER>.

4. The prepared Source Demo program will begin and take you on a completely automated five- to six-minute tour of the system.

Documentation and Instructions

The Source Manual is without question one of the finest pieces of documentation to be produced since the first microcomputer sprang to life back in 1976. Superbly organized and presented, written in an easily understood, conversational style, it does an admirable job of describing the system's many features and telling you how to use them. It is also something of a living document, for it has been designed to grow and change as The Source itself does. As new features and services are added, all Source subscribers automatically receive updated pages to be inserted in the Manual's three-ring binder. There is no charge for this service.

Curiously, the only serious flaw in the Manual is the fact that it *is* a manual and thus contains nothing of what professional educators like to call "programmed instruction." The manual presents you with virtually everything you need to know to use the many features of The Source, but it offers little guidance on *how* to use them, which ones to try first, and how to methodically master the system. It's like a cookbook containing lots of interesting recipes but no instructions on cooking in general and no battle-plan for the feast.

It is also worth noting that not all Source programs and features are presented in equal detail. Some occupy several pages, with accompanying examples, and some are treated in single paragraphs. This was probably unavoidable, given all there is to cover, and it is not a serious problem since additional documentation, instructions, and examples are available for every feature online.

For example, virtually every program will give you the opportunity to type in Y or YES to the question: "Would you like instructions?" And you can always get quick, informative summaries of most features by typing HELP followed by the feature name. This online documentation may duplicate, supplement, or amplify the text in The Source Manual. You may or may not find these instructions necessary, since many programs can be used by choosing items from a menu or answering on-screen prompts.

When a new program is added, The Source will announce the fact on the system and suggest using the online documentation associated with the program until new manual pages can be prepared and mailed. You will find these announcements in the "Today" section, one of the choices offered on the "Welcome to The Source" menu that greets you when you sign on.

Online Tip: In some cases you will find it convenient to view the task of learning to use a particular Source program as a two-step process. Sign on and download the instructions for a particular program. Then sign off and read the instructions before going back in to try your hand at the program. This approach will be especially useful in the Games section, since the Source Manual merely provides the general command needed to start any game.

You might also want to consider using the documentation you download to customize your Source Manual. The instructions can be printed out and inserted at the appropriate points in your Manual. The Source Manual is also a good place to keep printouts of your electronic correspondence with other subscribers.

As your manual grows, you may even want to replace the original Source three-ring binder with one of greater capacity.

Customer Service and Support Publications

You can call Source Customer Support for help and answers to your questions whenever the system is online Monday through Friday. Customer Support hours on weekends and holidays are somewhat shorter. In addition, you can contact the system monitor whenever you are online by using the CHAT function.

Source Customer Support

Phone Numbers
(800) 336-3300 in the continental United States.
(703) 734-7540 in Virginia and outside the continental United States; Canadian customers may call collect.

Online Help from System Monitor
Type: CHAT TCA088 and hit <ENTER>

Hours
24 hours a day

There are two support publications that every Source subscriber receives free of charge: *Sourceworld* and *Source Digest*. *Sourceworld* is a monthly newsletter designed to keep users up-to-date on the latest system features. It also includes user profiles and ideas for making the most of your subscription. *Source Digest* is a 5" × 9", 50-page subject and service index. With *Source Digest* you can look up subjects like arms control, property for rent, or Standard & Poor's Hourly Index and find the command you should type to go immediately to that section of The Source.

Moving About Within the System

There are at least five major ways to move around within The Source system. You will find explanations and instructions for each technique in The Source Manual, but unfortunately, you will not find them all in the same place. Consequently, without a bit of guidance, it may take you a while to discover all of them. The techniques are, in increasing order of convenience (and complexity):

Technique	*Source Manual Page*
1. Menus	1-12
2. Menu selection number strings	1-14
3. Commands	1-8
4. Command strings	Scattered throughout
5. Command Output (CO) files	15-8

The Source is like the Red Queen's chessboard in *Alice Through the Looking Glass*. There is a "square" for each feature or program, and the "chessboard" stretches for miles in every direction. The square or programs themselves may be divided up into smaller, more specific "squarelets." Your goal is always to reach a particular square or squarelet from wherever you happen to be on the board.

The Menu Approach

The menu approach is the easiest way to reach your destination, and it is the technique all beginners should use. As soon as you sign on to The Source, you will see the greeting or "Entry Menu." Choose option 3, The Source Menu, and you will be guided through successive menus until you reach the program you want. Figure 3.3 illustrates the way you would use the menu approach to check your mailbox on The Source.

Menu Selection Number Strings

The menu approach is fine if you are just getting to know the system, but wending your way through the various menus that are presented is a relatively slow process. To speed things up a bit, you can skip the menus and just enter the selection numbers. For example, look at the last line of the "Welcome to The Source" menu in Figure 3.3. Instead of entering selection 3, you could have typed the following command: MENU 613. If you have been reading your computer manuals, you know that a "string" is any series of letters or numbers on the same line, and that's exactly what this is. Typing in this particular string would have taken you to your goal of checking your mailbox ("3 Unread, 1 Unread Express, 4 TOTAL" in Figure 3.3) without presenting any of the other menus.

To fully understand what's happening, it is important to know that you can make The Source Main Menu appear at any time, regardless of where you are in the system, by typing MENU. So by entering the command MENU 613, you are actually saying to the system, "Give me The Source Main Menu. Then give me selection 6 from that menu, followed by selection 1 from the Mail and Communications Menu that follows, followed by selection 3 from the Mail Menu that follows *it*." The main difference between using the menu approach and menu selection number strings is that with the latter, none of the menus appears. You are taken directly to your goal.

Commands and the Command Level

If you look at the "Welcome to The Source" menu in Figure 3.3, you'll see that selection 4 will take you to the Command Level. When you choose the Command Level, the following symbol appears on the screen: ->. This is called the Command Level prompt, and whenever you see it, you will naturally be expected to enter a command.

> **Online Tip:** Important for beginners. Should you ever see the Command Level prompt (->) on your screen and be uncertain as to what to do, type the word MENU and hit <ENTER>. This will immediately present The Source Main Menu, your entry point for the "menu approach" to moving about the system. Indeed, *anytime* you think you may be lost, type MENU—even in response to on-screen messages like -MORE- or -END-.
>
> If you are caught in the midst of an on-screen printout that you can't seem to stop, send a <BREAK> by hitting whatever key or keys your personal computer requires. This will stop the program and return you to the program prompt. To leave the program and return to the Command Level, type either QUIT or STOP. Once at the Command Level, you can type MENU and hit your <ENTER> key to get to The Source Main Menu.

Figure 3.3. The "Menu Approach."

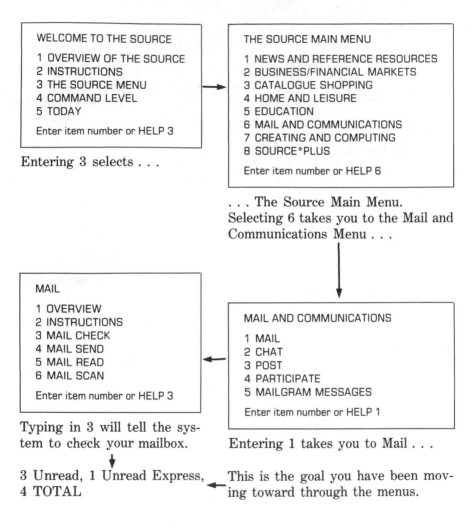

WELCOME TO THE SOURCE

1 OVERVIEW OF THE SOURCE
2 INSTRUCTIONS
3 THE SOURCE MENU
4 COMMAND LEVEL
5 TODAY

Enter item number or HELP 3

Entering 3 selects . . .

THE SOURCE MAIN MENU

1 NEWS AND REFERENCE RESOURCES
2 BUSINESS/FINANCIAL MARKETS
3 CATALOGUE SHOPPING
4 HOME AND LEISURE
5 EDUCATION
6 MAIL AND COMMUNICATIONS
7 CREATING AND COMPUTING
8 SOURCE*PLUS

Enter item number or HELP 6

. . . The Source Main Menu.
Selecting 6 takes you to the Mail and
Communications Menu . . .

MAIL

1 OVERVIEW
2 INSTRUCTIONS
3 MAIL CHECK
4 MAIL SEND
5 MAIL READ
6 MAIL SCAN

Enter item number or HELP 3

MAIL AND COMMUNICATIONS

1 MAIL
2 CHAT
3 POST
4 PARTICIPATE
5 MAILGRAM MESSAGES

Enter item number or HELP 1

Typing in 3 will tell the system to check your mailbox.

3 Unread, 1 Unread Express, 4 TOTAL

Entering 1 takes you to Mail . . .

This is the goal you have been moving toward through the menus.

The menu approach lets you wend your way toward your goal by following paths on the ground. But the Command Level puts you into the air above the chessboard and lets you swoop down on the square or squarelet of your choice. The only requirement is that you know the coordinates of your target.

For example, if you select the Command Level option from the Welcome menu and then type the command: MAILCK (for "Mail Check") at the -> prompt, the system will automatically generate the "3 Unread, 1 Unread Express, 4 TOTAL" sentence from Figure 3.3 on your screen. You can type POST to go immediately to the bulletin board. You can type UPI to go immediately to United Press International. And so on. Each of these "squares" can be reached with the menu approach or with menu response number strings. But direct commands are always quicker. And the commands you need are all provided in The Source Manual.

Command Strings

This technique is quite similar to the menu response number procedure described above. The difference is that it is even more sharply focused. The thing to remember is that both menu-related techniques will always take you to the *beginning* of a program or feature. The same is true of single commands. All three techniques will put you on the desired square of the Source chessboard. Command *strings* put you on a *particular part of the square* or on a particular squarelet.

To take a simple example, if you type in the command MAIL at the Command Level, the next thing you will see on your screen is this:

SEND, READ, OR SCAN:

If you then type in SCAN, the system will provide you with a numbered list of the letters you have received, who sent them and when, and the subject they address. (Subjects are entered by the sender in the course of preparing the letter. The other information is provided by the system itself.)

However, you can skip this intermediate step by entering the command string MAIL SCAN at the Command Level prompt. The underlying idea is the same as that of the menu response number string technique. But with command strings you can be even more precise in your specifications. In both cases, you must either be familiar with the required commands or menu selection numbers, or have a list of the strings to enter. You can find both types of lists in The Source Manual and in *Source Digest*.

Command Output (CO) Files

This technique is tucked away in the "Creating and Computing" section at the back of the Manual, and if you don't dip into that section, you will never hear about it. The Manual will tell you everything you need to know to create and use CO files, but here's the general idea.

A CO file is nothing more than a particular command string that has been given a name and recorded in your personal Source "filing cabinet." It is designed to save you the trouble of typing in a particular command string every time you want to reach a particular part of The Source. Instead of the commands themselves, you merely type CO FILENAME at the Command Level prompt. And, of course, "FILENAME" can be any name you choose. For example, suppose that you wanted to scan the first few lines of the latest UPI sports stories for the state of California. Here is the command string you would have to enter:

```
->UPI S CA S * SB
```

However, if you had recorded the above commands in a CO file and decided to call the file S (for "Sports"), you could merely type:

```
-> CO S
```

The Source Manual explains this particular example in more detail. But the principle is clear: If you use certain features of The Source regularly, you can save a lot of time and keystrokes by creating CO files.

Crucial Commands and the Genindex Format

You can get a list of all Source commands and what they do by typing DATA SYSCOM (for system commands) at the Command Level prompt. However, of all the commands at your disposal, there are three that are absolutely crucial, particularly to a beginning user. They are <BREAK> (or your computer's equivalent), QUIT, and OFF.

They are all the more important because of the way the on-screen prompts tend to channel your thinking. For example, when you see the prompt "Enter item number" or HELP at the bottom of a menu, you naturally assume that you have only two choices. And when you see the word –MORE– at a pause in the on-screen printout, you naturally assume that your only option is to hit your <ENTER> key. But this is not the case. *You have other options.*

Some Source programs work a little differently, but in general, here is what to do. Think of the <BREAK> key (or your system's equivalent) as a *brake* key. Any time you're in the middle of an on-screen printout that you want to end, "put on the brakes" by sending the system <BREAK>. That will stop the printout and give you some kind of on-screen prompt. At this point you will still be "within" the program or feature you have selected. To get out of that particular program or feature, type QUIT and hit <ENTER>.

QUIT will return you to the Command Level prompt (->). And from there, you can enter MENU to go to The Source Main Menu, or enter some other command or command string.

The third crucial command is OFF. This is what you must type to officially "stop the meter" when you want to sign off The Source. Source computers are constantly looking for input from your terminal. If they do not see anything coming in for a period of three minutes, they will automatically sign you off the system and stop the meter. However, if you don't officially sign off, you will be charged for up to three minutes of additional connect time. The important thing to remember is that to sign off, you *must* be at the Command Level. So, whether you are using the menu or the command approach, type <BREAK> if necessary to stop a program. Then type QUIT to go to the Command Level. Then, when you see the prompt (->), type OFF. The Source will respond with the number of minutes you have been online, the time, date, and other information described in The Source Manual.

Useful Commands for All Programs

There are a number of other commands you will find especially helpful. The command [<CONTROL> <S>] will *stop* an on-screen display from scrolling up your screen, so that you may read it. The command [<CONTROL> <Q>] will get the display moving again.

Possibly even more important are the commands for moving *within* a particular program or feature. For example, even though there are no on-screen instructions to do so, if you enter the letter <P> at many prompts or whenever you see the word –MORE–, the system will usually return you to the previous prompt. The previous prompt is whatever question you responded to in order to get into the portion of the program you now want to leave. Entering the letter <M> will usually take you to The Source Main Menu. These commands apply to virtually all Source programs.

When using Genindex format programs, entering the command NO CRT instead of a simple <ENTER> when you see the word –MORE– will eliminate any subsequent pauses in the on-screen printout or scroll.

For example, suppose that you are using the menu approach and have arrived at the following menu:

```
                    HOME AND LEISURE

                    1  GAMES
                    2  ADVICE & HOROSCOPES
                    3  TRAVEL & DINING
                    4  ENTERTAINMENT
                    5  HOME FINANCE

                    Enter item number or HELP 4
```

You have chosen selection 4, Entertainment, and this causes the following menu to appear:

```
                    ENTERTAINMENT

                    1  WEEKLY BESTSELLERS LIST
                    2  MOVIE REVIEWS
                    3  MUSIC NEWS
                    4  TV PREVIEWS
                    5  SOAP OPERA TUNE IN

                    Enter item number or HELP 5
```

In spite of your B.A., M.A., and Ph.D. degrees from prestigious universities, you find soap operas irresistible, so you choose number five. You will see something like this:

00 Aug 19-- 8-26-00__975__For release beginning 8-00-00 UNITED Feature Syndicate JON-MICHAEL REED TUNE IN TOMORROW What's happening By Jon-Michael Reed

ALL MY CHILDREN: Ray was paroled after squealing on his cellmate who was killed during a prison escape engineered by Ray. Donna went into a tailspin to learn Chuck is marrying Carrie. Langley convinced Opal to keep their engagement under wraps and that Phoebe married him for his money. Erica insisted she's not sexually interested in Kent but was jealous he's dating his secretary, Ingrid. Jenny's boss, Evelyn, demanded an intro to Erica who ran into Jenny. Ellen refused to attend the opening of Mark's play. Rick babysat Emily Ann while Estelle worked.

ANOTHER WORLD: Julia was slightly injured when someone mysteriously pushed her down some stairs on the movie set. Diana resented Rachel who refused to

-MORE- P

"Another World" is just not your cup of tea, so rather than hitting <ENTER> to continue the synopsis, you enter <P>. This causes the previous prompt to appear, and your screen will look like this:

ENTERTAINMENT

```
1  WEEKLY BESTSELLERS LIST
2  MOVIE REVIEWS
3  MUSIC NEWS
4  TV PREVIEWS
5  SOAP OPERA TUNE IN
```

Enter item number or HELP

At this point you can look at the latest *Publishers Weekly* bestsellers list, take in a movie review, make some other selection, or type QUIT to return to the Command Level.

Finally, it can be very helpful to have some idea of what the Genindex format is all about. This too is explained in The Source Manual, but a very brief summary may make it easier to understand. Basically, some—but not all—Source programs and features are organized into "paragraphs." Each paragraph deals with a particular topic. Each has a label. And each has a unique number. Within the New York Guide program, for instance, the paragraph containing information about New York City art galleries is labeled "Art Galleries" and is numbered paragraph P001. In the Washington Metro Guide program, paragraph P014 is titled "L'Escargot" and contains information on that Washington restaurant.

To retrieve information from any Genindex program, *you must always type in a paragraph number.* The only question is how you go about obtaining the correct number for the information you are after and how sharply you focus your search. The art gallery paragraph mentioned above, for example, will give you all of the information on *all* of the galleries in the program. But if you know the right paragraph number, you can zero in on just those galleries in Soho or just those that specialize in graphics.

The Source Manual contains a list of the programs that are organized on the Genindex format. But as a rule of thumb, if you ever enter a program and see the following prompt, you will know that the Genindex format applies:

ENTER A SUBJECT, A PARAGRAPH NAME, "STOP,"
OR "HELP" FOR INSTRUCTIONS:

If you enter a subject, the system will search the entire list of paragraph *titles* for a match. When it finds one, it will show you the title and the paragraph number and then repeat the above prompt. At that point, just enter the paragraph number and you'll be on your way.

This is fine if you use the program infrequently. But to get the most out of a Genindex program, you ought to have a complete list of all paragraphs including their titles and their numbers. That way, you can get into the program, check your list for the specific paragraph of interest, and enter its number at the prompt. As The Source Manual points out, you can generate such a list by typing either INDEX or CONTENTS at the prompt. If you are going to download and save a list for future reference, CONTENTS is the command to use since it includes *every* paragraph in the program.

The INDEX is a broader listing and is more useful if the system cannot find a match for the subjects you enter at the prompt. When you use it for this purpose, be sure to have pad and paper ready to note the paragraph numbers as the index scrolls by. Here is what your screen will look like when you request an index of the New York Guide program:

INDEX

```
.ART GALLERIES . . . . . . . . . . . . . . . . . . . . . . . . . . . . . . . . . . . . . . . . . . . . . . . . . . . . . P001
UPTOWN GALLERIES
   MODERN. . . . . . . . . . . . . . . . . . . . . . . . . . . . . . . . . . . . . . . . . . . . . . . . . . . . . . . . . . P002
   TRADITIONAL . . . . . . . . . . . . . . . . . . . . . . . . . . . . . . . . . . . . . . . . . . . . . . . . . . . . . P003
   GRAPHICS . . . . . . . . . . . . . . . . . . . . . . . . . . . . . . . . . . . . . . . . . . . . . . . . . . . . . . . . . P004
   GREENWICH VILLAGE . . . . . . . . . . . . . . . . . . . . . . . . . . . . . . . . . . . . . . . . . . . . . . P005
   SOHO. . . . . . . . . . . . . . . . . . . . . . . . . . . . . . . . . . . . . . . . . . . . . . . . . . . . . . . . . . . . . . P006
.ATTRACTIONS IN THE BIG APPLE . . . . . . . . . . . . . . . . . . . . . . . . . . . . . . . . . P007
.BOOK STORES . . . . . . . . . . . . . . . . . . . . . . . . . . . . . . . . . . . . . . . . . . . . . . . . . . . . . . P008
```

Using Your Source Communications Options

The communications options The Source places at your disposal are all well-documented and easy to use. In each case, you are prompted through the entire process and can thus learn to use the basic features of a particular option in about two minutes.

Online Tip: Want to send an electronic letter right away? Do this:

1. Sign on and enter selection 4, Command Level, from the "Welcome to The Source" menu.
2. When the Command Level prompt (–>) appears, type the words MAIL SEND and hit <ENTER>.
3. When you see TO: on your screen, type in TCA088. (Be sure to use a zero and not the letter "O" between "A" and the first "8".) This is the address/account number for Source Customer Support, but of course you may use any other address you like.

4. The SUBJECT: prompt is your chance to be creative. Type in a single word or a short phrase.
5. Type your letter.
6. When you have finished, hit <ENTER> to generate a fresh blank line. Then type .S ("dot S") and hit <ENTER>.

Done! Your letter is now in your correspondent's Source mailbox and ready to be read, regardless of where you are in the country or in the world.

Mastering the more advanced features will take a bit longer. But it is well worth the effort, because some of the communications options offer you an astonishing degree of sophistication. For example, in addition to allowing you to send a simple letter, the SourceMail feature includes options for sending "carbon" copies to additional individuals, blind copies, and letters with "acknowledgment requested" attached. You can send the same letter to an entire mailing list of individuals. You can type in the letter on Monday but specify that it be delivered on some other day, such as Friday. You can require the recipient to use a password to read your letter. You can load entire blocks of text from your personal filing cabinet by typing .L ("dot L"), followed by the name of the file you want to include. You can even run the whole thing through the Source spelling-checker with the command .SP ("dot SP").

These are just some of the options available to you when *sending* mail. There is an equally impressive list of options at your disposal when *scanning* or *reading* your mail.

The Synergistic Possibilities

Electronic mail; a keyword-searchable electronic bulletin board; a classified, searchable directory of Source users; a well-developed computerized conferencing system; and the ability to send a Western Union Mailgram™ from your keyboard arc all powerful options in and of themselves. But think of what you can do if you *combine* these options and get them working together to achieve a single goal.

Used together, for example, your Source communications options enable you to search for, identify, and communicate with all of your fellow Source subscribers who share a particular interest. There are tens of thousands of Source subscribers, but using your communications options, you can perform your search and send a letter to each identified individual in a single evening.

The possibilities are limited only by your own imagination. Just for fun, consider this brief example. Suppose that you want to start a science-fiction club complete with a monthly newsletter, a book exchange, SF convention coverage, and a mechanism for swapping member-written short stories. And suppose that you are starting from ground zero—that is, the club currently has only one member, you. Here is one way you might use your Source communications options to get things started.

• Step 1.
Use the DISEARCH option to search the Source directory for listings of individuals who have specified "Science Fiction," "SF," or (shudder) "SciFi" as one of their interests. The on-screen printout will look something like this, and it may include 25, 50, 100, or more names:

```
STD000/Bill/VA/Apple, Science Fiction, History, Girls!
TCB000/Tangela/CA/S-F/Intergalactic Government/Intellivision
TTY00/Gail/NJ/Writing/SF:Zelazny, Niven, Wolfe, etc./Atari
```

• Step 2.
Use your word-processing program or create a file of all of the account numbers generated by DISEARCH. Then, following the instructions in the "Creating and Computing" section of The Source Manual, upload that list into your personal filing cabinet. We'll call the file LIST.

• Step 3.
Write a letter proposing your idea for an SF club and upload it into your Source filing cabinet. We'll call the file LETTER.

• Step 4.
Go into the SourceMail program. The Source Manual will tell you how to send the same letter to everyone on your mailing list. But about all you have to type will be LIST and .Load LETTER. This will send your letter to everyone on the list.

• Step 5.
Next, go to the Source bulletin board (POST) and search it for any messages about "Science Fiction," "SF," and the like. Here is the kind of printout you can expect to see on your screen:

```
Keyword(s) or <H>elp:Science Fiction
  Searching . . .
  15 entries valid.

  <N>arrow, <E>xpand or Return for all: Hit <ENTER> or <RETURN>
  Wait . . .
```

Category: SCIENCE FICTION
Subject: FIRST EDITION "STARSHIP TROOPERS"
From:TCE000
Posted:00 SEP 11:24 pm

<N>ext,<PO>st, or Return for text: Hit <ENTER> or <RETURN>

I am looking for a first edition
of Heinlein's *Starship Troopers*.
Must be in good condition. Top-
dollar paid. Contact me via SMAIL.

Lyle Monroe
TCE000

A listing in DISEARCH is completely voluntary. Consequently, notices like this on the bulletin board may generate additional people to contact about your club. Since you have already got your letter in your personal filing cabinet, you have only to type in the additional account numbers to send these individuals your letter.

• Step 6.
Place your own message on the POST bulletin board under the subject "Science Fiction." To increase the chances of interested individuals reading your message, you might want to POST the same notice under the subjects "SF" and "SciFi" as well.

• Step 7.
Next, go into the Source's teleconferencing area by typing PARTI (for PARTICIPATE) at the Command Level prompt or by following the menus (see Chapter 10). Here you will probably find at least one ongoing "conference" on science fiction. Conference members in PARTI contribute their thoughts and ideas for everyone else to read and comment upon. The discussion process takes place over time, and as a new member you will be able to read all previous contributions to the conference. And, of course, you will be able to make your own comments.

A PARTI conference on science fiction will be a good place to locate additional people and to solicit suggestions on your club. You may even find individuals who would be interested in helping you organize and run the organization.

This is just a brief glimpse at how you can use your Source communications options synergistically to quickly and easily accomplish things that were undreamed of only a few years ago. Obviously, you could use all of these options to exchange messages, send electronic newsletters, distribute member-written short stories, and even send notices of club dues once you get your club started.

Online Tip: Another communication option to consider is the Source's User Publishing program. If you have something to offer that might reasonably be of interest to other Source users (a newsletter, short stories, poetry, essays, a tips and advice column), you may be able to arrange to have your creation "published" on The Source. Published works of this sort are available to all Source subscribers at no additional cost. (Type PUBLIC at the Command Level prompt to see what is available.) But you as the creator/author will be paid a *royalty* of 9 percent or more. The royalty is calculated on the gross billing for the amount of time a Source user spends reading your contribution. Popular features can generate payments of several hundred dollars a month for their creators.

Getting to Know the System

As a new Source subscriber, you shouldn't worry if you feel overwhelmed by all of the possibilities open to you. That's a perfectly natural reaction considering all that you have to choose from. The trick is to relax, congratulate yourself for being on the cutting edge of the Information Age, and then sit down and look at The Source Manual. Make sure that you also pick up a pad and pen. There will be lots of things you will want to try on the system, and if you don't write them down, you can easily forget to do them.

Once you have a general feeling for The Source, you might want to try the following four-session approach to getting to know the system. The procedures to follow for signing on to the system through Telenet, Tymnet, and DataPac are illustrated and explained in The Source Manual. However, some things have changed since the Manual was written. You will not be explicitly prompted to "Please type ID . . ." Instead, you will see a carat or a "greater-than" sign (>). Simply type in your ID and other information as described in the Manual.

Before you sign on, make sure that you know how to generate a BREAK on your computer. Page number 1-4 describes how to do this on most machines. If you are using a Xerox 820 and ASCOM communications software, however, you will use [<CONTROL> <B>] to issue a BREAK. If you are using a communicating CPT word processor, you will use [<CODE> <STOP>] to send a BREAK, and [<CODE> <=> <;>] to send the ESCAPE signal needed to get out of CHAT on The Source. These are unusual situations, but if something similar applies to you, be sure to contact your manufacturer for more information.

Online Tip: Unfortunately, the system settings printed in The Source Manual may *not* be complete, depending upon the edition you have.

Manual	*Will Also Work*
300 or 1200 baud	300 or 1200 baud
Full-duplex	Full-duplex
No parity	Even parity
8-bit ASCII Code*	7-bit ACSII Code*
1 stop bit	1 stop bit

*Refers to "word" or "character" length setting

Session Number One

• Step 1.

Make sure that it is a weekend, a holiday, or after 6:00 PM your local time. These are the times when the Source's $7.75 per hour rates (as opposed to $20.75/hour) are in effect. Follow The Source Manual instructions for signing on via Telenet or Tymnet.

Enter selection 4 from the Welcome menu to go to the command level and type PASSWD or DATA PASSWD as described in The Source Manual. Follow the instructions for changing your original password to something of your own invention. Then *write it down* some place where you can find it easily.

• Step 2.

When you have finished changing your password, the Command Level prompt will appear. Type DEMO SOURCE for a five-minute tour of The Source. The demonstration is completely automated. All you have to do is watch.

• Step 3.

At the Command Level prompt (−>), type the word MENU and hit <ENTER>. This will cause The Source Main Menu to appear. Follow the menu options as the spirit moves you. Just remember that you can always return to the Main Menu by typing <M> or MENU at most prompts. If that does not work, type QUIT to get to the Command Level and *then* type MENU.

• Step 4.

Go to the Command Level by typing QUIT at one of the menu prompts. Then set your system to capture incoming data, and type DATA SYSCOM for a listing of Source Commands; DATA LIBALL for a quick list of Source library ("canned") computer programs; DATA SYSDOC for a list of specialized programming manuals you can order; INFO INFO for a complete listing of Source features and programs (takes a while to scroll out); and so on. The Source Manual explains how to get additional information with DATA, INFO, and HELP commands.

> **Online Tip:** In September of 1982, The Source installed a new operating system with additional features not detailed in the original Source Manual. Under the new system, you can obtain information on virtually any Source feature or program by typing HELP followed by the name of the program or feature.

• Step 5.

When you want to sign off, go to the Command Level and type OFF. The system will respond with information about how much time you have used and say BYE.

Session Number Two

• Step 1.

Sign on and select the Command Level option from the Welcome menu. Then set your system to download incoming data and type HELP POST to get online information on how to use The Source bulletin board.

• Step 2.

Following the instructions in The Manual and in the material from HELP POST, search the bulletin board for notices about your computer equipment. You will probably want to save the results, so set your system to capture data.

Here is but one example of the kind of helpful information you can expect to find—in this case, for owners of Texas Instruments (TI) computers.

<C>ategory,<U>ser ID,<D>ate,<K>eyword: K

Keyword(s) or <H>elp: Type TI as your keyword
Searching . . .
8 notices valid.

<N>arrow, <E>xpand or Return for all: Hit <ENTER> or <RETURN>
Wait . . .
Category:TI-99/4
Subject:SIGN-ON HINT!!!!!
From:TI0000
Posted:30 APR 2:42 am

<N>ext,<PO>st, or Return for text: Hit <ENTER> or <RETURN>

Discovered a great way to speed up Source sign-on. As soon as you get the COPYRIGHT SOURCE TELECOMPUTING CORPORATION message, do a BREAK (Control slash "/", despite what the TE 2 book says). This will bring you to Source Command level, but you won't be able to do anything yet. Type TEXNET, then type SOURCE when you get the "*" prompt in Texnet. Try it!

Henry TI0000

• Step 3.
Type QUIT at the POST prompt to return to Command Level. Then type HELP DISEARCH. This will give you information on searching the Source user directory for subscribers using a particular kind of computer, expressing a particular interest, or located in a particular state.

When the HELP DISEARCH information has finished printing out, you will be returned to the Command Level. Type DISEARCH to actually get into the program. Set your machine to download. Then search the directory. You might search for people who like to CHAT, people who are interested in The Source, people who use your own brand of computer, or use some other category.

• Step 4.
Finally, for this session, you might want to try your hand at CHAT. You can get into CHAT by typing the word at the Command Level.

But if you have never done it before, it is the best approach through the menus since the system will prompt you through the process.

At the Command Level type MENU 62. This will take you to the following:

```
CHAT

1 OVERVIEW
2 INSTRUCTIONS
3 BEGIN CHAT
```

Online Tip: Whenever you use CHAT, remember to always hit your <ENTER> key *twice* to tell the other person that you are finished typing and awaiting a reply. This is like saying "over" when using a two-way radio.

Session Number Three

• Step 1.
Review the DISEARCH listings you downloaded last time to get an idea of the kind of topics people enter and the phrases they use. Then give some thought to the interests you might like to include in your own listing. You only have a limited amount of space to work with, so try to make every word count.

When the system searches for listings containing a keyword, it looks for a matching series of characters. Thus if you search for listings containing the word "telecommunications," the system will find and display not only listings with that exact word, but also listings containing "communications."

Thus if you want other people who are interested in telecommunications to be able to find your listing, entering "communications" as one of your interests will probably do the trick, and save you four characters. You might even be able to enter just "communicat" and save four more characters of space. You can then use those eight character spaces to include an additional interest or topic in your listing.

• Step 2.
Sign on and type DIRECTADD at the Command Level. This will take

you to the portion of the Source Directory used to add your listing. Follow the on-screen instructions and put yourself on the list.

Remember, directory listings are completely voluntary. And you can add, delete, or change your listing at any time.

• Step 3.
Review the Directory listings you downloaded in the previous session to find the account numbers of people you think you might like to write. Then type MAIL SEND at the Command Level and send them an electronic letter.

Session Number Four

• Step 1.
By now you're becoming very comfortable with The Source, and are ready to do some serious exploring of your own. By now you may also have some mail in your Source mailbox. So sign on, and type MAILCK (for "mail check") at the Command Level.

• Step 2.
You're on your own! But at some point in this session, make sure that you check the PARTICIPATE computerized conferencing section by typing PARTI at the Command Level prompt. This is a Source feature you won't want to miss.

When you enter PARTI for the first time, be sure to set your equipment to capture incoming data. The PARTI introduction contains a number of pages of instructions that you will want to download and review to get maximum benefit from the feature.

• Step 3.
At some other point, either in this session or later, be sure to type PUBLIC at the Command Level. This will transport you into the realm of User Publishing on The Source. There is always a lot of activity there, and there are many features to explore.

For the Experienced User

As you use The Source, it is worth keeping track of the shortcuts and other tips you discover. The Source Manual includes a number of suggestions for shortcuts as they apply to various programs. But these are just the beginning. You will discover many of your own, and you will meet others on the system with tips and advice to share. Two ways to find these "Sourcerers" are to search for individuals expressing an interest in The Source in their directory listings (DISEARCH) and to search the bulletin board for messages containing "Source" in their subject line. You will also find at least one conference on The Source in the PARTI section, and one or more electronic magazines on using The Source in the PUBLIC or User Publishing area.

With these online resources at your disposal—plus the advice provided by Source Customer Support—you will be able to develop an extensive list of tips and advice customized to your interests and needs.

There are a number of things, though, that you should be sure to look into after you have gotten to know your way around the system. Most of these can be found in the "Creating and Computing" section at the back of the Manual. There you will find detailed instructions on how to use the Source Editor (word processor) when creating text files or writing a letter, plus valuable information on how to make the most of your personal filing cabinet on The Source.

One type of file worthy of special note is the C_ID file explained on page 15-9 of the Source Manual. This is an "automatic execute" file that will "run" each time you sign on to The Source. For example, suppose that, like most Source users, the first thing you do after you sign on is to check your mailbox. As you know, the standard procedure is to enter Selection 4 Command Level from the Welcome menu and then type in MAILCK. With the proper C_ID file, however, you can skip the Welcome menu entirely and order the system to check your mailbox the moment you sign on.

You will not be in a position to create a truly sophisticated C_ID file until you have become familiar with The Source and the various commands and command strings necessary to accomplish each task. But an automatic mail-check file is relatively easy. Here's what to do:

1. Sign on to The Source and select the Command Level.

2. At the Command Level prompt (->), type the word ENTER and then C_ID. This tells the system, "Okay, I want to start a file, and I want to call it C_ID." (If your computer cannot generate an underline, type SID instead of C_ID. In fact, there's no reason why you can't use SID, whether your computer generates underlines or not.)

3. The system will pause and then come back with the word ENTER. It will then give you a blank line to begin writing. (This is a function of the new operating system mentioned earlier. Your Source Manual may indicate that BEGIN will appear, but this is no longer the case.)

4. Type MAILCK and hit your <ENTER> key *once.*

5. Then hit your <ENTER> key *twice* in a row.

That's all there is to it. The two successive <ENTER>s in Step 5 close the file and tell the system to record your work in your personal filing cabinet. From now on, each time you sign on to The Source, the system will immediately check your mailbox for any unread letters.

Here are a few points to keep in mind when using this feature:

- For obvious reasons, there can be only one C—ID (or SID) file per account number. (If you had two or three of them, how would the system know which one to execute when you sign on?)

- You can disable the C—ID file by typing one or more <BREAK>s as soon as you sign on. This will stop whatever program you have set up to run at sign-on and put you at the Command Level.

- You can erase the file at any time. Go to the Command Level and type in DELETE C—ID (or SID). That will wipe it out.

- Finally, there are two commands to use for checking to make sure that your C—ID file was recorded properly. At the Command Level, type FILES for a directory of your personal filing cabinet. If you see C—ID (or SID) listed, you will know that it was indeed recorded. To actually look at or "list" the file, type TY C—ID (or SID) at the Command Level. Consult your Source Manual for instructions on how to *edit* an existing file.

Complete Automation

One thing The Source Manual does not tell you is that you can use a C—ID file to collect information and then *automatically sign off the system.* You *must* be familiar with the command sequence or sequences required to obtain the information. But if you know the sequence and how the information program runs, you can add QUIT and OFF to your C—ID file. This will make it possible for you to sign on and walk away from your machine, if you like. Everything will run automatically. When all the information has been retrieved, the C—ID file will issue a QUIT to return to the Command Level. It will then issue an OFF—just as if you were sitting at your keyboard and entering those commands yourself. That will sign you off the system and stop the meter from running, automatically.

Finally, let's look at what you can do with a C—ID file if you have the right equipment and software for your computer. Suppose that you have investment interests and that you want to check the latest Dow Jones and Standard & Poor's averages daily. You are most interested in the figures that come in over the UPI wire every day at 3:22 PM. But unfortunately, you cannot always be at your computer terminal at that time. The answer is clearly to completely automate the information collection process, and here's how.

You will need three components, in addition to your personal computer and a C_ID file on The Source containing the words QUIT and OFF at the appropriate points. All of these components are described in Chapter 2, and they include:

• An auto-dial modem

• Communications software capable of:
    Telling the modem what number to dial
    Automatically logging you onto The Source
    Automatically capturing incoming data. (Depending upon the specific program, the software may simply load the information into a buffer in the machine, or it may be able to automatically write the buffer to disk.)

• A digital clock like the Hayes Stack™ Chronograph or a device of similar capabilities.

You will have to read the instructions for each component, of course. But basically, you will be able to set the clock to turn your system on at the correct time and have the software load in automatically. The software can be made to automatically tell the modem to dial The Source. The software itself will then log you on to the system. At that point, your C_ID file will take over and generate the stock averages you're after. When the figures have stopped, the C_ID file will get you out of the program and log you off The Source.

In the meantime, your computer will be taking it all in and saving the information either in a buffer or on a floppy disk. Let's assume that your software can record the information on disk. In that case, the clock device could shut your machine off after an appropriate period of time.

When you return—hopefully before the stock market closes—you will have all the information you need on disk in your machine. You will only have to boot up the system and look at the file—then call your broker!

RCV—*The Secret Source Command*

The normal procedure for uploading a file to The Source is to type in the word "Enter" at the Command Level prompt and wait for the system to respond with "Enter text." When the upload is finished, you hit two carriage returns (<ENTER>) to close the file. This usually works fairly well, but it means that all of your text must be single-spaced. If your text contains a carriage return at the end of the first line, followed by a carriage return to generate an empty line, The Source will read this as your signal to close the file. And that's what it will do. (*Note:* If you are having trouble uploading in this manner, see Appendix B for some Telenet and Tymnet commands that can help.)

If you want to send someone something that is double-spaced, your only alternative is to upload the file single-spaced, use the Source Editor to double space it, and then re-save it in your filing cabinet. Then you can use the "dot-Load" command to insert the text into your letter. This is a nuisance. Worse, it's time-consuming; and when you're online, time is money.

For this reason you may be interested in a little-known command that will alleviate the problem. The command is RCV, and it tells the system that you want to sent text a line at a time. It's easy to use. Simply type RCV FILENAME at the Command Level prompt. The FILENAME, of course, is whatever name you have chosen to give the file. (If you don't specify a filename, The Source will prompt you for one: "Name of file to save in?")

The system will respond with a question mark (?). At that point, you are free to commence the upload. When you have finished, type this command:

```
$$DONE
```

to close the file. You will find that the whole thing works like a charm.

In addition to making it possible to upload double-spaced text, the RCV command also stops the system from checking for the ASCII characters for erase (backspace) and the "@" sign, something it does under most circumstances. This can be particularly important if you want to upload computer programs that contain these characters.

Should You Sign Up?

With its many features and services and its round-the-clock availability, The Source represents the first full realization of an information utility. But it is not cheap. Studies show that the average individual user spends approximately $25 per month on The Source. Many "Source addicts" spend much more.

When considering the charges, however, it is important to realize that the rates The Source charges are not excessive in relation to the costs of providing its information and services. For example, prior to

August 1982, the midnight-to-7:00 AM charge was $4.25 per hour. But at that rate, the firm was losing 25¢ for every subscriber connect hour. The new rate is $1.50 higher ($5.75) for that time period, and presumably it enables The Source to make a profit.

There is no question that The Source provides value for what it charges. Indeed, by information industry standards, it is a real bargain. The question is: Do you really need or want this bargain? Perhaps CompuServe or the Dow Jones News/Retrieval Service would better serve your needs. Only you can answer that question. But, while Chapters 4 and 5 will describe these two services in greater detail, here are some points of comparison to help you decide whether to subscribe to The Source.

The least expensive rates for access to the Dow Jones News/Retrieval Service range from $9.00 to $36 per hour, depending on the DJNS database you access. DJNS is absolutely unbeatable when it comes to financial news. If this is a primary interest, and if you can only subscribe to one utility, DJNS is the one to pick. DJNS, however, offers no recreational features and it has nothing to compare with the communications options you will find on The Source.

At $5.00 per hour, CompuServe is the cheapest alternative. But you should be aware that CompuServe began by offering computerists and other high-tech hobbyists the opportunity to write and run programs on mainframe computers during the evening hours. (Information and other services were added later.) To a large extent, these origins are still reflected in the firm's general approach and in the type of subscribers you will meet on the system.

It is a subjective judgment, but CompuServe is somewhat more difficult to use than The Source. To get the maximum benefit out of a CIS subscription, you are expected to know about computers and computing. And since the initial documentation supplied to CIS subscribers is less than extensive, you are often left to figure things out on your own. (Other instructional manuals for various CIS features are sold separately and must be ordered from CIS headquarters, since they are not carried in stores.)

CompuServe has many features comparable to The Source (and many that are uniquely its own). For lots of people, CIS provides all of the information and communication services they need. But the system is still available only at night and on weekends, and is likely to remain so for the foreseeable future.

Finally, you might want to sample all three information utilities before making up your mind. You can do so for about $26 and net a CIS and Dow Jones subscription while you're at it. First, buy the Radio Shack Universal Sign-Up package mentioned in Chapter 4. This will give you a subscription to CompuServe and DJNS (and an hour's free time on each service). Then go to a computer store and charge the $100 Source subscription on a major credit card.

The Source's $100 initiation charge is completely refundable within 30 days. You are liable for only the connect time you use. If you access The Source after midnight, you can spend an hour on the system for $5.75. If you decide against subscribing, you can return your manual to the computer store and have them remove the charge from your credit card. Your total cost for this comparison shopping: $25.75.

The only catch is that once you sign on to The Source, you may never want to sign off.

...4...

CompuServe
The Nighttime Utility

CompuServe, Inc., the Columbus-based subsidiary of H&R Block, Inc., began as a remote data processing "time-sharing" service in 1972, and that is still the firm's primary orientation. For a fee, business and governmental organizations are offered telephone access to the company's large DEC 2050, K1-10, and KL-20 computers to run their payrolls, handle their accounting, and do everything else that a mainframe computer can do. Time-sharing saves individual clients the expense of buying and maintaining their own machines, and it makes a tidy profit for the service provider. The firm's revenues have typically grown at a compounded annual rate of over 20 percent.

The only problem is that once the workday rush is over, many time-sharing computers have a lot of idle capacity. Their circuits are warm, and they're still gobbling electricity. But they are not earning any income. It's not an unusual problem, but in August 1979 CompuServe came up with an unusual solution. The firm began to make its computers available to hobbyists and other individuals with computing expertise. Most of these folks built their own machines, either from a kit or from parts they acquired and assembled on their own. Thus for a very modest investment, an individual could sign on to CompuServe during the idle evening and weekend hours and "play" with a huge bank of mainframe computers.

The system was called MicroNET. For a one-time hookup charge of $9.00 and a cost of $5.00 per hour, an individual not only received 128K of personal storage space on the system, but could write and run programs in X-Basic, Fortran, Pascal, Macro-10, APL, and other computer languages, run a variety of standard CompuServe programs, and communicate with other users through electronic mail.

The idea caught on, and soon CompuServe began to add features like stock quotes, news and weather information, and magazine articles. These additional features evolved into what the firm calls the "Video-

90

tex" (no "t") or "Display" portion of its product. In 1980, a separate CompuServe Information Division was created within the company, and today Videotex and MicroNET are the two principal parts of the database now called the CompuServe Information Service (CIS).

The one-time hookup charge has risen to $19.95 and CompuServe is still available only at night and on weekends. But the cost per hour of use is still just $5.00. Since 1979 its subscription base has grown and grown, until by early 1983 it numbered over 32,000. New subscribers are signing up at a rate of about 1000 a month.

America's Do-It-Yourself Database?

Perhaps the most important point to remember about CompuServe as it now exists is that providing information and services to personal computer users is still a secondary or even tertiary business for the firm as a whole. And, as *Business Week* recently pointed out, it is "aimed almost exclusively at sophisticated users who already own personal computers." These are the hobbyists, CIS's original customers. This will undoubtedly change. But because of this hobbyist orientation and perhaps most of all because of its exceedingly low prices, subscribers do not receive much in the way of documentation and instructions when they sign up. The *User's Guide* supplied with your subscription, for example, contains only eight pages with generous portions of each devoted to either white space or photographs.

This has led some to call CompuServe "America's do-it-yourself database." This is probably an unfair characterization. After all, where else can you do so many things for less than 9¢ a minute?

You will find much of the documentation you need to use CompuServe *online* instead of in your subscription package. Most programs in the Display or Videotex area offer online explanations and command summaries if you want them. For more information on using CompuServe, you can call Customer Service via a toll-free number (except in Ohio) every evening of the week until midnight.

Online Tip: Take advantage of the online documentation offered by CIS to create your own customized user's guide. A notebook with dividers for the instructions and commands that apply to each program module, combined with a methodical approach to downloading and printing out the information you need, can save you a lot of time and money. In some cases, the documentation you can buy from CIS is nothing more than a printout of these same online instructions.

With the help of Customer Service, this chapter, and a little ingenuity you should be able to access and use CIS relatively easily. And it is clearly worth whatever effort may be involved, for CIS has a great deal to offer you, including a highly unique online CB Simulator that may alone be worth the price of your subscription.

What's Available on the System?

CompuServe has a feature for everyone from food coupon clippers to aircraft owners and pilots to businesspeople—not to mention computer buffs, game players, and everyone else with a desire for online information and services. What follows is a brief survey of the major areas of interest and some of the features that are available in each. The list is by no means comprehensive, but it will give you a fairly good idea of what you have at your command as a subscriber to this utility.

Communications

- Electronic Mail. Known as EMAIL on the system. Allows you to send, receive, and file or delete letters and messages to and from any other CIS subscriber.

- User Directory. Allows you to search for other subscribers by account number, name, city, type of computer equipment, or interests. Directory is made up of only those people who have voluntarily entered their information.

- National Bulletin Board System. Known as BULLET. Lets you post public messages of three types (NOTICE, SELL, and WANTED) on an electronic bulletin board that can be searched for keywords and read by anyone on the system.

- FEEDBACK. Feature to let you send comments, suggestions, and questions directly to the CIS staff. Also used to order CIS documentation manuals and other products.

- CB Simulator. Connects your system to a special "multiplayer host" computer. Gives you access to 36 to 40 "channels" to carry on real-time conversations with people all over the country.

- Special Interest Groups (SIGs). Electronic clubs to exchange views, tips, information, software, and so on. Most maintain their own bulletin boards within the group. Interests covered include: aviation,

CP/M, ham radio, LDOS, Apple computers, PDP-11 computers, TRS-80 computers, players of CIS Space War and Decwars, UCSD Pascal, TRS-80 Color Computer, CIS CB users (Netwits), health care, software authors, and literary pursuits. More are being added all the time.

News and Information

• News, Weather, and Sports from the Associated Press Newswire.

• Electronic Newspapers. Online editions of the *Washington Post*, the *Columbus Dispatch*, the *St. Louis Post-Dispatch*, and the *Middlesex Daily News*.

• Electronic Magazines. Features, tips, advice, and product reviews drawn from the pages of *Popular Science, Better Homes and Gardens*, and *Popular Electronics*.

• Feature Reports. May or may not be available elsewhere. Include "Gandolf's Report" on fashion, "The Future File" (technology and its impacts), and "The Small Business Report."

• American Self-Health Association. Called "Health Tex." Emergency and non-emergency health information. File updated daily to include most recently published health-related information. Personalized nutrition program and access to discount shopping available to those who join.

Business and Finance Information and Services

• Archer Commodities. Specialized reports on a wide range of specific commodities.

• Business Information Wire (BIW). Product of The Canadian Press (CP), Canada's national newsgathering cooperative of 111 daily newspapers. Constantly updated information on business subjects. Available to businesses and prime CIS account holders during the day for a $50 subscription and prime-time rates. Available to regular CIS subscribers at night at normal CIS rate.

• Commodity News Service (CNS). Updated every 20 minutes. Tracks news and price activity on all major commodity exchanges.

• Federal Reports. Articles and reports on recent legislation and its impact, particularly on financial and investment climate.

• MicroQuote. Current and historical information on more than 40,000 stocks, bonds, and options. An extra-cost service. But prices are modest. To find the stock symbols for 25 companies, cost is 25¢; to read a report on a given issue, cost is $1.25; and so on.

You can use the filing options of CIS's MicroNET to create a portfolio of stocks to be updated each time you use MicroQuote.

• QuickQuote. High, low, closing, volume, and net change on more than 9000 securities. Updated throughout the trading day. Extra cost on the order of 2¢ per quote.

• Standard & Poor's General Information File. Detailed descriptive and financial information on 3000 major publicly held companies. Extra cost of 25¢ to read report on each company. Report includes: business summary, important business developments, product/service contribution to revenue/profits, and selected financial items. Also corporate address and phone. List of directors, principal officers, and stock transfer agents, five-year earnings per share growth rate, and S&P-assigned dividend rank.

• Value Line Database II. Product of Arnold Bernhard & Company. Same firm conducts weekly Value Line Investment Survey (a different product). Requires separate agreement. Approximately 1600 companies listed. Approximately 400 data items each. Cost is 8¢ per data item received. Volume discounts available.

• CIS Business Wire. Contains 40 to 50 news releases from major organizations and companies.

• FINTOL (Financial Analysis Tool). One of several computer programs located in the MicroNET area of CIS. Contains modules for calculating loan payment and amortization, compound interest, sum from a periodic investment, sinking fund deposit, present value of cash flows, present value and internal rate of return (projects), depreciation analysis, and compound growth rate.

Personal Computing Information and Services

• Newsletters. Currently newsletters for users of Atari, Commodore,

Microsoft, RCA, and Tandy Radio Shack computers and software. Sponsored by the companies. Enables you to send questions and comments directly to manufacturer.

• The Micro Advisor. Provides information on microcomputing. Enables you to submit questions for answer by experts.

• Direct Download of Software. Enables you to buy software and have it downloaded into your computer while you are online. Programs available for TRS-80 and Apple computers. Financial and investment management, games, word-processing programs, and more. Price range from $14.95 to $125. You are prompted through the entire download process and your account is charged automatically. Special Apple and TRS-80 Videotex software required to use this feature. Both are available at Radio Shack stores.

• Free Software. Also for direct download into your machine. Located in the Public Access section of MicroNET. Can keyword search all available listings for programs of interest. No charge. Software is written and offered by individual CIS members for the benefit of all.

• 128K of Storage. Every CIS subscriber automatically receives this much space on the system (equivalent to between 18,000 and 25,000 English words) as a personal private filing cabinet. More is available at extra cost. Can be used to store letters received in EMAIL, programs written by you, or programs and text written by others (through file transfers).

• Programming Power. MicroNET section of CIS gives you access to DEC mainframe computers, plus access to large number of programs, including a word processor, a number of file editors, and a whole range of computer languages. *The CompuServe Personal Computing Guide* ($3.95) is an absolute must for using this feature. Order through the FEEDBACK option.

• Automatic Placement on Log-in. Using the MicroNET or Computing area of CIS, you can arrange to be immediately placed in the CB section, the EMAIL section, or other section of your choice every time you log in, without having to enter any commands to do so.

Electronic Banking

• CompuServe has a growing bank-at-home program. Current banks include the United American Bank (Tennessee) and the Shawmut Bank of Boston (Massachusetts). System tells you how to establish an account. (See Chapter 9 for more information on electronic banking.)

Electronic Shopping

• Comp-U-Store Division of Comp-U-Card. Online access to descriptions and prices of over 50,000 products offered at discounts from 10 to 40 percent. (See Chapter 9 for more information on electronic shopping.)

Computerized Conferencing

• Done through the SIGs (Special Interest Groups). A still-developing system. But CB option permits real-time conferencing of many individuals. (See Chapter 10 for more information on computerized conferencing.)

Fun and Games

• Travel and Leisure. In planning stages. Will ultimately offer airline schedules between 1200 major cities; worldwide yacht, recreational vehicle, and vacation home exchange service; tour and cruise specials; airport arrival conditions; calendars of local community events. Planned to be available 24 hours a day.

• Trivia Unlimited, Categorically Trivial, and so on. Quizzes composed by Professor Howard Millman of the University of Maryland. Absolutely addictive. Ten-question warmup quiz. Followed by "sudden death" quiz. Miss three and you're dead. End of test displays current top scorers on system.

• Space War, Decwars, Megawar, and Adventure. "The star's gravitational field has swung you far beyond your intended orbit. . . ." And many, many more online games. Played in CB section so can accommodate up to ten real-time players. Some are text games (like Adventure); some have simple on-screen rapid-fire graphics (like Space War).

• Art Gallery. Order high-density computer line printer art. Golden Gate bridge to Mr. Spock to real spaceman, Neil Armstrong. Prices: $4.30 to $19.50. Sizes: Up to 8'4" × 8'8".

Other Services

- *World Book Encyclopedia*
  The entire 22-volume encyclopedia, including 31,000 subject entries and over 10 million words of text. You can search for relevant articles by entering as few as 2 characters or as many as 30. Other features include a Phonetic Spellings section to help you search using unusual or unfamiliar words; Facts in Brief, tables of key facts about states, provinces, and other demographic information; Cross References to direct you to other articles on the subject you have chosen; and categories called "Related Articles," "Questions," and "Bibliographies."

  Also: The World Book Challenge, containing quizzes on facts, figures, dates, and trivia; This Week in History, summary of what happened during the current week in the past; Flashbacks, features on relationships between current news and past events; and Talk-Back, your chance to type in questions and comments to the World Book staff. (See Figure 4.1.)

- The College Board. Made up of representatives of 2500 secondary schools. Provides online advice on selecting a college, what to do when, and how to prepare for the SATs.

- EMI Flight Planning. For aircraft owners and private pilots. Product of Engineering Management Information of Missouri. Will give you complete flight plan, regardless of whether or not you have RNAV equipment onboard.

- Refundle Bundle. Tips, advice, addresses, and other invaluable information from Susan Samtur, author of *Cashing In at the Checkout*. Appeared on "The Phil Donahue Show" demonstrating purchase of $80 worth of groceries for total investment of $2.50, thanks to refunds. How to send in proofs-of-purchase for cash and prizes. Online answers to letters.

– **Figure 4.1. Online *World Book Encyclopedia* on CompuServe.** –

The following example shows the main *World Book* menu on CompuServe and the results of a search for articles containing the word CHINA. No articles on CHINA were read. Instead, a more refined search was conducted for articles on the MING DYNASTY. And the resulting article was displayed and printed out.

Figure 4.1 continued

```
World Book                                          Page WBE-1
                    WELCOME TO
                 ONLINE WORLD BOOK
                  Copyright (C) 1982
                  World Book, Inc.
1. Online Encyclopedia
2. How to Use Online World Book
3. News Flashback
4. This Week in History
5. World Book Challenge
6. Product Information
7. World Book Talk-Back
 Last menu page. Key digit
or M for previous menu.. =!1


. Search term: CHINA


World Book                                          Search
CHINA
8 articles selected
1 CHINA
2 CHINA,
3 CHINA GRASS.
4 CHINA SEA.
5 CHINA SYNDROME.
6 CHINA-WOOD OIL.
7 CHINA'S SORROW.
8 CHINATOWN.
. Input a number or key
<ENTER> for more choices. =!
```

———————————————————————————— [Intervening menus not shown.]

```
. Search term: MING DYNASTY


World Book                       Page WBE-107132
```

MING DYNASTY ruled China from A.D. 1368 to 1644, a period of Chinese rule between two foreign conquests. It was preceded by the Mongol Empire and followed by the Manchu dynasty. Ming rulers restored traditional institutions, such as the civil service, which the Mongols had temporarily suspended. Chinese authority extended into Mongolia, Korea, Southeast Asia, and the Ryukyu Islands.

Ming means bright in Chinese, and the period was important especially in the arts. Ming architects built the imperial palace, which is in the area of Peking called the Forbidden City. Many buildings from this period are still standing. Artists produced beautiful porcelain, bronze, and lacquerware. Western traders came to China for the first time. Jesuit missionaries also came from Europe.

Please keep in mind that this is really only a brief sampling of what CompuServe Information Service has to offer. Many other modules exist and more are being added all the time. For an up-to-date listing of the programs you might access in the Display or Videotex area, type GO IND (for "Index") at the command level as explained in the "Moving About Within the System" section of this chapter.

What Does It Cost?

Prior to 1983, CompuServe subscriptions were available only through Radio Shack stores. However, with the expiration of CIS's contract with Tandy, subscriptions are—or soon will be—available through other outlets as well. The basic CIS subscription is $19.95. (Instructions on how to use the system are extra.) This is a one-time-only sign-up charge. It allows you to access the system during the standard hours of 6:00 PM to 5:00 AM (your local time), and all day Saturday, Sunday, and major holidays.

You will undoubtedly want to order some basic manuals and instructions (see the "Documentation and Instructions" section below). The total cost will depend on which manuals you purchase, but typically you should plan on spending an additional $30 or so. This brings the cost of your CompuServe subscription and instructions to about $50.

The subscription package will include at least one free hour of connect time. After that, time is billed at $5.00 per hour for 300 baud and $17.50 for 1200 baud. Connect time is calculated to the nearest minute, and there is a one-minute minimum per online session. A CIS subscription also automatically entitles you to 128,000 characters of mainframe storage. There is no charge for this and there is no monthly charge associated with your standard CIS subscription.

The only additional costs you may incur have to do with the way you access CompuServe. There is a $2.00 per hour surcharge for using your local Tymnet number in the United States. Canadian subscribers using DataPac/Tymnet will be charged an additional $8.00 per connect hour. You can also access CIS through WATS lines, but the surcharges are $20.00 per hour weeknights and $10 per hour weekends.

Fortunately, there *is* another alternative. As part of its remote data processing service, CompuServe, Inc., is working hard to develop ComLink, its own version of Telenet and Tymnet. The service is already available in nearly 200 cities and the total is expected to reach 300 by the end of 1983. Used during the day by remote data processing customers, the network is available—free of charge—at night to CIS subscribers.

> **Online Tip:** To obtain a list of ComLink phone numbers in your area, select the User Information option from the main menu that greets you when you sign on. Then choose Telephone Access Numbers from the next menu that appears.
>
> Better yet, phone CIS Customer Service before you sign on for the first time, and they will give you the telephone number(s) you need. Call (800) 848-8990 between 8:00 AM and midnight. In Ohio, call (614) 457-8650.

Most individual subscribers arrange to have their charges billed through their credit cards, but it is possible to open a VIP Account (handled by Bank One in Columbus) or to be billed directly. Both options cost an additional $3.00 per month. Prime Service (CIS during business hours) is also available after you have established your Standard Service account. This carries a monthly minimum charge of $2.00 and is billed at rates of $22.50 per hour for 300 baud and $35 per hour for 1200 baud.

Additional storage space on the system is available in 64K increments at a rate of $4.00 per week. And some programs (such as MicroQuote and QuickQuote) have transaction charges in addition to standard connect costs.

How Do You Sign Up?

As mentioned earlier, prior to 1983, CompuServe subscriptions were available only through Radio Shack stores. Today, however, that is in the process of changing and other outlets are being added. Many of these carry the CompuServe Starter Kit. The kit includes a prevalidated ID number and a password, a *User's Guide*, and other printed materials, as well as a binder to hold them. The ID number allows purchasers five free hours on the system. The package sells for $39.95.

For an updated list of computer stores offering CompuServe subscriptions, call CIS Customer Service at (800) 848-8990.

Subscriptions should still be available through Radio Shack, however, and there may be a very good reason for buying yours in this way. The $19.95 Radio Shack package includes subscriptions to both CIS and to the Dow Jones News/Retrieval Service and one free hour of connect time on each service. Purchased separately, the total cost could be as high as $70. "Radio Shack Videotex" packages that contain TRS-80, Apple II, or Apple II + communications software as well as subscriptions to the two services are available for $29.95. It will be very helpful to your Radio Shack salesperson if you can provide the appropriate product numbers, and here they are:

Subscriptions Only—No Software

Universal Sign-Up Kit. 26-2224 $19.95

Cassette Software and Subscriptions
(Each package $29.95)

TRS-80 Model I/III Package. 26-2220
TRS-80 Model II Package. 26-2221
TRS-80 Color Computer Package. 26-2222
Apple II Package (for Apple II and Apple II +). 26-2223

> **Online Tip:** These items are stocked in Radio Shack T500 regional warehouses, and any store should be able to order them for you. However, your chances of finding them on the shelf are best at one of Radio Shack's Computer Centers. Or failing that, at one of the regular stores that maintains a "computer corner." Phone before you go.

> **Online Tip:** At least one CompuServe feature *requires* the use of Radio Shack videotex software—the SOFTEX module that is designed to let you purchase and download software directly into your computer. The Radio Shack software packages include some sophisticated error-checking features to make sure that the software you buy online transmits properly. Radio Shack videotex programs also transmit a special signal to the CIS system. If the CIS computers do not receive that signal, you will not be able to get into the SOFTEX area.

Your package will contain a sealed page containing your CIS account number and password. Account numbers contain eight numbers and a comma (for instance, 70012,345) and passwords contain up to eight letters and a non-alphanumeric character like an asterisk. Passwords intentionally make no sense (for instance, SEDGE*PURSURER), but they will get you onto the system and can be used as long as any portion of your free connect hour remains.

Now for the tricky bit. Although you may think you signed up for a CIS subscription when you bought your package, what you actually did was to buy access to the system for an hour, or five hours if you purchased the Starter Kit. In order to activate your subscription, you must sign up again while you are online. None of this is explained in the *User's Guide*, but if you haven't signed up by the time the end of your free hour approaches, the system will ask you whether you want to do so. The online sign-up procedure is covered in the "Getting to Know the System" section later in this chapter.

Documentation and Instructions

In addition to the online documentation and user's guides cited earlier, it is also possible to order manuals dealing with specific parts of the system. This can be done while online through the FEEDBACK option of the User Information section. You are not charged for the time you spend in FEEDBACK, just for the manuals you order. Of the 27 manuals described in the January 1982 edition of *Today*, the CIS magazine, only 6 dealt with noncomputerist subjects. The rest bore titles like *DEC-10/20 Processor Reference*, *TOPS-10/20 APLSF Reference*, and *BLISS-10 Programming Reference*.

If you are a noncomputerist, and have not purchased the CIS Starter Kit, you should order the *User's Guide* ($2.95); the *CIS Personal Computing Guide* ($3.95) for the information it contains on the word-processing program you'll use when writing letters in EMAIL, and for its coverage of general MicroNET procedures; and—if you intend to try some online recreation—the *CompuServe Games Guide* ($5.95). (There are also guides available for the Fantasy Game and for the Decwar Game, $3.98 and $4.00, respectively.) You may also be interested in the guide to using the MicroQuote stock program ($4.95).

Online Tip: CIS sells an *Index of Services and Subjects* for a dollar. But you will be better off if you type GO IND at the Command Level prompt (= !) and download the complete index while online. At 300 baud it will cost you about a dollar in connect time, but it will be more up-to-date. It will also be on magnetic disk and easy to manipulate with your computer.

Online documentation is also available when you enter a program area, and it is worth taking advantage of. As we have said before, downloading and printing out this information and putting it in a notebook is an excellent way to create your own customized documentation manual.

Customer Service and Support Publications

As evidence of its commitment to online Videotex information and services, CIS has considerably augmented its customer service capabilities. A staff of a dozen people now answer some 10,000 questions and send out as many as 1600 FEEDBACK replies to customers via electronic mail each month. The average "please hold" time for telephone inquiries is 30 to 45 seconds, and the average turnaround time for responding to a FEEDBACK query is 48 hours.

You can reach CIS Customer Service by dialing the following numbers:

CompuServe Customer Service

Phone Numbers
(800) 848-8990 in the United States and contiguous countries
(614) 457-8650 in Ohio

Hours
Weekdays: 8:00 AM to midnight, EST
Weekends: 2:00 PM to midnight, EST

As a CompuServe subscriber, you automatically receive a free subscription to two CIS publications: *Today* magazine and the *Update* newsletter. *Today* is a glossy, four-color, 8½" × 11" magazine issued every two months. It contains articles on using CIS programs, a question and answer section, and other features. It also contains advertising for products offered by CIS and others. Most important of all, it usually contains a two-page pull-out subject index of what is available on the system.

Update is a four-page monthly newsletter containing announcements of newly added features, CompuServe press releases, and changes in ComLink phone numbers.

Moving About Within the System

The first thing you should be aware of is that there are two separate but closely intertwined areas of the CompuServe Information Service. These are the Display area and the MicroNET area. The Display area is where all the online Videotex features and information are located. The MicroNET area is where computer programs are run. Each area has its

—————————— **Figure 4.2. Selecting Menus.** ——————————

```
CompuServe          Page CIS-1

CompuServe Information Service

1 Home Services
2 Business & Financial
3 Personal Computing
4 Services for Professionals
5 User Information
6 Index

Enter your selection number, or H for
more information.. = !5
```

Entered 5, the selection number
for "User Information."

```
CompuServe          Page CIS-4

USER INFORMATION

 1 What's New
 2 Command Summary & Usage Tips
 3 FEEDBACK, Manuals, Products
 4 Changing Terminal Defaults
 5 Changing Your Password
 6 Reviewing Your Charges
 7 Changing Credit Card Info
 8 Telephone Access Numbers
 9 Current Rates
10 CompuServe Viewpoint

. Last menu page. Key digit or M for
previous menu.. = !4
```

Entered 4 for "Changing Terminal
Defaults."

```
CompuServe          Page CIS-6

You can change your terminal type for
this session or permanently with
DEFALT, or by going to the next page.
You can also establish your initial entry
into the CompuServe Information
Service, or command mode.
. . . Proceed to the next page to
change your terminal type or defaults.

Key S or <ENTER> to Continue. = !
```

own set of commands and techniques. As a CIS subscriber you will have access to both areas and will be able to move in and out of them at will. In some instances, the system will automatically transfer you from one to the other to execute a task. When the task has been completed, you will be returned to the area you started from. A third area, called the "Multi-Player Host," is used for CB communications and game-playing. It too is accessible from both Display and MicroNET.

At this point you should be thoroughly confused. If you aren't, then you're a born computerist and should go directly to the system. If you are puzzled, however, it will help if you think only of the Display area and pretend that the others do not exist. The only thing you will not be able to do is straight programming. The CIS system will move you in and out of the appropriate area automatically, depending upon what you want to do.

Menus, Pages, and the Command Level

Everything in the Display area exists on "pages." These are blocks of text containing 32 characters (left to right) per line, and 16 lines (up and down) per page. Each page has a specific number, and it is possible to get to any page on the system directly if you know what that number is. Normally, however, you will use the "menus," special pages containing two or more items for you to choose from. When you make a selection, either a second menu will appear or the text you want to read will begin to scroll onto your screen.

For a clearer idea of how this works, look at Figure 4.2. The first menu (Page CIS-1) is what you will see after you have typed in your account number and password and are logged onto the system. This is the CIS main or TOP menu. Notice the sentence at the bottom reading "Enter your selection number, or H for more information.. = !" Type the number 5 and hit <ENTER>, and the User Information menu (Page CIS-4) will scroll up your screen. This is called a "sub-menu." Selecting 4 for changing terminal defaults at the "equals/exclamation" (= !) prompt causes Page CIS-6 to scroll onto your screen. And so on.

As you explore the system, you will learn what programs and features are located under the categories offered on that first menu page and what sub-menus each of these selections will generate. Selecting the Home Services option from the main menu, for example, will generate the following sub-menu:

CompuServe   Page HOM-1

HOME SERVICES

1 News/Weather/Sports
2 Reference Library
3 Communications
4 Home Shopping/Banking
5 Groups and Clubs
6 Games and Entertainment
7 Education
8 Home Management
   Last menu page. Key digit or M for previous menu.. = ! 3

Entering selection 3 for "Communications" leads to this menu:

CompuServe   Page HOM-30

COMMUNICATIONS

1 Electronic Mail (user to user messages)
2 CB Simulation
3 National Bulletin Board (public messages)
4 User Directory
5 Talk to Us
6 Lobby Letters of America
7 Ask Aunt Nettie

  Last menu page. Key digit or M for previous menu.. =!

The CompuServe menus provide you with an easy way to get to know the system. But there is one other technique you need to be aware of to use the menus effectively. And that concerns the "commands" you can enter instead of selecting a number from a given menu. Each time a page or menu appears, it will scroll up and stop at the "equals/exclamation" prompt. Because this is the Display area of CompuServe, this is called the Display prompt. You may then hit <ENTER> to move on to the next page. *Or* you may type in a number of other commands.

The commands consist of single letters (followed by an <ENTER>, of course), and here's a brief summary of the ones you will use most often:

H (for Help)   Will generate a list of all available commands and short
     explanations of each.
T (for TOP)   Will immediately take you to CompuServe's TOP menu
     (Page CIS-1).
M (for Menu)   Will take you to the menu you used most recently.
F (for Forward)   Will display the next page.
B (for Backward)   Will display the previous page.
R (for Re-send)   Will cause the system to send you the current page
     again.

Three additional commands deserve special attention. These include the command to make the system send you pages of text without interruption, the command to *deliberately* interrupt and stop an on-screen printout, and the command to log off the system.

When text is being displayed, as when you are reading an article or news story, the system will stop after each 16 lines and prompt you with: "Key S or <ENTER> to Continue =!" If you hit <ENTER>, the next page will scroll up, and the same prompt will appear at its end. This can be a convenience when you are merely reading; hitting <ENTER> becomes like turning the page. However, if you are downloading a large file or a large quantity of text, it can be a real nuisance. *Hitting <S> instead of <ENTER> will eliminate the interruptions and cause the text to scroll smoothly to its end, regardless of how many pages it occupies.*

The second command is designed to solve the opposite problem: stopping an endless scroll of unwanted text. If you ever find yourself in this situation do this: *Hold down the key marked <CONTROL> and hit the letter "C".* A "Control-C" should stop any scroll and return you to the Command Level as indicated by the Display prompt (=!). (A Control-P may also work.) From there, you can enter one of the other commands or a GO Command, as explained below.

Finally, you may officially log off or sign off the system any time you see the Display prompt. Type in either OFF or BYE. This will close the book on your current session and, not incidentally, will stop the meter. The CompuServe system is programmed to wait for up to 15 minutes for some kind of input from your machine. If you do not officially log off, it has no way of knowing whether you are packing it in for the evening or whether you have just gone to fix yourself a sandwich. And you will be charged for the time between the moment you switch off your modem until the system automatically disconnects you.

A "menu-driven" approach is fine for new users. But since you must wait for each menu to scroll onto your screen, it is a slow way to move about within the system. Fortunately it is not your only alternative. In addition to all the other commands you may enter at the Command Level, you may also enter the word GO (or just the letter <G>) *followed by any page number.* For example, if you enter GO PAN, you will be taken directly to the first page of the Pan American travel section. Enter GO TMA-9, and the next page to appear will be The Micro Advisor. GO EMA takes you to the first page of the EMAIL section. And so on. You can get an index of all the major pages while you are online by selecting 6 for index from CompuServe's TOP menu.

Online Tip: You don't *have* to enter the hyphens in hyphenated page numbers. The system does not care. And remember, you may use a simple <G> instead of GO.

Online Tip: Notice that the letters in the page numbers tend to be abbreviations for the service or feature. If you cannot remember the exact number of the page you want to reach, you can always try typing in the abbreviation or the abbreviation followed by 1 for the first page of the section.

MicroNET, or Programming and Computing

Many CIS subscribers are able to accomplish everything they want to accomplish in the Display section of the service. However, there may be times—such as when you are using your storage space or transferring files to another user—when you will want to deliberately enter the MicroNET area. When you are in this area, you are in direct contact with the CompuServe mainframe computers, and your own machine becomes a terminal for them.

You can enter in at least three ways. First, you can start at the TOP menu and follow the sub-menus until you reach the page titled "Programming and Computing." This page will tell you to hit <ENTER> to enter the computer. Second, you can type in the commands MIC (for MicroNET) or EXI (for Exit Display) whenever you see the Display prompt (= !). And third, you can arrange to enter MicroNET automatically whenever you log in (this is done by setting "Terminal Defaults" as explained below).

In MicroNET the Display prompt is replaced by OK, and there generally are no menus. Commands to get a program started are preceded by an R for Request as in R INDEX or R FINTOL. After the program has begun, typing *HELP will give you a list of valid commands, and an asterisk (*) followed by any command will provide a brief description of its function.

Frankly, you shouldn't go into MicroNET *until* you know what you're doing. This is why the *CompuServe Personal Computing Guide* is absolutely essential. As mentioned earlier, you can order a copy through the FEEDBACK option on the User Information menu (Page CIS-4).

Online Tip: CIS Customer Service reports that many people go into MicroNET and are unable to get out. If this happens to you, type R DISPLAY at the OK prompt and hit <ENTER>.

Using Your CompuServe Communications Options

Electronic Mail

Electronic mail is one of the most important features of an information utility. It is something everybody uses, whether for business or pleasure or both, and it is a rare subscriber who doesn't check the mailbox during an online session. Unfortunately, the documentation supplied in some editions of the CompuServe *User's Guide* may not match what you see on the screen. If you have one of these older manuals, you should know that the Mini Editor they mention no longer exists. Instead you must use either FILGE or the ICS editor. The principal difference is that the ICS editor automatically numbers each line you enter and FILGE acts more like a word processor. Instructions for using each program are available online and in the *Personal Computing Guide*.

The important thing to remember about using CIS EMAIL is the overall concept of what is happening, and it applies regardless of the "editor" you select. To send a letter, you must first create a "file" (the letter itself) in your workspace. Every CIS subscriber is alloted a temporary workspace of about 16,000 words for use while online. This is your scratch pad.

When you want to compose a letter, the system creates a temporary file for your text and lets you compose on your scratch pad. When you are finished composing you simply select the menu option that lets you *send the file from your workspace.* You will then be prompted for the account number of your correspondent and a brief subject label (for instance, "reply to your note," "congratulations," or "Help!").

Online Tip: You should probably select the FILGE editor when sending your first letters, even if you are not completely familiar with all of its sophisticated editing commands. You will be fine if you remember two points:

1. You can rub out any mistake and retype the correct characters on any line—as long as you do so *before* you hit your <ENTER> or <RETURN> key.
2. Most important of all, to get out of FILGE and tell the system that you are finished writing, type in /EX at the far left of a fresh line and hit <ENTER>. This will cause the next menu to scroll up and you will then be able to send the letter from your workspace.

Online Tip: For best results, try to remember to hit your <ENTER> or <RETURN> key after every 32 characters. You may do so sooner, of course, but if you type beyond the 32 mark, the system may drop any additional characters on the line. Your correspondent will then have to puzzle out what you have written.

User Directory

To send mail, the first thing you need is someone to send it to. The second thing you need is the person's account number. You can find both in CompuServe's User Directory section on page HOM-4. That page will present options for locating other users who are in the directory, for adding your own name to the list, and for changing or deleting your listing.

Other users can be located by any item in their CIS listing: name (usually just first name), account number, city, state, brand of computer, or expressed interests. It's a great way to find an expert, a colleague, a neighbor, or just an electronic pen pal. Listings are entirely voluntary and the procedure for using this feature is well-documented online.

The system will notify you of how many individuals are in the directory whose listings match the search criteria you have specified. It could be 15. It could be 206. But whatever it is, you will then be given the option of reading the listings or not. Here are three typical examples:

```
70000,000 WILLIAM
TARZANA, CA
APPLE            APPLE II+
TELECOMMUNICATIONS

70000,000 STEVE
SEATTLE, WA
NORTH STAR     HORIZON 2D
FLYING/USSR/WRITING/PHOTO

70000,000 CHRIS
NEW YORK, NY
APPLE          II+/Z-80
JAZZ/WRITING/BLACK HISTORY
```

Online Tip: You will undoubtedly want to put your name on the list to enable other users to find you. However, before entering your listing, it is best to search for and read several that are already on the system. This will give you a better idea of the words people use to describe their interests and can guide you in creating a listing that will be easy for individuals sharing your interests to find.

The National Bulletin Board (BULLET)

This feature will allow you to post and read three kinds of bulletins: "wanted," "for sale," and general "notices." And it will allow you to locate and/or read notices in each of these categories by ordering the system to scan for bulletins containing a particular keyword in their subject line (the entire text of a bulletin is *not* scanned).

This feature may be selected from the menu on page HOM-30, and shortly after you make your selection, you will be advised to order the

CIS *User's Guide* before using the bulletin board. This is rather puzzling, since the *User's Guide* referred to contains fewer than 100 words of description on this feature and none of the commands you must use. You will be much better off if you continue with the program, since it is well documented online and since it will tell you how to ask for help or more information on any command.

Here are all of the bulletin board commands. You can get more information on each of them by first typing HELP and then the command:

SCAN	READ	INDEX	VIEW
COMPOSE	POST	EDIT	ERASE
CHECK	EXIT	AGE	OFF

And here is a brief sampling of the output generated by the INDEX command. The output provides the bulletin number, the account number of the person who placed it, and the subject line words describing the bulletin. If you enter this command, be sure to have a pad and paper ready since you will later have to enter the number of the bulletin(s) you want to read (READ #).

```
245   70000,000  24-Apr-00  INVENTORS
257   70000,000  24-Apr-00  OSBORNF1
258   70000,000  24-Apr-00  ASYLUM
261   70000,000  27-Apr-00  LAMBDA
206   70000,000  22-Apr-00  DBASE
187   70000,000  27-Apr-00  AMWAY
161   70000,000  19-Apr-00  VIC-20
127   70000,000  17-Apr-00  BANKRUPT?
 27   70000,000  18-Apr-00  APPLE
  6   70000,000  24-Apr-00  BBS
306   70000,000  20-Apr-00  EPSON
```

CB Simulator

CB is one of the most innovative and exciting features on CompuServe or any other information utility. As mentioned previously, there are 40 "channels" you can "talk" on. Individuals use CB-like "handles" like "Charlie Chaplin," "Octaplus," "Sexy Lady," and so on ad infinitum. And you can "talk" on one channel while monitoring up to three additional channels.

The CB feature is well documented online, and you really must read the instructions before you join in. CB is located under the Communications heading, and the first time you try it, you should go through the menus to get there. This will enable you to request the necessary instructions. Later, you can GO directly to Page CIS 39, the CB entry point on the system.

When you begin CB, you will enter on Channel 19. But you may then switch to any channel you like. To see which channels have the most activity, type /STA (for "status"). This will tell you what channel you are tuned to, which channels you are monitoring, and the number of people on each of the other channels. To tune to a different channel, you merely type /TUN, followed by the desired channel number. To see a display of all CB members' handles and the channel they are using, type /UST.

The short CB sample in Figure 4.3 will give you an idea of how this feature works and what you can expect to see on your screen. If you read this segment through, you will see that there are several conversations going on at once. And you will rejoice with Biker as he finally gets Cupcake's attention.

——— Figure 4.3. A CB Sampler: Midnight Confessions ——— and Passionate Replies.

/STA   <-------- Gives current CB status.

(1)9,(5)7,(8)3#,(33)4   <-------- Channel 1 has 9 users, 5 has 7 users, etc. We are tuned (#) to Channel 8.

/TUN 1   <-------- Now tuning Channel 1 to see what's happening there.

(1,<<<**BYTE**>>>) NITE ALL   <-------- (Channel number, CB handle) followed by message.

(1,GAMBLER) NITE BYTE
(1,SEXY SALLY) NITE BYTE HON TALK IN A
FEW
(1,CUPCAKE) HI AGAIN!
(1,Biker *-*>) Cup, I said I love U . . . U
ignoring or no copy?
(1,SEXY SALLY) HIYA CUP
(1,CUPCAKE) HIYA SALLY!
(1,GAMBLER) MS.D> = YOU WANT TO TALK?
(1,<<<**BYTE**>>>) GONEE
(1,Biker *-*>) Cup, sorry U are ignoring me . . .
(1,CUPCAKE) BIKER-NO IM NOT . . HAVENT SEEN U!
(1,SEXY SALLY) ANYWAY ALL GOT TO GO
(1,007 Secret Spy) CLEVELAND OHIO
-- ROCK AND ROLL CAPITAL OF THE WORLD!
(1,CUPCAKE) NITE SALLY!
(1,**MS*D**) HI 007 AGAIN
(1,CUPCAKE) BIKER-IM SORRY . . MUSTA
GOTTEN LOST

> **Online Tip:** Frequently individuals will meet on Channel 19 and then mutually agree to switch to a different channel, where there is less activity, to carry on their conversation. Remember, if you are on a channel with 25 users, the lines typed by each one will appear on your screen as they are typed.

Getting to Know the System

A Three-Session Approach

As you may have guessed by now, there are lots of things for you to discover and explore on the CompuServe system. You have many hours of enjoyment ahead of you. But to make the most of your time on the system it can help to get started on the right foot. There are a number of "housekeeping" chores to take care of when you are new to the system, and the sooner you dispose of them, the sooner you will be free to start your explorations.

You may want to start out by planning three separate online sessions. In your first session you can take care of your housekeeping chores. After you have had a chance to read and digest the material you downloaded in the first session, you can then sign on and do a little exploration. In the third session, you will be up to speed and be ready to locate other users, read bulletin board messages, and send electronic mail.

Session Number One

Step 1: Logging onto the System. The first thing you should do is to call CIS Customer Service to see if there is a ComLink (CIS's own network) telephone number near you. You *can* use Tymnet or DataPac, but both services tack on a surcharge. Unless you must dial long distance to use them, there are no charges associated with ComLink numbers.

If you use Tymnet or DataPac, you'll be asked for your terminal identifier. The terminal ID for virtually every personal computer is "A." If you are unsure what ID to use, call Tymnet Customer Service at (800) 336-0149 for information.

Next, check your computer and software documentation to make sure that you know how to generate a Control-C. This is the first command you will want to enter as soon as a connection has been established.

> **Online Tip:** The actual keystrokes used to generate a Control-C will depend on your hardware and software. On the Radio Shack Color Computer, the <BREAK> key will do it for you. On the

Online Tip continued

TRS-80 Models I and III, initiate the control function by holding down the <SHIFT> and <DOWN ARROW> keys, then hit <C>. Atari, Commodore, and Heath machines all have <CON-TROL> keys, but some Commodore models use software that re-defines some of the keys. If this applies to you, try the <F1> key.

In all cases, check your documentation first. Then, if you are still having problems, call CIS Customer Service.

Now set your system to the following parameters:

Baud: 300
Parity: even or no parity
Stop bits: 1
Word (or character) length: 7, if even parity; 8 if no parity

Set your modem to "originate mode" and "full-duplex." Dial the appropriate number, and when you hear it issue a high-pitched tone, switch on your modem. You will now be connected to a network, and the first thing you should do is to send a Control-C.

If you are coming in through Tymnet, you will then be asked for your terminal identifier. As mentioned, in most cases you simply need to type in the letter "A" and hit <ENTER>. Next, you will see the prompt: PLEASE LOG IN. At that point type in CIS02. You will then be asked for your CompuServe ID number and password.

Making your connection through one of CIS's own numbers is easier. Here, once the connection has been established, a simple Control-C will immediately generate a prompt for your ID and password.

Online Tip: If after the connection has been established, you hit the <ENTER> or <RETURN> key twice as you might when using Telenet to access The Source, you will be prompted for the "host" name. If this happens, type in CIS, and the procedure will continue as described above. This is generally not the best way to enter the system, so if you can, send a Control-C instead.

When you see the prompt "User ID:," type in your CIS number. When you see the prompt "Password," *carefully* type in your password. *Your password will not appear on your screen.* This is a security measure, in case someone is looking over your shoulder, but it can be a little disconcerting to be typing along and seeing nothing on the screen.

Step 2: Terminal Type and Official Sign-Up. The very first time you sign onto CompuServe, you will immediately be asked for your "terminal type." This will enable the CIS system to know what to expect from your machine in the way of signals and what signals to send you. There are five selections: VIDEOTEX–compatible, TRS-80 with MNEXEC, Teleray 1061, VT100, and "other." You can request an explanation of terminal types before making your selection, but you will probably want to select VIDEOTEX–compatible.

The second thing you will be asked your very first time online with CIS is "Do you wish to sign up for continued service?" At this point, you may either sign up or begin using the free hour included with your subscription to explore the system. You can't lose by signing up, since there is no monthly minimum charge for a CIS subscription. The sooner you sign up, the sooner you will start receiving CIS newsletters and *Today* magazine. Even more important, though, you will not be able to order any CIS manuals through FEEDBACK until your credit card information requested at signup has been verified.

The system will prompt you through the sign-up procedure. You will be asked for your name, address, phone number, and billing option (which credit card). And at the end of the process, you will be authorized to use an additional two hours. These hours are not free, but they will allow you to use the password that came with your subscription until you receive a letter containing a second password from CIS, normally about 10 days after you have signed up online.

When you receive your new password, one of the first things you should do is change it. This is done through the User Information menu, and the system will tell you how to do it. The only thing to remember is that all CIS passwords must contain at least one non-alphanumeric character (for instance, #, *, &, and so on).

Online Tip: CompuServe quite rightly cautions against using your name, initials, or any other words that might easily be associated with you when deciding upon a password. When you post messages on the bulletin board or leave contributions in the Public Access area, for example, the name and account number you enter will appear for all to see.

You can change your password by accessing the User Information section (selection 5 on the CIS Main Menu that greets you at sign-on.)

Step 3. Downloading the Index. You will now have three hours (one free, two billable) to play with, and one of the first things you should do is to download the entire CompuServe Index. You can select this option from the TOP menu, or type in GO IND-1 at the Display command prompt (= !).

The index looks like this:

```
Access: ....................................Go PCS-30
Access phone numbers:...........................CIS-4
Adult education:............................Go HOM-70
Adventure game: ...........................Go HOM-60
Advertising:
For sale:..................................Go HOM-30
Notices: ..................................Go HOM-30
Want ads: .................................Go HOM-30
```

It continues for the equivalent of 12 pages at 55 lines apiece, or nearly 700 lines. As you can imagine, it is invaluable for exploring the system.

With the Index in hand, you will have no problem at all spending your allotted three hours in exploration.

Session Number Two

Step 1: Ordering Your Manuals. CompuServe requires from 7 to 10 days to process subscriptions and verify credit card information. Until that happens, you will not be able to order your *User's Guide* or anything via FEEDBACK. So you will want to enter your order as soon as you are permitted to do so.

Step 2: Downloading Documentation and Sampling CB. In the meantime, you will want to explore the system using the Index for guidance. When you see a program you think you might use frequently, it is a good idea to set your own system to capture incoming data and download any instructions that are offered online. Write them to disk. Print them out. And put them in a notebook for future reference.

You will probably also want to have a fling at CB. As mentioned previously, you will need the online instructions to use your CB "radio" effectively. But you can listen in and take part immediately, if you like. Just remember that the command /TUN followed by a number from 1 to 40 will put you "on the air" on that channel. The command /STA will show you how many people are on what channels. And the command /EXI (for "exit") will get you out of CB.

From the TOP menu, select the Home Services option. Then choose Communications from the sub-menu that appears. And, finally, choose CB Simulation from the next menu. Or type in GO HOM-30 wherever you happen to be at the time.

Step 3: Other Recommended Programs. There are so many fascinating and enjoyable things to choose from that it is difficult to make definitive recommendations. However, you will undoubtedly enjoy the CIS quizzes (Trivia Unlimited, Categorically Trivial, and others.) But be warned: Besides making you feel stupid, they can be addictive.

What was Justine's last name on "American Bandstand"?

Answer ? Smith
Wrong. The correct answer is Corelli.
Her partner was Bob Clayton.

What timed show did Bud Collier host?

Answer ? Beat the Clock
Right. Roxanne was his assistant.

Bonus What is the rent on Illinois Avenue with four houses? (Monopoly of course)

Answer ? 360
Wrong. Better luck next time.

Press <ENTER> to continue . . .

Other suggestions include:

• "GO-ing" to page HOM-40 to look at the Comp-U-Store "shop-at-home" program. Actually purchasing through Comp-U-Store requires a membership fee, but there is a demonstration program you can run to see what it is like.

• GO to page PCS-10 in the Personal Computing Services section to read the Atari, RCA, Tandy, or Microsoft newsletters *and* The Micro Advisor for general answers on personal computers.

• Finally, be sure to check the Reference Library section on page HOM-20 for movie reviews, the Refundle Bundle, and selections from *Popular Science* and other publications

Session Number Three

By now, you probably feel fairly comfortable with the system, and you will be ready to use the communications options. You might start by scanning the User Directory (GO HOM-30) for the first names and account numbers of CIS subscribers using the same kind of computer or sharing one of your interests. Or you might scan the Bulletin Board for notices of interest and the account numbers of the subscribers who have posted them. (Be sure to have your pad and pen ready to copy down account numbers.) Then you could "GO EMA" to reach the electronic mail page and send those individuals a letter. CompuServe subscribers are a friendly lot, so the chances are very good that in a day or so there will be a reply in your own mailbox.

For the Experienced User

There comes a time when you begin to "think system," that is, you suddenly find that you and your machine—or database—are on the same wavelength. When that happens, you often know without being told how the system or database will do something, and what *you* will have to do to get it to perform.

When you reach that stage of intimacy with CompuServe, you are ready to take advantage of some of the system's more advanced features. Individuals with programming skills will be able to access the power of mainframe DEC computers. And with a bit of work and the CIS *Personal Computing Guide*, virtually anyone can learn to transfer files from his or her own storage area into someone else's and vice versa.

Terminal Defaults: Fine Tuning and Automatic Entry

It would be impossible to present all of the advanced capabilities you can take advantage of as an experienced user. But there are two possibilities that will be of interest to virtually everyone: customizing your terminal defaults, and downloading interesting programs from the huge collection of free, user-contributed software available in the system's Public Access area.

Default is one of those words you have to get used to in personal computing. It simply means that, in the absence of specific instructions to the contrary, the settings will be thus and so. As you will recall, the very first time you sign on to CompuServe you must specify your terminal type (VIDEOTEX–compatible, TRS-80 with MNEXEC, and so on). Although this is all that is necessary to use the system, it is really only one of many settings you may select.

For example, the system's default setting is to produce pages measuring 32 characters across and 16 lines from top to bottom. But if you like, you can set your terminal defaults so that the system sends you pages measuring 64, 72, or 80 characters across and anywhere from 1 to 128 lines per page. You can also set things up so that you are automatically placed in CB, EMAIL, MicroNET, or some other CompuServe area as soon as you log in, without having to deal with menus or enter a GO command.

To change your terminal defaults, select the User Information option from the TOP menu and select the appropriate option from the submenu that will then appear. This will lead to page DEFALT-1 (sic):

```
CompuServe      Page DEFALT-1

Options:

0  To exit DEFALT
1  Change terminal type
2  Change initial page
3  Change EMAIL waiting action
4  Change terminal parameters
5  Set/clear BRIEF mode
6  Change Auto IRUN
7  Display terminal settings
```

If you look for any mention of terminal defaults in the printed documentation you order, your quest will be in vain. Brief explanations are available online, however, and the system will notify you of your current default setting in each case—before asking you to choose a specific setting.

Selecting "Change terminal type" activates the same program used during your very first sign-on. "Change initial page" allows you to decide whether you want to automatically enter CompuServe in the Display area or in the MicroNET computing area each time you sign on. "Change EMAIL waiting action" lets you instruct the system to automatically put you into the EMAIL section whenever you log in—if and only if you happen to have mail waiting. This makes it easy to read and answer any letters you may have.

We will deal with the "Change terminal parameters" option in a moment. The "Set/clear BRIEF mode" option is for experts only; it enables you to suppress certain menus when using the system, and consequently requires a thorough knowledge of CIS commands. "Change Auto IRUN" also requires some expertise. With this option you can tell the system to automatically run a particular program whenever you enter the MicroNET computing area. The program can be one that you have written yourself, or it can be one of the standard MicroNET programs like MQUOTE. If you specify this particular program, for example, the MicroQuote program will begin to run each time you enter MicroNET, whether by default or by typing in MIC or EXI at the Display prompt.

The last option, "Display terminal settings," will show you the results of all the default settings you have entered, including most of what you did under selection 4, "Change terminal parameters." The display looks like this (asterisks added):

```
          Permanent Terminal Settings are:

            Terminal Type       : VIDEOTEX
          * Terminal Width       : 64
          * Lines per Page       : 16
          * Form Feeds           : REAL
          * Horizontal Tabs      : SIMULATED
          * DELAY after C/R      : 0
          * DELAY after L/F      : 0
          * Parity sent by CIS   : EVEN
            Initial Service      : DISPLAY
            EMAIL action         : ENTER
            EXPERT mode          : OFF
            AUTO-program
              RUN                : *NONE*
            Key <ENTER> for next page:
```

Those settings we have marked with an asterisk are entered under the "Change terminal parameters" option. Under this same option, you may decide how you would like to have incoming and outgoing letters displayed (all upper- or all lowercase, or mixed), whether you want any blank lines in the CIS transmitted text to show up on your screen, and whether the <RUBOUT> or <BACKSPACE> key can be used to delete any character you have typed.

Downloading Free Software

Many CompuServe users are either professional or amateur programmers, and many of them have contributed their programs to the Public Access section of CompuServe for others to download and use. Unfortunately, no published instructions exist for this CIS feature, but some documentation is available online.

The first thing you must do is to enter the Public Access area. And this can be done either by typing in the word ACCESS when you are in the MicroNET area, or by typing in GO PCS-40 at the Display prompt. Once there, the first thing you should do is get the list of commands that are used and the explanations that accompany them. You can cause the system to send you explanations by typing a question mark (?) followed by any command. Here are the commands used in ACCESS:

```
Valid commands:
CAT  - catalog
COP  - copy to disk
TYP  - type a file
DOW - download a file
KEY  - search keyword list
SUB  - submit a file
DEL  - delete a file
EXI  - exit from ACCESS
HEL  - explains ACCESS
```

If you want to locate and download programs of interest, the commands to concentrate on are CAT, KEY, and TYP, COP, or DOW. The CAT command will give you a complete listing of all of the software and text files in ACCESS. (ACCESS also includes articles, essays, and other user compositions as text files.) Listings generated by CAT include the account number of the person who submitted the file, the name of the file, and the number of times someone else has looked at or "accessed" it to date. Files that have not been accessed by anyone within 30 days of the date of submission are purged (erased!) by the system. Typical listings look like this:

```
[70000,0000]
USEFUL.COM    08-Jul-82 2655
        Accesses: 67  19-Sep-82

[70000,0000]
APPLE1        19-Sep-82 1870
TRANS.ATR     19-Sep-82 1870
```

The KEY command will allow you to search for programs containing keywords in the special descriptions that have been supplied by the person who submitted the file. As the online documentation points out, entering KEY APP will find APPLE, APPLICATION, and APPROX-IMATION if these words exist in the submitted descriptions. Using various combinations of commands will enable you to conduct an even more precise search, and this is explained in the online documentation.

Important commands not mentioned in the online documentation include those used to stop a scrolling output, to restart a scroll, and to return to the ACCESS prompt where you will be able to enter another command. To accomplish each of these things, here is what you should enter:

To temporarily stop the onscreen scroll: [<CONTROL> <S>]
To restart the scroll: [<CONTROL> <W>]

To return to the ACCESS prompt: [<CONTROL> <P>]
To leave the ACCESS area entirely: [<CONTROL> <C>]

Whenever you locate a program or a text file that you would like to have, you can order the system to provide it using the COP, TYP, or DOW commands. The COP command copies the file to your personal storage space on the system. The TYP command sends the file to you immediately, and if you have your system set to capture incoming information, you can record the file on one of your own disks. Here is a brief example of the kind of thing you can expect to see on your screen when you enter a TYP command followed by a file specification (in this case, a program for an Apple computer):

Access: TYP APPLE1

```
10 DIM HEX$(16),DEC$(23),NUM$(10),W$(4),BIN$(8),BNY$(8),
TRANS(8),A$(2)
15 DATA 128,64,32,16,8,4,2,1
20 FOR n = 1 TO 8:READ B:TRANS(N) = B:NEXT N:POKE 201,14
25 PRINT CHR$(125)
30 HEX$ = "0123456789ABCDEF":DEC$ = "@ABCDEFGHI!!!!!!!JKLMNO"
```

> **Online Tip:** The lack of printed documentation can make this feature rather challenging to use. But you can always call CIS Customer Service for instructions or for answers to particular problems.

Should You Sign Up?

The answer is an unequivocal "yes!" For only a few dollars more than the cost of most printer ribbons—and considerably less than most software packages—you and your communicating computer can leap into the Information Age with CompuServe. Depending upon the subscription package you buy, you will have from one to five free hours on the system. If you find that it does not meet your expectations, you need never sign on again. There are no monthly minimums or other charges.

No database is perfect, and CompuServe does present its share of problems to the noncomputerist user in particular. But as this chapter has shown, there are ways to get around those problems. And CIS appears to be aware of the difficulties it presents and to be working to improve things. For example, Jeffrey M. Wilkins, the firm's president, was quoted in a recent issue of *Business Week* as saying that CompuServe will upgrade its service to match market needs. Other company officials predict that the consumer information market will eventually be CompuServe's largest business.

In the meantime, there is only one thing more to be said: At prices like these, how can you lose?

...5...

The Dow Jones News/ Retrieval Service
Money Matters, an Encyclopedia, and More

The Dow Jones News/Retrieval Service (DJNS) is a news and financial database in the process of becoming an information utility. Owned by Dow Jones & Company, publishers of the *Wall Street Journal, Barron's,* and a number of Canadian newspapers, the database was begun as a joint venture with Bunker Ramo Corporation in 1974. Originally it provided only stock-market information to brokerage houses and professional investors, and each subscriber had to be "hard-wired" via a direct line to the DJNS computers. The service was very expensive and not generally available to the public.

In the summer of 1977, the News/Retrieval database was added to give customers access to summaries of the latest news appearing in Dow Jones publications. Rates were reduced, and it became possible to access the service through local Telenet and Tymnet numbers. Then in 1979, Dow Jones bought out its partner, reorganized the service, and began adding new databases and features. In 1980, DJNS announced an agreement with Apple Computers that enabled Apple owners to subscribe. In 1981, some of the individual databases were reformatted to permit owners of TRS-80s and Commodore Pet computers to use the service. And when the IBM Personal Computer was introduced in the fall of that year, one of the first software packages made available by IBM was The Dow Jones Market Analyzer™.

As this brief historical summary demonstrates, the Dow Jones News/ Retrieval Service is *serious* about attracting microcomputer users.

124

DJNS is also aggressively expanding its offerings to include databases that will be of interest to a wider market than businesspeople and stock brokers. Relatively recent additions include, for example, Cineman movie reviews, Comp-U-Store, sports and worldwide weather information, news from United Press International, and one of the first online encyclopedias available anywhere. An electronic mail service will be added in the near future, and the number of new databases is constantly growing.

To emphasize its new orientation as an information utility for everyone, at least one DJNS brochure follows "The Parks Family" through a typical day online. The brochure starts with fourteen-year-old "Tim" accessing DJNS at 6:32 AM to get the previous evening's baseball scores and team standings, and it ends at 8:00 PM with young "Mary" calling up the latest movie reviews. Along the way wife "Eleanor" relaxes with a mug of coffee as she reads the "What's News" column from the *Wall Street Journal* Highlights Online database, husband "Bob" searches for news and investment information, and Mary uses the online encyclopedia to research her school report.

Slickly published and lush with four-color photographs, this brochure is as significant for what it says about the information industry as for what it says about Dow Jones. It marks the first fully developed presentation of online services as a *utility* that family members can access the way they "access" tap water by turning a spigot.

Given its reputation as a provider of financial information, this lavishly produced vision is not the kind of thing one would expect from Dow Jones. But then, as a utility in the making, the firm is actively repositioning itself. And as the largest of the three information utilities—over 60,000 subscribers—it is the one best able to afford it. Dow Jones is growing at the rate of 2000 per month, but this may accelerate. The firm predicts that it will have 250,000 subscribers by the end of 1984.

What's Available on the System?

News and General Information

• Dow Jones News. Drawn from the *Wall Street Journal, Barron's*, and the Dow Jones News Service (sometimes called the "Broadtape"). Includes over 80 news categories, information on over 6000 companies, and over 50 industries. Also includes information on over 700 individual Canadian companies listed on the Toronto Stock Exchange. News currency ranges from 90 seconds after the filing of a story by a Dow Jones reporter to 90 days after publication. Normally searched by entering subject code. But stories 10 days or older can be found via Free Text Search (described later in this section).

• World Report from United Press International. Front-page stories, plus other national and foreign news. Updated continuously from 8:00 AM to 7:00 PM EST. The command / /NEWS brings up the report's "front page" containing the top five stories of the moment, and you select the number of the story you want to read. Other news available as well.

• *Wall Street Journal* Highlights Online. Available each business day at 7:00 AM EST. Contains headlines and summaries of front-page and back-page stories, descriptions of editorials and commentaries, summaries of both "Heard on the Street" and "Abreast of the Market" features.

• Weather Reports. Temperature tables showing highs, lows, and one-word forecasts ("cloudy," "thshwrs," or whatever) for individual cities in five U.S. regions, Canada, Europe, Latin America, Asia, and Australia, and the Middle East and Africa. Also National Weather Forecast and National Weather Wrap-up.

Recreational Features

• Cineman Movie Reviews. Reviews of 50 current movies, updated every Friday. Includes categories for new releases, current movies, and coming attractions. Not keyword-searchable.

• Sports Report. News stories, team standings, amateur rankings, statistics, and scores for *all* professional, collegiate, and top amateur sports.

• Comp-U-Store. Online access to descriptions and prices of over 50,000 products offered at discounts from 10 to 40 percent. (See Chapter 9 for more information on electronic shopping.)

Financial Information

• Current Quotes. Direct from the trading floors of the New York, American, Midwest, and Pacific Stock Exchanges. Current stock exchange and money market price quotes for all common and preferred stocks and warrants, corporate and foreign bonds, mutual funds, options, and U.S. Treasury issues. Due to stock exchange requirements and regulations, there is a mandatory 15-minute delay while the markets are open. OTC ("over-the-counter") market quotes updated six times daily between 11:00 AM and 5:00 PM EST. OTC volume updated once each business day at 6:00 PM EST.

- Historical Quotes. Provides past prices for common and preferred stocks and warrants traded on the New York, American, Midwest, and Pacific Exchanges, as well as on the OTC market. Includes daily quotes for the past year, quarterly summaries beginning with 1978, and monthly summaries from 1979 to the present.

- Corporate Earnings Estimator. Drawn from estimates and forecasts provided by over 1000 professional market research analysts at 45 top brokerage firms. Provides forecasts of *earnings per share* for 2400 companies. Database is provided by Zacks Investment Research, Inc., and is updated weekly.

- Disclosure II. A product of Disclosure, Inc. Information drawn from data filled with the Securities Exchange Commission (SEC). Includes business and descriptive data on approximately 6000 publicly held companies; extracts from 10-K, 10-Q, and 8-K forms; proxy statements; and more. Extra cost: $4.00 per company during prime time; $2.00 after 6:01 PM, your local time. Note: These charges apply whether you select all items from the Disclosure menu or only one item.

- The Media General DataBank. A product of Media General Financial Services, Inc. Over 58 different statistics on each of over 3200 individual companies. Plus composite data on 180 industry groups. Price/ Earnings ratios (P/E) provided include current and five-year average (high or low). Price and volume figures, price to common stock equity, betas up and down, percentage of shares outstanding, return on total assets, and more.

  Planned enhancements for this database include a screening feature in which you tell the system to give you the names of all the stocks meeting the criteria you specify (such as "all stocks with a P/E ratio of X and a five-year growth rate of Y"). A new Dow Jones–published software program for the Apple II called Market Microscope allows you to accomplish much the same thing with your own computer. Similar programs for the IBM/PC and other computers are planned.

- Weekly Economic Survey from Money Market Services, Inc. Consists of commentary and analysis; median forecasts of monetary and economic indicators; and bar charts illustrating the distribution of forecasts around the median. Information drawn from surveys of economists and money-market professionals from 40 to 50 leading financial institutions. Topics covered include money supply, Fed funds rate, consumer price index, and unemployment rate. Updated weekly. (See Figure 5.1.)

- Weekly Economic Update. Prepared by DJNS editors. Consists of statistics, analysis, and commentary on the past week's economic events, plus a look at the month ahead.

- "Wall $treet Week" Online. Complete transcripts of the four most recent PBS programs. Divided into four categories. Includes Louis Rukeyser's opening commentary, unbearable puns and all; the panel discussion; viewer questions and panel responses; and the guest interview. Particularly useful if you missed a statistic during the program or forgot to set your Betamax to record.

Special Features

- Free Text Search. Allows you to search for any keyword or combination of key words contained in any summary of any article published by *Barron's*, the *Wall Street Journal*, or the Dow Jones News Service. Database goes back to 1979 and contains over 150,000 news stories, interviews, and reports. There is a lag of about 10 days between the time a story first appears on the Dow Jones News database and when it becomes available through the Free Text Search database as well.

   Important Points:

   This service involves a physical link to the computers of Bibliographic Retrieval Services (BRS), and since BRS is not available during the weekends, neither is Dow Jones Free Text Search. This may already have changed, however, as BRS is contemplating Saturday and possibly Sunday service. For more information on BRS, please see Chapter 6.

   One of the most powerful of the DJNS features, Free Text Search has always been comparatively expensive. However, rates were cut in September 1982. The cost is now 60¢ per minute between 6:01 AM, your local time, and 4:00 AM EST (or 3:00 AM Central time, 2:00 AM Mountain time, and 1:00 AM Pacific time). During prime time,

─────── Figure 5.1. Weekly Economic Survey Charts. ───────

```
              WEEKLY ECONOMIC SURVEY
                 OF OCT. 00, 19—
                COPYRIGHT (C) 1982
              MONEY MARKET SERVICES, INC.

     A SURVEY OF FORECASTS BY ECONOMISTS AND MONEY-MARKET
     DEALERS AT 40 TO 50 LEADING FINANCIAL INSTITUTIONS
     PREPARED WEEKLY BY MONEY MARKET SERVICES, INC.,
     BELMONT, CALIFORNIA.

              (01) FORECASTS OF THE CHANGE (IN BLN. OF DOL.)
PCT.OF                IN M1 DURING THE WEEK ENDED SEPTEMBER 29
TOT.RESP.             TO BE REPORTED FRIDAY, OCTOBER 8
  |
  |                             XXX
20+                            XXX                    MEDIAN =
  |                            XXX                    −$1.5 BLN.
  |                            XXX   XXX
  |                     XXX    XXX   XXX   XXX
  |                     XXX    XXX   XXX   XXX
10+                     XXX    XXX   XXX   XXX
  |                     XXX    XXX   XXX   XXX   XXX
  |              XXX    XXX    XXX   XXX   XXX   XXX                          XXX
  | XXX   XXX   XXX    XXX    XXX   XXX   XXX   XXX   XXX                     XXX
  | XXX   XXX   XXX    XXX    XXX   XXX   XXX   XXX   XXX   XXX   XXX
 0+ ---- + ---- + ---- + ---- + ---- + ---- + ---- + ---- + ---- + ---- + ---->
 −4.0  −3.5  −3.0  −2.5  −2.0  −1.5  −1.0   −.5    0    +.5   +1.0 MORE

              (02) MONEY MARKET ATTITUDE INDEX
PCT.OF                (SCALE: −5 = BEARISH TO +5 = BULLISH)
TOT.RESP.           XXX                             ----N-O-T-E-S----
  |                 X:X                             "XXX" REPRESENTS
  |                 X:X              MEDIANS:        ATTITUDE TOWARDS
30+                 X:X              BILLS   = 0     THE BILLS.
  |                 X:X    :::       COUPONS = 0     ":::" REPRESENTS
  |          :::    X:X    X:X                       ATTITUDE TOWARDS
  |          X:X    X:X    X:X                       THE COUPONS.
  |          X:X    X:X    X:X                       "X:X" REPRESENTS
15+          X:X    X:X    X:X                       OVERLAPPING DATA.
  |  X:X     X:X    X:X
  |          X:X    X:X    X:X
  |  XXX     X:X    X:X    X:X    XXX
  |  X:X     X:X    X:X    X:X    X:X    X:X    :::
 0+ ---- + ---- + ---- + ---- + ---- + ---- + ----
 −3     −2     −1     0     +1     +2     +3    +4
```

the cost is $1.20 per minute, the same as the charge for many other DJNS services.

You absolutely must have the DJNS *Free Text Search Manual* to use this feature. The manual is free, but you must request it by calling Customer Service. Be sure to do so as soon as you become a subscriber, whether or not you plan to use the feature immediately.

- The *Academic American Encyclopedia*. The online version of the 21-volume work created by Aretê Publishing Company, Inc., and now published by Grolier, Inc. Contains over 28,000 articles. Updated twice a year. Keyword searchable by article, title, or subject heading. Very easy to use. Just 60¢ a minute during prime time and only 30¢ a minute after 6:01 PM your local time. (See Figure 5.2.)

- //INTRO. Online information about the Dow Jones News/Retrieval Service as a whole, plus announcements concerning various individual databases. There is no charge for the time you spend in the //INTRO program.

— **Figure 5.2. The Academic American Encyclopedia Online!** —

```
ACADEMIC AMERICAN ENCYCLOPEDIA
   COPYRIGHT (C) 1982
ARETE PUBLISHING COMPANY, INC.

THERE ARE TWO WAYS TO FIND INFORMATION
IN THE ELECTRONIC ENCYCLOPEDIA:

PRESS     TO

1         SEARCH BY THE PARTIAL TITLE
             OF A SUBJECT HEADING

2         SEARCH BY THE COMPLETE TITLE
             OF A SUBJECT HEADING
   1
ENTER ONLY AS MUCH OF THE TITLE AS YOU
ARE SURE OF. INCLUDE ALL PUNCTUATION.
ENTER THE LST NAME FIRST, FOLLOWED BY
A COMMA, A SPACE AND THE FIRST INITIAL.
USE SINGULAR WORDS, NOT PLURAL WORDS.

FOR EXAMPLE, YOU CAN:

ENTER     REAGAN, R  OR  REAGAN, RON
TO FIND   REAGAN, RONALD
```

ENTER   TRADE ASSOCIATIONS
TO FIND   TRADE ASSOCIATIONS

ENTER QUERY

  Space Shuttle
                    PAGE 1 OF 1
PRESS FOR

1   SPACE SHUTTLE
_____
  PRESS RETURN TO VIEW THE SELECTIONS
    AGAIN OR ENTER A NEW QUERY.
  1
                    PAGE 1 OF 1
PRESS FOR

1   SPACE SHUTTLE
2   COMPONENTS
3   TESTING
4   CREW AND PROGRAMS
5   TYPICAL MISSION
6   BIBLIOGRAPHY
7   SEE ALSO
  2

                  PAGE 1 OF 3
COMPONENTS.
   THE SPACE SHUTTLE CONSISTS OF THE
ORBITER, THE EXTERNAL TANK, AND TWO
SOLID ROCKET BOOSTERS. THE ORBITER,
WITH A LENGTH OF 37.3 M (122.4 FT) AND
A WINGSPAN OF 23.79 M (78 FT), CARRIES
THE CARGO AND CREW AND IS THE ONLY
COMPONENT THAT ACTUALLY REACHES ORBIT.
THE FORWARD PART OF THE ORBITER WILL
CONSIST OF AN UPPER FLIGHT DECK
CONTAINING THE DISPLAYS AND CONTENTS
THAT WILL BE USED TO PILOT, MONITOR,
AND CONTROL THE VEHICLE, AND A LOWER
CABIN, CONTAINING THE LIVING QUARTERS
OF THE ASTRONAUTS. THE LOWER CABIN WILL

                  PAGE 2 OF 3
BE CONNECTED BY AN AIRLOCK TO THE
PAYLOAD, OR CARGO, BAY, 18.3 M (60.0
FT) LONG AND 4.6 M (15.0 FT) IN
DIAMETER, WHICH WILL TAKE UP THE MIDDLE
AND GREATEST PART OF THE FUSELAGE. THE
TAIL SECTION OF THE ORBITER WILL

Figure 5.2 continued

CONTAIN THE THREE MAIN ENGINES AND THE
PROPELLANT LINES BRINGING LIQUID OXYGEN
AND LIQUID HYDROGEN FROM THE EXTERNAL
TANK.
   THE SOLID-FUEL ROCKET BOOSTERS, EACH
45.5 M (149.2 FT) LONG, WILL FUNCTION
FOR ONLY TWO MINUTES BEFORE THEY ARE
SEPARATED FROM THE CRAFT AND RETURN TO
THE ATLANTIC OCEAN. THE EXTERNAL TANK,

PAGE 3 OF 3
47 M (155 FT) LONG AND 8.38 M (27.5 FT)
IN DIAMETER, WILL PROVIDE PROPELLANTS
TO THE ORBITER'S THREE ENGINES, AND THE
TOTAL LIFTOFF WEIGHT WITH FUEL IS
ALMOST 2 MILLION KG (4.5 MILLION LB).
THE OVERALL LENGTH OF THE SHUTTLE
SYSTEM ON THE LAUNCH PAD IS 56.1 M
(184.0 FT), COMPARED TO 110.7 M (363
FT) FOR THE SATURN V.

-END OF TEXT-

What Does It Cost?

The DJNS pricing scheme is not the easiest thing in the world to understand. In the first place, there is a one-time-only startup fee of $50, but you may or may not have to pay it, since a number of special deals and promotional offers are available. For example, if you own an Apple and you purchase the software program called the Dow Jones Portfolio Evaluator for $50, the signup fee will be waived. The software package includes a free subscription to DJNS. This is only one example. Various other offers are available for different software designed to run on different computers and for a number of modems.

Any kind of communications software can be used to access DJNS, however, and if you are happy with what you are currently using, you might want to consider the deal offered by Tandy Radio Shack stores. For a total cost of $19.95 you can obtain subscriptions to *both* the Dow Jones News/Retrieval Service and CompuServe. The item to look for is Radio Shack's Universal Sign-Up Kit. The Radio Shack product number is 26-2224, and it contains only subscriptions, no software. Like many other packages, this one offers an hour of free time on the service.

Generally, the price you pay for using DJNS is determined by two things: the time of day and the specific database you access. Non–prime-time rates are less expensive. Non–prime time begins at 6:01 PM your local time, but it ends at 4:00 AM EST. Non–prime-time rates also apply over the weekend and on major holidays, but the hours the service is available are reduced slightly (see Figure 5.3.)

The rates for accessing individual databases vary from a high of $1.20 per minute ($72/hour) to 15¢ per minute ($9/hr). (See Figure 5.3 for a rate table.) But DJNS has introduced at least two special plans: The Executive Membership and the Blue Chip Membership. The Executive Membership is designed for high-volume (more than 150 minutes per month) prime-time users. In return for a monthly subscription payment of $50, all rates at all times are reduced by one third. The Blue Chip Membership is designed for non–prime-time use. In return for a once-a-year fee of $75, subscribers save one third on the standard non–prime-time costs. (Under certain circumstances the annual fee may be reduced to $50.)

Both plans entitle you to a guaranteed six hours of free time on each *new* database over the course of the year. Regular subscribers usually receive only half an hour of free time to explore each new database.

DJNS bills you directly, providing an itemized accounting of your use of the system each month. There is no option for charging your connect time via MasterCard or Visa.

─────── Figure 5.3. DJNS Rate Schedule. ───────

	Prime Time	*Non–Prime Time*
Dow Jones News Weekly Economic Update *Wall Street Journal*	$1.20	20¢
Free Text Search	$1.20	60¢
Current Quotes Historical Quotes	90¢	15¢
Disclosure II Corporate Earnings Est. Media General Weekly Econ. Survey	$1.20	90¢
//INTRO	FREE	

Figure 5.3 continued

	Prime Time	Non–Prime Time
UPI News		
Encyclopedia		
Movie Reviews		
Sports Report	60¢	30¢
Weather Report		
Wall $treet Week		

Notes
1. These are prices per minute.
2. These prices apply to 300-baud communications; 1200-baud rates are 70 percent higher.
3. Telenet and Tymnet charges are *included*. There are no extra charges.
4. There is an additional fee for using Disclosure II. The extra costs are $4.00 per company during prime time and $2.00 per company during non–prime time.
5. Executive Membership rates are a third less at all times. Blue Chip Membership rates are a third less during non–prime time.

Online Tip: The financial information and analysis available online is so extensive and so current that—if you know what you're doing—you can virtually eliminate the need for a "full-service" brokerage firm and the services its higher fees support.

There are a number of software packages designed to completely automate the information-collection process. You just tell your computer what stocks or other investments you are interested in and press a button. Your computer will then dial the phone, sign on to the database, collect and record the information, and then sign off and hang up the phone.

Many sophisticated investors find that online services provide all the information they need to make investment decisions, enabling them to have all of their trades handled by "discount" brokerage firms for considerable savings on every transaction.

How Do You Sign Up?

If you buy a modem or software package that includes a DJNS membership, you can be online in half an hour. You merely call Customer Service and read them the information they will request from the sealed envelope that comes with your purchase. In other cases, you can simply call and ask for an application.

Documentation and Instructions

Dow Jones has got you covered. You will receive the DJNS *Fact Finder* manual describing the various services with your subscription. The manual also details the Telenet, Tymnet, and DataPac sign-on procedure, and it gives you all of the codes you will need to retrieve news and other information about specific American and Canadian companies, bonds, mutual funds, and industry groups on the Dow Jones News Service database.

Online Tip: In addition to the user's manual you should also ask Customer Service to send you a copy of the *Free Text Search Manual,* as mentioned earlier. There is also a free booklet on Disclosure II and information on using Media General. You may have to specifically ask for these and any other publications, however. Also, since Media General is such an extensive database, you might find it worthwhile to write to the firm directly for *their* manuals. The address is:

Media General Financial Services, Inc.
P.O. Box C-32333
Richmond, Virginia 23293
(804) 649-6587

In addition you will find online instructions. You can obtain these instructions for any database by typing two slash marks (the normal DJNS symbol) followed by the name of the database, followed by the word "Help." For example, //MEDGEN HELP, //ENCYC HELP, and so on.

Customer Service and Support Publications

Customer Service is available from 9:00 AM until 11:00 PM EST on weekdays and from 9:00 AM until 5:00 PM EST on Saturdays. The numbers and address are:

(609) 452-1511 in New Jersey
(800) 257-5114 in other states and Canada

Dow Jones News/Retrieval Service
P.O. Box 300
Princeton, New Jersey 08540

The main support publication is *Dowline*,, a quarterly magazine intended to keep subscribers up-to-date on new databases, new features, new ways to use DJNS, and announcements of software for accessing and using DJNS information.

Moving About Within the System

It's surprising, but the operating system and command structure offered by Dow Jones News/Retrieval Service is merely adequate. It is a kindness to say that it is less than sophisticated. For example, there is no "Command Level" prompt equivalent to those found on The Source and CompuServe, and on-screen printouts simply stop with no instructions as to what you should do next. As we'll see, your ability to stop and start an on-screen printout or issue a <BREAK> command will depend upon whether you access DJNS through Telenet or Tymnet.

This does not mean that the system is difficult to use. It's just that you should not expect any of the refinements available on other databases and information utilities.

You can use either a "menu approach" or a "command approach" to access DJNS. When you sign on, here is what you will see:

```
DOW JONES NEWS/RETRIEVAL
   COPYRIGHT (C) 1982
DOW JONES & COMPANY, INC.
   ALL RIGHTS RESERVED.

TYPE //INTRO FOR INFORMATION
ABOUT OUR WORLD REPORT AND
OTHER NEW OFFERINGS, OR //MENU
FOR A DATA BASE LIST.
ENTER QUERY
```

At this point you *must enter a command* of some sort. It may be either of the two suggested or the command to go directly to the database of your choice. The command / /MEDGEN, for example, will take you directly to the Media General database. If you are new to the system, you should type / /MENU to look at the Master Menu:

```
MASTER MENU
COPYRIGHT (C) 1982
DOW JONES & COMPANY, INC.

TYPE    FOR

  A     DOW JONES BUSINESS
           AND ECONOMIC NEWS
  B     DOW JONES QUOTES
  C     FINANCIAL AND INVESTMENT
           SERVICES
  D     GENERAL NEWS AND
           INFORMATION SERVICES
```

Each of these selections will take you to a sub-menu containing selections for the specific databases in each grouping. For example, entering <A> at this point will produce this:

```
DOW JONES BUSINESS
AND ECONOMIC NEWS SERVICES

TYPE       FOR
//DJNEWS   DOW JONES NEWS
//FTS      FREE-TEXT SEARCH
              OF DOW JONES NEWS
//UPDATE   WEEKLY ECONOMIC
              UPDATE
//WSJ      WALL STREET JOURNAL
              HIGHLIGHTS ONLINE

FOR HELP, TYPE CODE AND HELP.
(EXAMPLE: //DJNEWS HELP)

ENTER     FOR
  T       TOP OF SECTION
  R       PREVIOUS PAGE
```

The specific procedures for using these and all other DJNS databases are well explained in the manual. In general, it's fair to say that DJNS makes it easy for you to obtain the information you want. But once the information starts to scroll onto your screen, you may have difficulty stopping or controlling it. On other systems, for example, hitting your <BREAK> key will stop an information scroll and produce a prompt for you to enter a new command. But if you access DJNS via Telenet and you hit your <BREAK> key, the system will "hang" and you will have no choice but to disconnect and redial. Unfortunately, there is no warning of this in the Dow Jones *Fact Finder* system manual. On the other hand, if you access DJNS via Tymnet, both the <BREAK> key and the <?> key will interrupt a printout for you. The manual does not mention this either.

Here are some other points to keep in mind when using DJNS:

• If you are reading a story and decide that you do not wish to continue, you will have to wait until the system pauses and displays -MORE- on your screen. *Do not try to send the system a "Break,"* since this will cause it to lock up on you. Although you are not prompted to do so, at that point you may hit <ENTER> to continue and enter any of the R, T, M, P, or other commands described in the manual. Or you may enter one of the double slash (//) commands to go to a different database.

• You must use stock symbols, numerical industry group, and other codes to obtain information from several DJNS databases. But there is no way to obtain these symbols and codes online. You must look them up in the manual before signing on.

• You may find that you cannot erase incorrectly typed commands with your <BACKSPACE> key. If you make a correction and hit <ENTER> you will get an INVALID QUERY message and must start again. This is the only prompt you will receive.

Online Tip: It is not documented in DJNS instruction manuals, but here's how to stop and restart an on-screen printout. If you access DJNS via Telenet, type [<CTRL> <S>] to *stop* a story from scrolling. Type [<CTRL> <Q>] to start it again. (Control - S sends an "X-OFF'" and Control-Q sends an "X-ON.")

If you access DJNS through Tymnet, things are just a little bit tricky. Look at the Tymnet log-in instructions in your DJNS manual. When you are asked to PLEASE LOG IN, type the command [<CTRL> <R>]. Nothing will happen, but you will have just told Tymnet to watch for your stop/start (X-ON/X-OFF) commands. Now proceed as usual by typing DOW1;; or DOW2;; . The same Control-S and Control-Q commands described for Telenet will now work for you. Remember to repeat this procedure each time you log on through Tymnet.

Online Tip: To tell the system to scroll continuously through the item you are reading, instead of stopping and informing you that there is -MORE-, hit your <ENTER> key once for each page in the story. The number of pages in a story appear just before the actual printout begins. The system will "remember" your ENTER commands and continue to scroll to the "-END-."

Online Tip: Most important of all, the command to stop the meter and log off the system is DISC. No slashes. You can normally log off any time the system stops, either at -MORE- or -END- or when you would otherwise choose a menu selection.

Getting to Know the System

Since individual interests and needs vary so, it's difficult to make specific recommendations for getting to know DJNS. Probably the single feature that everyone will want to try is the online encyclopedia (//EN-CYC). (Please see Figure 5.2.) You might like to take a look at the bar charts that will appear on your screen when you access the Weekly Economic Survey from Money Market Services (//MMS) (Figure 5.1.) You might also consider looking up the symbol for a single stock in the DJNS manual and then collecting all of the information available on it from all applicable DJNS databases.

The one thing you should probably not do if you are new to the system is to try the Free Text Search feature. If you haven't sent for and studied the *Free Text Search Manual*, you could easily burn up a large portion of any free time that came with your subscription and have nothing to show for it.

Other than that, you will find *all* DJNS databases interesting (even the weather!) and relatively easy to use.

For the Experienced User

The DJNS system is not sophisticated enough to support most advanced techniques. However, many of the newer software packages designed for accessing DJNS are very sophisticated indeed. Used with an auto-dial modem, most DJNS-related software will dial the phone and automatically log you on to the system. Many will also automatically retrieve specified information on the stocks you have chosen. And it is *user-purchased personal computer software* that is responsible for the

squiggly graphs and trend lines you will see in some DJNS photographs
(only bar charts are available online.)

The newer packages, however, also harness your computer's power to
process the information after either you or your machine have signed
off. Highly developed and detailed charts, graphs, and analytical reports can be generated to aid you in your investment decisions. DJNS-
related software is available for Apples, Ataris, Commodores, IBMs,
Radio Shacks, and other machines. And increasingly, it is available from
Dow Jones *itself*.

Other Points to Keep in Mind

• If you use Tymnet to access DJNS, you have a choice of entering
either DOW1;; or DOW2;;. The response time on DOW2;; is faster.
However, if you are using auto-log-in software, you will *not* be able to
use DOW2;; and must stay with DOW1;;.

• Dow Jones uses IBM 4341 computers as hosts.

• Save money! There is an extra charge for using Disclosure II to retrieve information on a company (see Figure 5.1). The charge goes
into effect each time you enter a company name. Therefore, make sure
you get all the information you want on a company at the same time.
If you don't do this and find that you must reenter the company name,
you will be charged again.

• Columns per screen. If your system will display at least 72 columns
(lines of 72 characters across), you can obtain up to *five* market quotes
at a time. Likewise, if you find that quotes are scrolling off your
screen, you can arrange to receive only one quote at a time, followed
by a -MORE- message. Ask Customer Service about this when you
first call them for your password. If you are a current user and want
to take advantage of these features, call Customer Service and they
will change the information in the system that is associated with your
account number.

• Finally, it would not hurt to ask Customer Service about the possibility of ordering back issues of *Dowline*. You receive a subscription
to this quarterly magazine as a subscriber, but the back issues contain
information about the system that you may be able to use.

Should You Sign Up?

As mentioned earlier, Dow Jones is in the process of adding databases and services designed to make itself appealing to a broader segment of the public. One should never underestimate a company with so many resources and so much management and marketing skill. However, it seems unlikely that DJNS will be able to effect this transformation from financial database to full-featured information utility anytime soon. For one thing, its operating system will have to be completely overhauled and probably replaced to make the system more "user-friendly." This is not a task to be taken lightly under any circumstances, but accomplishing it while simultaneously adding (and debugging) new features and services would be exceptionally challenging.

There is also the fact that DJNS is getting something of a late start in the information utility business. CompuServe and The Source are already in the field with advanced electronic mail, computer conferencing, real-time communications, and many other programs designed to appeal to the same potential subscribers.

Both CIS and The Source charge considerably less for comparable features. For example, DJNS charges $18 an hour to access its online encyclopedia between 6:00 PM and 4:00 AM EST. But for $5.00 an hour you can use the *World Book Encyclopedia* on CompuServe during that same time period. The Source does not have an encyclopedia, but all of its services are available for $7.75 per hour from 6:00 PM until midnight and for $5.75 an hour from midnight until 7:00 AM.

The upshot would seem to be that if you are interested in a full-featured information utility, the time is not yet as far as DJNS is concerned. However, if you are an investor using a communicating computer, there isn't any question. You *must* subscribe to the Dow Jones News/Retrieval Service. The Source and CompuServe are good in most financial areas, but nothing comes close to the information available on Dow Jones.

To get the full benefit out of your subscription, you will almost certainly have to have a software package designed to analyze the information you obtain. A package capable of *automatically* accessing DJNS to obtain the information you seek, and of analyzing it as well, would be even better. As mentioned earlier, software packages like these are available for every major brand of personal computer. Call DJNS Customer Service at (800) 257-5114. They range in price from about $150 to about $300 and include:

Dow Jones News and Quotes Reporter
Dow Jones Portfolio Evaluator

Dow Jones Market Analyzer
Dow Jones Investment Evaluator
Dow Jones Portfolio Management System
Dow Jones Market Microscope

With an appropriate software package and a DJNS subscription, there is virtually no limit to the kind of information you can develop to help you make investment decisions. Investment information has always been the primary strength of Dow Jones, and is likely to remain so for many years to come.

...6...

DIALOG, BRS, and ORBIT
The Encyclopedic Databases

The encyclopedic databases can be thought of as vast storehouses of highly detailed, specific information on an exceptionally wide range of topics. One might say that their breadth is exceeded only by their depth, and in this they differ from the information utilities. With some exceptions, information utilities are designed to provide information on many different topics without telling you more than you usually need, or want, to know. The encyclopedics, in contrast, are designed to give you information *in depth*. The utilities also offer online shopping, banking, and communications options, but the encyclopedics generally specialize in information and only information.

It is convenient to think of DIALOG, BRS, and ORBIT, the three major databases of this type, as suppliers of information; but the encyclopedics are really the *delivery mechanisms* for individual databases supplied by information providers or, in information industry terms, "IPs." In this respect, they are rather like "information department stores." Each organization decides which "products" it wants to carry, and each has its own billing department, special offers, and unique in-house features. Consequently, just as you are able to find the same brand of blue jeans in every major department store, you can also find the same database on two or more encyclopedics. But the reverse is true as well, for DIALOG, BRS, and ORBIT each have certain exclusive offerings.

The Power and the Potential

Regardless of their differences, though, all three encyclopedic databases have at least one thing in common: They each place an astounding amount of knowledge and information at your fingertips. It is only a slight exaggeration to say that if there is anything you want to know—from a comprehensive list of all current applications for Teflon® to a description of the lush plant life that once covered Antarctica—you can find it on an encyclopedic database. And if it is not there today, it probably will be tomorrow, since new information and new individual databases are constantly being added. If knowledge is power, the collective potential represented by these three organizations is all but incalculable.

Interestingly, none of them is a new creation. DIALOG officially began operation in 1972; ORBIT, in 1974; and BRS (for Bibliographic Retrieval Service) in 1976. What is new—and profoundly significant—is the increased *availability* of the information stored in these treasure houses, made possible by the personal computer.

In the past, encyclopedic databases have been available only to librarians, professional researchers, large companies, and other institutional or corporate entities able to justify and afford the equipment needed to access them. Recognizing this, the databases have traditionally marketed their services only to this select audience. As a result, most people are not even aware of their existence, let alone all that they have to offer.

Today, all of this is changing. Thanks to the microchip and the personal computer, everyone—businesspeople, high school and college students, doctors, lawyers, scientists, homemakers, professors—can now search through tens of millions of books, reports, articles, indexes, and abstracts—for the exact fact, figure, or phone number they need.

A sizable portion of the world's knowledge is now easily accessible to a sizable portion of its people—or will be in the very near future. This is the *real* potential represented by DIALOG, BRS, ORBIT, and encyclopedic databases to come. The impact will not be felt for several years. But by the time high school students routinely switch on their computers to research a class report, the widespread availability of in-depth information will be seen to be a phenomenon as significant and sweeping as the computer revolution itself.

First Impressions

As a prospective user of any of these databases, the biggest obstacle you will have to overcome is your reaction to the sheer size of what confronts you. DIALOG, the largest of the three, offers over 175 databases and contains in excess of 55 *million* units of information or "records." It is *mammoth*—so large that its name should probably be carved in sand-colored stone like the title of "Ben Hur" or some other epic movie. BRS and ORBIT, with between 60 and 80 individual databases apiece, aren't exactly cozy little enclaves either.

There is also the fact that when you're dealing with the encyclopedics, you're in the information industry's major leagues, complete with "Boolean operators," "word stems," "limit commands," and fat operations manuals filled with descriptions of advanced precision features.

These are databases designed for professional researchers, and it is perfectly natural to conclude that you have no business being there.

But that would be a mistake. The basic search commands are not difficult to learn. And unless you are a professional fact finder, you will not *need* all of the advanced variations. What's more, the *same* commands apply to all of the individual databases on a given system. Taken together, they are like a toolbox that can be used to open and search virtually any file. With a little practice, you will be able to move from one individual database to another with very little effort.

The encyclopedics themselves will help you. Each of them offers free connect time, either for practice or for exploring a newly added database. Each has several extra-low-cost "practice files" for you to use, as well as a master index file to help you decide which individual databases you should consult for the information you need. Regular workshops and training sessions are also offered. And Customer Service is only a toll-free call away if you run into trouble.

The important thing is not to allow yourself to be overwhelmed. If you spend a bit of time mastering the basic commands and a bit of time applying them to the databases of your particular interest, you'll be amazed at what you can do. You may not be ready to apply for a professional researcher's union card, but viewed from this perspective, each of the giant encyclopedic databases becomes eminently manageable. And they are likely to become even more so in the future: DIALOG, BRS, and ORBIT all have plans underway to address the needs of the personal computer owner.

Two Kinds of Output: Bibliographic Citations and Abstracts

The encyclopedics present their information in two major formats: bibliographic citations and abstracts. A *bibliographic citation* provides two things. First, it will usually give you an indication of the kind of material to be found in the book, article, report, or other item it refers to. This can help you decide whether that particular item is worth pursuing. And second, it will give you everything you need to know to find the item in a library. (See Figure 6.1.)

——————— **Figure 6.1. A Bibliographic Citation.** ———————

The database ABI/INFORM, a product of Data Courier, Inc., was searched on DIALOG for references to "perfume," "fragrance," and "scent." ABI/INFORM contains over 500 magazines and journals—everything from *Accounting Review, Interface Age,* and *Real Estate Law Journal* to *Word Processing & Information Systems.* One of several possible bibliographic citations generated as a result of this search is

Figure 6.1 continued

displayed below. Notice that in addition to some special codes, the article title, the author (Anonymous), the magazine *(Product Marketing)*, the volume and issue number, and the date of publication (March 1980) are all included.

```
80007611   ID No. 80007611
Price/Samples, Best Sales Lures for Fragrance
Anonymous
Product  Marketing  v9n3  S32,S34,S39  Mar 1980
Coden: PMARDX ISSN 0090-2454 Jrnl Code: PDM
```

If the particular work referred to by the bibliographic citation looks promising, you can then order the system to give you an *abstract*. An abstract is a summary of the information contained in the work, and most of the time it will contain all of the facts and figures you are looking for (see Figure 6.2).

―――――――――――――― **Figure 6.2. An Abstract.** ――――――――――――――

The article mentioned in the bibliographic citation in Figure 6.1 looked interesting, so an additional command was entered to generate an *abstract* of the article. In most cases, this fact-filled summary would eliminate the need to review the actual article. However, if you wanted to receive a photocopy of the article—perhaps to look at the graphs mentioned in the last line of the abstract—you could order one by typing in the appropriate command or by calling the encyclopedic database toll-free.

```
80007611   ID No: 80007611
Price/Samples, Best Sales Lures for Fragrance
Anonymous
Product  Marketing  v9n3  S32,S34,S39  Mar 1980  Coden:
PMARDX  ISSN 0090-2454  Jrnl Code: PDM
Doc Type: JOURNAL PAPER
```

According to a survey by Newsweek of consumer fragrance buying patterns, special pricing and in-store sampling constitute the most effective ways to sell to women who buy their own fragrances. The majority (53.6%) purchased cologne, while 19.5% preferred perfume. This group of women buying their own perfumes are more likely to buy them in department stores as opposed to drugstores. Natural sprays are preferred over aerosols by a huge majority of 93.7%. Pricing is the most influential factor in purchase decisions, followed by company name, cost, and packaging, and when women buy a perfume for the first time, it is usually because they tried it in a store via a free sample. The fact that a product is imported influenced the buying decisions of only 6.1%. Male respondents buying fragrances as gifts often select a brand according to the recommendation of friends, but 24% of male respondents stated that advertising was the major impetus for their choice. Graphs.

What About "Full Text"?

It's important to realize that as a rule the encyclopedic databases do not offer the entire text of newspapers, magazines, or other items. Some "full-text" items are available online from BRS, but they are exceptions. The reason is money. The full text of a single magazine article, for example, could easily occupy 30 or 40 times the computer storage space of a bibliographic citation and abstract. Even with the rapidly declining cost of computer memory, storing the complete text of most items is prohibitively expensive.

This is not really a drawback, however, since a computerized search of the full text of an article or articles would simply require too much time to be practical in most cases. To say nothing of the time *you* would have to spend going through the article to find the information you want.

Unless you are reading to savor the author's style, you will undoubtedly prefer having a quick, fact-packed summary to reading the full text. Presenting information in abstract form may be a practical necessity as far as the computer is concerned. But it is also part of what you are paying for, since someone has to sit down and prepare the online summaries that can save you so much time.

If you find that you need an actual copy of the article, book, or other source document—perhaps to get a look at accompanying charts, graphs, or illustrations—you can place an order for it while you are online with any of the encyclopedic databases. You can also phone a toll-free number. Or, if you are close to a good library, you can use the bibliographic listing you have downloaded from the database to find the document there.

Using an Encyclopedic Database—An Overview

A session on an encyclopedic database always begins by selecting the individual database you want to search (chemistry, patent law, American history, the magazine index, or whatever). You enter your selection, and a few seconds later the title of the individual database will appear. Now you're ready to type in a query.

From here on, it's a two- to three-step process. First, you conduct your search by telling the computer to look for certain keywords in the database. Each time you enter a search command, the system "goes away" to look for items that match the words you specified. When it "comes back," it will tell you how many matches or "hits" there are in the database you are searching.

The number of hits can range from zero to several thousand or more. It all depends upon how sharply you focused your inquiry. Using the encyclopedic's search commands, you continue the process until you have narrowed things down to an acceptable number of hits.

At that point, it's time to see what you've got. This is the second step. Normally, you'll want to type the command that will cause the system to display a bibliographic listing for each of your hits. As mentioned earlier, this will usually tell you whether a particular hit is worth pursuing.

Online Tip: Whenever you access an encyclopedic database, make sure that you have your printer toggled on, since you will find it convenient to refer to the printout of your session while you are online. For example, if the system notifies you that you have 10 hits on a particular topic, that notification will scroll off your screen when you request the first bibliographic listing or two. But if it was printed by your printer as it first appeared, you will be able to find it again easily.

Let's suppose that you got 10 hits for your topic and that you have ordered up bibliographic citations for all of them. Of these, three look especially promising. That is, based upon the bibliographic citation and your knowledge of the field and perhaps even the specific publications mentioned, you feel there is a good chance that an abstract of each of these three articles will contain the facts and figures you're looking for.

So you enter the command that says, "Give me the abstracts for bibliographic citations 1, 3, and 7." This is the third step in most searches. Within seconds, information similar to that shown in Figure 6.2 will begin to scroll up your screen. If you have toggled your printer on and/ or set your computer to capture incoming data, you will have a permanent record of the information.

At this point, you may enter the commands to order a photocopy of the entire article or other publication, start another search in the same database, move on to another individual database, or sign off the system.

What Does It Cost?

The cost of searching an individual database offered by an encyclopedic is largely determined by the information provider—that is, by the organization that assembled the information in the database and supplied it to DIALOG, BRS, or ORBIT. To return to the department store analogy for a moment, the price of a digital watch, a shirt, or a handbag is always based on the wholesale price charged by the manufacturer. The department store adds a markup to cover its expenses and profit, and offers the article to the customer at the total price. Similarly, each individual database offered by an encyclopedic carries its own price. Prices are expressed in cost per hour of use, and they range from a low of $25 per hour to $300 per hour or more. The actual dollar figure you pay is usually calculated to the nearest one-thousandth of an hour.

There are additional charges for each bibliographic citation you ask to see, and for each abstract. These too vary with the individual database. For example, the bibliographic citation from the ABI/INFORM database displayed in Figure 6.1 cost 10¢. The abstract associated with that same citation shown in Figure 6.2 cost 20¢. These are the ABI/INFORM rates, but they are typical. The prices charged by other databases range from a low of 8¢ to a high of $55 per item.

There are also charges for using Telenet, Tymnet, or some other telecommunications network.

All of which is to say that the encyclopedic databases are not cheap—at least not in an absolute sense. After searching DIALOG's File 15 (ABI/INFORM) for the topics "perfume," "fragrance," and "scent" and ordering a number of bibliographic citations and abstracts, for example, the following automatic cost summary appeared on the screen:

```
        4oct00 0:32:12 User00000
$12.85  0.176 Hrs File15 7 Descriptors
 $1.41  Telenet
 $1.30  10 Types
$15.56  Estimated Total Cost
```

A total cost of $15.56 sounds like a lot, and to be sure, it's nothing to be sneezed at. But in order to judge the value of the search, it is essential to realize all that it included:

• Five keyword searches of over 500 magazines and journals from all over the world. A total file containing over 190,000 "records" or units of information.

• Seven bibliographic listings of relevant articles, only one of which appears in Figure 6.1.

• Three fact-filled abstracts, only one of which appears in Figure 6.2.

Perhaps most significant of all, the entire search was conducted and all of the citations and abstracts were delivered in *under 11 minutes*. The cost was $15.56, but when you consider the alternative of driving to the library (or paying someone to do it for you) and consulting a variety of printed indexes, and then going to the library shelves to locate the appropriate volumes, reading the articles, and paying for photocopies, $15.56 begins to sound very reasonable indeed. When you add to this the fact that very few libraries are likely to possess reference books covering all 500 journals, let alone copies of the journals themselves, $15.56 begins to seem like a real bargain.

A Brief Look at What's Available on Encyclopedic Databases

The following list of individual databases will give you some idea of the breadth and depth of information you will find on the encyclopedics. DIALOG, BRS, and ORBIT all offer catalogs of their complete offerings, and you should definitely send for all three of them before deciding which ones are most appropriate to your needs. You will find the addresses for each encyclopedic later in this chapter.

General Interest

• Electronic Yellow Pages. Keyword searchable directory to over two million phone listings included in over 4800 U.S. telephone directories. Includes phone and address. May also include county, Standard Industrial Classification (SIC) code, office size, estimated city population, and indication of type of listing printed in the actual Yellow Pages (ordinary, boldface, display box, and so on). Information provided depends upon the file. Files include Financial Services, Professionals, Retailers, Wholesalers, Manufacturers, and five other directories. Available on DIALOG.

• *Academic American Encyclopedia*. Product of Grolier Electronic Publishing, Inc., this encyclopedia is now available on BRS. This is the same encyclopedia offered by Dow Jones, but BRS software makes possible at least one unique feature. In addition to allowing you to search the text for matches of one or more keywords, the BRS version permits "in context" display or printing. This allows you to select and view only those portions of the text containing your keyword or words, eliminating the need to read the entire article. According to BRS and Grolier, the feature is intended to make using the encyclopedia very convenient and economical. Available on BRS.

• CATAFAX Directory of Mail Order Catalogs. Over 4000 records. Monthly updates. If it's available via a mail order catalog, it's probably in this database. Listings include name, address, executive offices, frequency of publication, payment options offered (such as VISA or MasterCard), products, and so on. Available on DIALOG.

• Books in Print. R. R. Bowker Company's Subject, Author, and Title *Guides to Books In Print.* Plus *every other* Bowker *Books in Print* guide, including Guides to Forthcoming, Paperbound, Religious, Medical, Scientific and Technical, and Children's. Available on DIALOG and BRS.

• Magazine Index. Computer searchable index to over 370 popular magazines. Including all of those in the *Reader's Guide to Periodic Literature,* plus most of those found in *ACCESS* and *Popular Periodicals Index.* Nearly 600,000 citations. Updated monthly. Available on DIALOG.

• Microcomputer Index ™. Subject and index guide to magazine articles from more than 20 computer magazines, including general articles; book, software, and hardware reviews; new products; and more. Magazines include *Byte, Interface Age, InfoWorld, Personal Computing, Softside,* and *Dr. Dobb's Journal,* from 1980 to present. Updated quarterly. Available on DIALOG.

• International Software Directory. Computer searchable listing of all commercially available software for any type of mini- or microcomputer. Updated monthly. Includes two- to three-sentence description of each item, plus applications, purchase price, supplier's name. You can even order the actual software while online. Available on DIALOG.

• NEWSEARCH. Daily index of more than 2000 news stories, information articles, and book reviews from over 1400 newspapers, magazines, and periodicals. Much more extensive than anything available on the information utilities. Daily updates. Current month only. At the end of each month, the information is transferred to other databases (such as Magazine Index or Management Contents). Available on DIALOG.

- Book Review Index. Index of reviews published in over 400 periodicals from 1969 to present. Includes *Publishers Weekly, New York Review of Books,* the *London Times Book Review, Business Week, Money, Partisan Review,* and more. Available on DIALOG.

- Biography Master Index. Biographical information on over two million individuals in various fields of accomplishment. Corresponds to the eight-volume *Biography and Genealogy Master Index* published by Gale Research Company. Available on DIALOG.

- REMARC (REtrospective MAchine Readable Cataloging). Online version of the U.S. Library of Congress shelflist. Bibliographic listing and brief description. Includes all entries made from 1897 through 1978, or 83 percent of the entire list. Remaining 17 percent is on MARC (MAchine Readable Cataloging) database. Both available on DIALOG.

- Career Placement Registry. Designed to bring employers and job seekers together. Resumes, geographic, and occupational preferences, address, and so on. Contains two sections: Student (university seniors or recent graduates) and Experienced Personnel. Cost to student for placing resume on the service: $8.00. Cost to experienced personnel: $15 to $40, depending upon salary requirements. Database is available for searching by anyone, including over 10,000 companies in 55 countries around the world. Available on DIALOG.

Business and Economics

- ABI/INFORM. Bibliographic citations and abstracts from over 500 publications and journals worldwide. Monthly updates. (See Figures 6.1 and 6.2.) Available on DIALOG, BRS, and ORBIT.

- Standard & Poor's News Daily. Latest news on more than 10,000 public U.S. companies. Daily additions of 300–400 news stories. Available on DIALOG.

- Management Contents®. Articles from over 400 U.S. and international journals, proceedings, and transactions. Distinct business focus. Publications include *Across the Board, The Banker, Dun's Review, Sloan Management Review,* and *Wharton Magazine.* Available on DIALOG and BRS.

- BI/DATA TIME SERIES. Statistical data on industrial production, food consumption, labor force, and other matters for over 130 countries. "Time series" shows annual change in figure over a number of years. Available on DIALOG.

- ADTRACK. Index of all advertisements of a quarter page or larger appearing in 148 U.S. consumer magazines. Indexed by product name, company, and characteristics and content of the ad. Available on DIALOG.

Social Sciences and Humanities

- America: History and Life. Covers full range of U.S. and Canadian history, area studies, and current affairs. Covers ethnic studies, folklore, history, international relations, oral history, popular culture, and more. Quarterly updates. Available on DIALOG.

- Artbibliographies Modern. References to all modern art and design literature in books, dissertations, exhibition catalogs, and over 300 periodicals. Art history, biographies of artists, sculpture, ceramics, printing, etc. Since 1900. Updated quarterly. Available on DIALOG.

Chemistry, Medicine, and Biosciences

- CA Search. Everything contained in *Chemical Abstracts*. (A subscription to the printed edition now costs over $4000 a year.) Currently contains over 5,300,000 abstracts and is growing at rate of more than 400,000 a year. Biweekly updates. Available on DIALOG, BRS, and ORBIT.

- Excerpta Medica. Citations and abstracts from over 3500 biomedical journals published worldwide. All fields of medicine, and extensive drug and pharmaceutical coverage, environmental health, pollution control, forensic science, hospital management, public health, and more. Available on DIALOG.

- Biosis Previews. Citations from *Biological Abstracts* and *Biological Abstracts/RRM*. Worldwide coverage of research in the life sciences. Over 8000 primary journals, as well as symposia, reviews, preliminary reports, selected institutional and governmental reports, and more. Available on DIALOG, BRS, and ORBIT.

- MEDLINE (MEDLARS onLINE). Product of the U.S. National Library of Medicine. Corresponds to printed editions of *Index Medicus*, *Index to Dental Literature*, and *International Nursing Index*. Indexes articles from over 3000 international journals published in the

U.S. and 70 other countries. Monthly updates. Available on DIALOG and BRS.

Science, Technology, Engineering, and Patents

• MATHFILE. Online version of *Mathematical Reviews* from 1973 to present. Over 400 core journals in mathematics, plus selective indexing of 1200 more. Includes about 60 translation journals from Russian, Chinese, and other languages. Also reference books, conference proceedings, and dissertations. Available on DIALOG.

• Compendex. Worldwide coverage of nearly 3500 journals, publications of engineering societies and organizations, conference papers and proceedings, and selected government reports and books. Corresponds to printed edition of the *Engineering Index*. Updated monthly. Available on DIALOG, BRS, and ORBIT.

• INSPEC. The largest English-language database in the fields of physics, electrotechnology, computers, and control. Non-English material also included. Corresponds to printed edition of *Physics Abstracts*, *Electrical and Electronics Abstracts*, and *Computer and Control Abstracts*. Monthly updates. Available on DIALOG and ORBIT.

• CLAIMS™. Many separate files, including Chemistry, Citation, Class, U.S. Patents, U.S. Patent Abstracts, U.S. Patent Abstract Weekly, and Uniterm. Millions of patent abstracts, some as far back as 1950. Available on DIALOG, BRS, and ORBIT.

Law and Government

• CIS. Congressional Information Service, Inc. Electronic edition of CIS's *Index to Publications of the United States Congress*. Hearings, working papers, reports, publications, findings of nearly 300 House, Senate, and Joint committees and subcommittees. Hearings publications include transcripts of testimony, exhibit reports, statistical data, and articles. Updated monthly. Available on DIALOG and ORBIT.

• GPO Monthly Catalog. Electronic version of the *Monthly Catalog of United States Government Publications*. Over 100,000 records. Updated monthly. Available on DIALOG, BRS, and ORBIT.

• Federal Index. Covers proposed rules, regulations, bill introductions, speeches, roll calls, court decisions, executive orders, and contract awards, among others. The *Congressional Record, Federal Register,* and the *Washington Post* are also indexed. Available on DIALOG and ORBIT.

Education

• Comprehensive Dissertation Index. A subject, title, and author guide to nearly every American dissertation accepted by an accredited institution since 1861, the year academic doctoral degrees were first granted in the United States. Available on DIALOG and BRS.

• GRANTS. Lists over 2000 grants available from federal, state, and local governments; private foundations; and commercial organizations. Covers fields from archaeology to zoology. Monthly updates. Available on DIALOG and ORBIT.

• ERIC. The complete database on educational materials from the Educational Resources Information Center. Covers report and periodical literature on counseling and personnel services, career education, early childhood education, exceptional children, languages and linguistics, tests and measurement, reading and communications, and more. Updated monthly. Available on DIALOG, BRS, and ORBIT.

Encyclopedic Database Profiles
DIALOG

Address: DIALOG Information Services, Inc.
           Marketing Department
           3460 Hillview Avenue
           Palo Alto, CA 94304
Access: Telenet, Tymnet, TWX, Telex, Dialnet (in Europe)
Toll-free information numbers: (800) 982-5838 in California
                              (800) 227-1927 in other states and
                              Canada
Other information numbers: (415) 858-3785
                            334499(DIALOG)—Telex
                            910-339-9221—TWX
Customer service numbers: (same as toll-free numbers above)

Background

DIALOG Information Services, Inc., is a subsidiary of Lockheed Missile and Space Corporation. The service began in 1969 as a system designed to supply NASA with a computerized documentation collection program. Called RECON (Remote Console Information Retrieval System), the system was installed at NASA's Scientific and Technical Information Facility in Maryland and originally contained over half a million citations from documents dealing with the technical data developed as a result of the U.S. space program.

"Dialog" was actually the name of the special language used to search this database. But in early 1972, the name was capitalized and applied to the whole Lockheed information retrieval system. The service is accessed by more than 500,000 people each year in more than 50 countries.

Sign-up Procedure

DIALOG offers two types of accounts: the standard, full-service account, and a limited-service, low-cost KNOWLEDGE INDEX account. Both are accessible to anyone with a personal computer, but KNOWLEDGE INDEX is designed with the home user in mind. We'll consider the standard account first.

The Standard DIALOG Account

There is no charge for opening a standard DIALOG account. Merely phone or write, and you will be sent an application. Fill it out and mail it back and you will receive an account number, password, and information on the service. You will also receive $100 worth of free time on the system.

However, you will definitely need the *Guide to DIALOG Searching* offered by the service. The cost is $30, and it includes all available DIALOG "Bluesheets" (single-page descriptions of the individual databases). "Database Chapters," also available at a cost of $4.00 each, are more elaborate presentations of an individual database, including sample searches, explanations of how the database is set up, suggestions for how to search it most effectively, and so on. You can easily end up with a stack of material measuring 4 inches or more, so you may want to order one or more DIALOG binders at $8.00 each.

Altogether, you should plan on spending between $40 and $75 for the manual and additional documentation. Shipping charges are included, but prices for customers living outside of North America are higher.

Costs

Prices differ with the individual database you access. The highest-priced database (CLAIMS™/UNITERM) costs $300 per connect hour. The least expensive (ERIC) is $25 per hour. The average cost is probably close to $75 an hour, or a dollar a minute. This is for searching only; online bibliographic citations and abstracts are extra. These prices vary too, but they average 15¢ to 25¢ apiece.

There is also a charge of $6.00 per hour levied by the communications networks Telenet and Tymnet. In Canada, the Telenet surcharge is $5.00 and the Tymnet charge, $8.00.

You cannot charge your DIALOG time on a major credit card, but the service offers a variety of discounts for volume usage. If you are buying the service as an individual, for example, you will receive an automatic discount after five hours of connect time each month. The discount is $5 to $15 per hour, depending upon usage.

Customer Support and Additional Publications

Every active DIALOG subscriber receives the monthly *Chronolog Newsletter* containing information on recently added databases, tips for using individual databases, announcements of training sessions, and the like. The DIALOG *Pocket Guide* is also available at no cost. The brochure contains a quick summary of DIALOG search commands.

DIALOG is online 120 hours each week: midnight until 10:00 PM weekdays; midnight to 8:00 PM, Fridays; 8:00 AM to 8:00 PM, Saturday. All of these times are Eastern Standard Time. The service is not available on Sunday. Customer Service can be contacted by an "800" number whenever the system is up and running.

Training Programs

DIALOG has an extensive, ongoing training program. "DIALOG Day," for example, is a one-hour presentation of the service, including online demonstrations. These demonstrations are held the first Monday of each month at DIALOG's offices in Chicago, Houston, New York, Palo Alto, and Washington. There is no charge, but reservations are required.

A videotape called "DIALOG Information Retrieval Service—Worldwide Information on Command" is available (in Beta and VHS formats) for $25. And there is a full schedule of system seminars and "refreshers" running half a day to one and a half days. The one most people take is the one-and-a-half-day system seminar. Held in various cities on a regular basis, this seminar costs $65.

KNOWLEDGE INDEX—For the Home User

In November of 1982, DIALOG introduced KNOWLEDGE INDEX, a service specifically designed to respond to the needs of individuals who use personal computers at home, after regular business hours. A

KNOWLEDGE INDEX account gives you access to the following databases:

- ABI/INFORM. Over 500 publications, including *The Banker, Business Week, Canadian Business, Computer Decisions, Forbes, Fortune, The Futurist, The Harvard Business Review, IBM Systems Journal, The Journal of Applied Psychology, Money, Satellite Communications, Telephony,* and *Vital Speeches.* (See Figures 6.1 and 6.2.)

- AGRICOLA. Comprehensive worldwide coverage of agriculture and related subjects.

- Engineering Literature Index. Keyword-searchable index to literature (3500 journals) of the field.

- ERIC. (See previous section.)

- GPO Publications Reference File. Used to locate and identify Government Printing Office (GPO) publications for purchase.

- INSPEC. (See previous section.)

- Magazine Index. (See previous section.)

- MEDLINE. (See previous section.)

- National Newspaper Index. Front-to-back page coverage of *The Christian Science Monitor, The New York Times,* and the *Wall Street Journal.* Everything but the weather charts, stock market tables, crossword puzzles, and horoscopes.

- NEWSEARCH. (See previous section.)

- PSYCINFO. Covers over 900 periodicals and 1500 books, technical reports, and monographs to provide comprehensive worldwide coverage of the world literature on psychology.

- Standard & Poor's News. (See previous section.)

Additional databases will be added to KNOWLEDGE INDEX in the future. In the meantime, as DIALOG promotional literature points out, the KNOWLEDGE INDEX enables you to "evaluate the new computer products on the market, locate movie and book reviews, help your children with their homework, track the performance and activities of companies in which you may own stock, check on the latest therapies for arthritis, and much more."

KNOWLEDGE INDEX is available from 6:00 PM until 5:00 AM (your local time), Monday through Friday; from 8:00 AM to midnight on Saturdays; and from 3:00 PM until 5:00 AM on Sundays. The access cost for all KNOWLEDGE INDEX databases is $24 per hour (compared with an average, standard DIALOG account cost of about $75 per hour, regardless of time of day).

There is an initial sign-up fee of $35, but it entitles you to two free hours of connect time (a $48 value) and a complete self-instructional guide to using KNOWLEDGE INDEX. KNOWLEDGE INDEX accounts are completely separate from standard DIALOG accounts, and perhaps best of all, there is no direct billing. Everything is done through major credit cards.

When you consider all the information KNOWLEDGE INDEX places at your disposal for just 40¢ a minute, it's clear that this new DIALOG service represents an impressive value. When you consider that $35 buys you the manual and two hours of connect time, with no future obligation, the offer is almost irresistible. For more information, you can call the following toll-free numbers:

(800) 352-0458, Extension 415 (in Arizona)
(800) 528-0470, Extension 415 (in Alaska and Hawaii)
(800) 528-6050, Extension 415 (in other states and Canada)

BRS (Bibliographic Retrieval Services)

Address: Bibliographic Retrieval Services
1200 Route 7
Latham, NY 12110
Access: Telenet, Tymnet, Uninet
Toll-free information number: (800) 833-4707
Other information numbers: (518) 783-1161 (Latham, New York, headquarters)
(215) 527-4116 (Philadelphia field office)

Customer service numbers: (same as toll-free number and Latham, New York, number above)

Background

Bibliographic Retrieval Services was founded in May 1976 and was acquired by Indian Head, Inc., in October of 1980. BRS offers upwards of 70 individual databases as well as a number of other interesting services.

For example, BRS offers the *full text* of both the *Harvard Business Review* and the various Predicasts, Inc., business databases. Predicasts is also owned by Indian Head, which is undoubtedly one of the reasons why the BRS version is "full-text" and the DIALOG version consists of bibliographic citations and abstracts.

You can sign onto BRS and access the Dow Jones News/Retrieval Service. But only the DJNS *news* database is available, and it is usually about 10 days behind because of the time required to transport the magnetic tape containing the information to BRS headquarters. You can also access the New York Times Information Bank II, and the online version of the California Union List of Periodicals. These three services are billed separately at a rate that is somewhat higher than you would be charged for accessing them directly. The BRS flat rate for using DJNS, regardless of time of day, is $80 per hour for non-academic users, plus Telenet or Tymnet charges of $7.00 to $11 per hour. Accessing DJNS directly, in contrast, costs $72 per hour in prime time and just $12 per hour in non-prime time, including all Telenet and Tymnet charges.

BRS also has a rudimentary electronic mail and bulletin board feature that allows subscribers to contact each other and announce meetings of user's groups and other events.

Sign-up Procedure

For years the least expensive way one could subscribe to BRS was to sign a contract pledging to use at least 25 connect hours over the course of a year at a total cost of $750. That works out to $30 an hour. In addition to these connect hour charges, there are royalty charges for the individual databases, plus communications network surcharges. It was not a bad deal by information industry standards, but there was always that $750 guarantee.

In June of 1982, however, BRS introduced its Hourly Access Plan. In return for an initial payment of $50, individuals can now use BRS at any time for a basic connect hour rate of $35. Database royalties and communications network charges are extra, but there is no required guarantee and the $50 is applied as a credit to your account for any searching done within the first three months.

Then in November of that year, BRS added "BRS/After Dark." This program requires an initial registration fee of $50, and it entitles you to access BRS between the hours of 6:00 PM and midnight EST at a basic connect hour rate of $6.00. All of the BRS databases are included, and an online personal computer newsletter, an expanded electronic mail system, and an electronic shopping service are planned, as is a program for purchasing software online for direct download into your own machine.

Assuming you opt for one of the $50 services, your only additional sign-up cost will be $18 for the *BRS System Reference Manual* that explains commands and techniques to be used in searching the databases.

Costs

There are three components to the price you pay for using BRS: the basic connect hour rate (explained above), the database royalty, and telecommunications network surcharges.

As with the other two encyclopedics, the royalties charged vary with the individual database. Because BRS offers a number of basic connect hour rates, their rate card shows the database royalties and adds them to the various basic hourly charges to arrive at the total hourly figure. The highest royalty is $75 an hour for the database EIS: Digests of Environmental Impact Statements. The lowest is no royalty at all for ERIC, BRS/Pre-Med, and several others. Bibliographic citations and abstracts cost between 5¢ and 25¢ apiece.

The Tymnet surcharge is $11 per hour for access from the continental United States (Tymnet/DataPac fees are higher). Telenet is $7.00 an hour, and Uninet is $6.00 an hour.

Customer Support and Additional Publications

In addition to the basic manual, you may also buy a training workbook ($15) and a guide to searching the MEDLARS database ($9.00). There are also separate guides to each of the individual databases at $3.00 each. Subscribers also receive the monthly BRS Bulletin free of charge. For customer support, there is an "800" number (800-833-4707).

Training Programs

BRS maintains a regular series of workshops, training programs, and seminars in many cities in the United States and Canada. The cost for the full-day introductory session is $35. Sessions devoted to using specific databases are $50 per session. You can call Customer Service for the latest schedule.

ORBIT

Address: ORBIT Information Retrieval System
SDC Search Service
2500 Colorado Avenue
Santa Monica, CA 90406

Access: Telenet, Tymnet
Toll-free information numbers: (800) 352-6689 in California
                              (800) 421-7229 in other states and
                              Canada
Other information numbers: (213) 453-6194
                           (213) 820-4111 ext. 6194
                           65-2358—Telex
                           910-343-6643—TWX
Customer service numbers: (same as toll-free numbers above)

Background
   The ORBIT Information Retrieval System is the product of the System Development Corporation (SDC), a subsidiary of the Burroughs Corporation. SDC began operation of the first online bibliographic information retrieval system in 1965. And in 1974 a separate division, SDC Search Service, was formed with ORBIT as its chief product.
   ORBIT offers 80 individual databases and some 55 million citations and abstracts. Many of its databases are found exclusively on ORBIT. These include: Accountants, a product of the American Institute of CPAs; APIT, petroleum refining patents from eight countries; COLD, which covers all disciplines dealing with Antarctica; MONITOR, an index to the *Christian Science Monitor;* and SPORT, which covers the literature of training, sports medicine, international sports history, and other sports topics.

Sign-up Procedure
   There is no charge for opening an ORBIT account. Send in an application, and the firm will send you an account number and password. However, you will need an *ORBIT User Manual* ($40) and other information (about $17), for a total of $57. You may also want to order manuals for the individual databases at $7.50 each.
   ORBIT does not provide any free connect time with your subscription. However, as an individual user, you might be interested in the firm's Workbook Package. This includes an ORBIT workbook containing step-by-step instructions and exercises you can practice on your own, as well as $300 worth of connect time for selected databases. The cost is $125. This fee also includes the *User Manual,* the *Quick Reference Guide*, and five manuals (of your selection) for individual databases. Purchased separately, these items would cost $92.50.

Costs
   As with all the encyclopedics, specific costs depend upon the individual database accessed. ORBIT's costs range from a high of $125 per hour for the CHEMDEX files to a low of $40 for ERIC and AGRI-

COLA, the online version of the *Bibliography of Agriculture*. Only 15 of ORBIT's 80 databases offer online printouts of citations and abstracts, and rates range from 5¢ to $1.00. Offline printouts will be generated and mailed to you at a cost of 10¢ to $2.00 apiece.

In addition to these charges, there is a charge of $8.00 per hour for accessing ORBIT via Telenet or Tymnet.

Customer Support

Use the toll-free customer support numbers given at the start of this section.

Training Programs

ORBIT offers a regular schedule of training programs. The New-User program is either a one-day or a one-and-a-half-day affair designed to introduce you to ORBIT and online searching in general. The cost is $100 for the one-day version and $125 for the longer session. In both cases, the fee is credited to your account for use in searching the databases over the following six months.

A variety of seminars for the trained searcher is also available. These often concentrate on specific subject areas (business, chemistry, patents, or whatever), and cost $50 for a half-day session and $100 for the full-day version. These fees are not credited to your account.

New-User training and seminars are offered in cities all over the United States. Customer Service can give you a complete schedule.

Should You Sign Up?

Businesspeople, professionals, scientists, students, and anyone else with a continuing need for information will find DIALOG, BRS, and ORBIT invaluable. The wealth of information they provide, and the speed with which it can be obtained, make the encyclopedics the only sensible way to research certain topics.

Using an encyclopedic database instead of going to the library is rather like writing on a word processor instead of on a typewriter. The word processor is considerably more expensive, and you will have to spend some time learning to use it effectively. But the machine can triple or quadruple your productivity.

Libraries (and typewriters) still have their place. But when you need information on where to *find* information, nothing can match an encyclopedic database. Your decision on whether to sign up or not and which encyclopedic to choose will obviously depend, first, on your need for information, and second, on your need for the particular kinds of information each database provides.

If you think a subscription to an encyclopedic might be useful, you should contact all three of them to request more information about the databases they offer, what each individual database costs to use, and the provisions that have been made for inexpensive online practice.

It's worth remembering that opening an account on DIALOG and ORBIT costs you nothing. You pay only for the user's manuals ($30 and $40, respectively). For $50, and another $18 for the manual, you can have an "After Dark" account on BRS. Simply subscribing to an encyclopedic is thus not that expensive.

Since there are no standing monthly charges, it is possible to open an account and sample an encyclopedic relatively inexpensively. If you find that you don't like it or decide that you have no need for its power, you will not be committed to any continuing expenses. Best of all, unless you cancel your subscription, the encyclopedic will always be there for you should your needs change.

...7...

The Information Bank® and NewsNet™
News and Specialized
Business Information

The Information Bank® and NewsNet™ are two databases that fall somewhere between the encyclopedics and single-subject databases and the information utilities. The information they offer is specialized, but it is nevertheless of interest to large numbers of people, particularly in business. A service of The New York Times Information Service, Inc., The Information Bank® gives you electronic access not only to the *full text* of the *New York Times* but also to nearly 120 other publications, virtually none of which is available from any other service. For its part, NewsNet™ offers you full-text, online versions of some 150 specialized newsletters drawn from nearly 30 different industry groups and interest areas.

The convenience of being able to dial up a newspaper, magazine, or newsletter is important, of course. But as with all databases, "computer searchability" is the source of their real power. Why turn your hands black with ink smudges paging through old issues of the *Times* looking for that article you know you read on noncaloric left-handed sugar molecules? Why search for and photocopy 20 individual pages from individual newsletters to build a file on the latest financial, tax, telecommunications, or publishing issue?

Neither activity makes much sense when you can run a keyword search on every issue of the *Times* from 1980 to the present, and retrieve the complete text of the article on your personal computer or word processor. And not when NewsNet will let you keyword-search *all* the newsletters in any category or in the entire database for the up-to-date, expert information you want.

Let's look at each of them in more detail.

The Information Bank

The Information Bank was started by the *New York Times* in 1969 as a first tentative step into the realm of electronic publishing and information retrieval. Originally, only abstracts of stories appearing in the paper were available. But since then the database has grown to include not only the full text of the *Times* but abstracts from a wide variety of other publications. In most cases these journals go back for at least 10 years, and like all Information Bank databases, they are constantly updated.

New York Times Information Service (NYTIS, pronounced "nite-us") staffers produce over 12,000 new abstracts every month. Even in an electronic age, it is a surprisingly labor-intensive process. At a time when the newsroom of every major newspaper is at least as technologically advanced as the one portrayed on "Lou Grant," one would think that getting the daily *Times* ready to go online would be a simple . matter of transmitting copy directly from one reporter's or editor's terminal into the database.

But it doesn't work that way, and for a very good reason. Some professional researchers would disagree, but for many, part of The Information Bank's power lies in the fact that the service adds special index words to each article to make retrieval both easier and faster. That involves human judgment and input, and it is one of the reasons why NYTIS maintains a relatively large staff.

Another reason centers on the preparation of article abstracts. Other organizations rely heavily on the firms that supply their databases to do much of the preparation work. But NYTIS takes pride in the fact that no similar organization is as heavily involved in the preparation of the material it offers. Of course this is at least partially out of necessity, for electronic abstracts of *The National Review, Astronautics*, and *Consumer Reports* probably would not exist if NYTIS didn't prepare them.

What's Available on the System?

• The Information Bank. Although the entire *New York Times* service is sometimes referred to by this name, The Information Bank is actually but one of seven individual NYTIS databases. In addition to abstracts of the *New York Times* from 1974 to the present, the database also contains abstracts from over a dozen other newspapers and about 40 other publications (see Figure 7.1 for a complete list).

The Information Bank can be searched in two ways. You can select words from the "controlled vocabulary" words found in the *NYTIS Thesaurus*. Or you can conduct a "free text search," which will cause the computer to scan the entire text of each abstract for a match with the keyword you have entered. Searches can be limited by time frame, of course. A controlled vocabulary search causes the system to look at just the index "target" words that NYTIS staffers have added to each abstract (see Figure 7.2). This often speeds the process. In addition, since the *Thesaurus* words deal in overall themes, a controlled vocabulary search can often retrieve important articles that might otherwise be passed over for lack of an exact keyword match.

Importantly, the NYTIS operating system allows you to use *both* techniques simultaneously.

———————————————— **Figure 7.1.** ————————————————
The New York Times Information Bank Publications List.

The *New York Times*
Virtually all news and editorial matter from the final Late City Edition, including all Sunday and regional feature sections. Current issues are processed within four to five days of publication. Front page and leading business news items, available within 24 hours of publication.

Other Publications

General Circulation Newspapers:

Atlanta Constitution
Chicago Tribune
Christian Science Monitor
Houston Chronicle
Los Angeles Times
Miami Herald
San Francisco Chronicle
Seattle Times
Washington Post

Business Publications:

Advertising Age
Automotive News
Barron's
Business Week
Dun's Business Month
Editor and Publisher
Financial Times (Canada)

Financial Times (London)
Forbes
Fortune
Harvard Business Review
Japan Economic Journal
Journal of Commerce
Wall Street Journal
Women's Wear Daily

International Affairs:

Economist (London)
Far Eastern Economic Review
Foreign Affairs
Foreign Policy
Latin American Weekly
Manchester Guardian
Middle East
Times (London)
World Press Review (formerly
   Atlas)

Figure 7.1 continued

Science Publications:	Consumer Reports
Astronautics	Current Biography
Aviation Week and Space	National Journal
Technology	National Review
Bulletin of Atomic Scientists	New York
Industrial Research	New Yorker
Science	Newsweek
Scientific American	Sports Illustrated
	Time
Other Periodicals:	U. S. News and World Report
	Variety
Atlantic	Washington Monthly
California Journal	

• The *New York Times* Online. This is the system's second major database, the one that offers the complete text of the *New York Times* from 1980 to the present. Usually you can count on having access to major front page, business page, and metropolitan section stories within 24 hours of publication. The rest of the issue will be available online within two days.

The database does not include advertising, stock market quotes, shipping announcements, and similar items appearing in the paper. But it does include all news stories and features, editorials, opinion columns, and letters to the editor. Articles and other items are available both in abstract form and in full text, and the database is controlled-vocabulary searchable.

Notations are included indicating any maps, charts, or photos that appeared with the article, and although these are not included in the text you see on your screen, complete microfiche or microfilm records are available.

• Advertising/Marketing Intelligence (AMI, pronounced "amy"). This database is a joint project of the *Times* Information Service and J. Walter Thompson, the giant advertising agency. AMI contains about 65 publications dealing with the consumer product field, advertising, and marketing. It can provide you with a concise, informative abstract containing facts and figures on everything from the announced advertising budget of a competitor to the latest sales projections for automobile hood ornaments.

Here is a sample of the publications the database covers:

Advertising:

Ad Day
Advertising Age
Madison Avenue
"Who's News" from the
  Wall Street Journal

Food:

Beverage Industry
Progressive Grocer
Chain Store Age (Supermarkets)

Broadcasting/Communications:

Broadcasting
Cablevision
Media Decisions

Public Relations:

O'Dwyer's PR Newsletter
Public Opinion
Public Relations Review

There are also publications and categories for retailing, pharmaceuticals, transportation, and market research and product development. The database provides abstracts only, and it is searchable by both controlled-vocabulary and free text.

- SUMM. Each weekday at 8:30 AM (EST), NYTIS subscribers all over the country fire up their terminals to read the online morning news summary that becomes available at that time. The information is drawn primarily from the day's edition of the *New York Times*, and it is a "read only" service. Typically, the terminal operator in a subscribing office will generate a printout and route photocopies of it to key executives.

   The morning edition is one of three such summaries that make up this NYTIS offering. A summary drawn from the Business Day section of the daily *Times* and several other sources is also available at 8:30. Then, at 1:00 PM, the afternoon business update goes online. Unlike the morning summary, this contains information from a number of sources in addition to the newspaper itself.

- Deadline Data on World Affairs. This database offers you access to what is in effect a powerful online geopolitical encyclopedia. The information is produced by DMS, a large consulting/research firm in Greenwich, Connecticut. It includes military and governmental data, the most recent population statistics, cultural information, economic data, statistical profiles, names, addresses, and positions of political leaders, and much more—for every country in the world, every state in the

United States, and every province in Canada. In addition, the database contains information on every major international organization from the United Nations to OPEC.

The information is drawn from a sweeping variety of sources—literally tons of official documents, commission reports, newspapers, newsletters, and other publications are digested and entered each month. What's more, this database offers full text retrieval.

- Disclosure II. This is the same database found on DIALOG and on the Dow Jones News/Retrieval Service. Updated weekly, it contains the annual and quarterly financial statements and management reports for 8500 publicly held companies. (For more information, see Chapter 5, The Dow Jones News/Retrieval Service.)

- Globe Data. Finally, there is Globe Data. This is essentially a controlled-vocabulary searchable index to the *Boston Globe* newspaper.

Sample Output

NYTIS abstracts are intended to be "informative," as opposed to "indicative." That is, they are designed to present the classic "who, what, why, when, and where" information of a news reporter's lead paragraph, as well as any important facts and figures that may appear in the body of the article. This often makes it possible for you to find the information you're looking for without reading the whole text, where the whole text is available. And it saves you from having to go elsewhere to look up the article, as would be the case if the abstract merely indicated where it could be found. (See Figure 7.2.)

— **Figure 7.2. Sample Abstracts from the Information Bank.** —

The New York Times Information Bank was queried for references to "personal computers" dating from 1980 to 1982. The result was a 62-page printout containing abstracts from virtually every newspaper and business, science, and international publication in the database. Listed below are three representative samples.

The letter codes at the far left of each abstract stand for "accession number" (ACN), "microfiche number" (MF), "bibliographic citation" (BC), "abstract" (AB), "subject descriptors" (SD), "organization descriptors" (OD), and "geographic descriptors" (GD).

The various "descriptors" are important because they are the terms included in the NYTIS *Thesaurus*—the guide you must use for "controlled vocabulary" searches. Only words that are on the controlled vocabulary list can be used as descriptors or as keywords when searching the database.

****

ACN
    0811820276
MF N/A.
BC JAPAN ECONOMIC JOURNAL (JEJ), 1982-07-20, PAGE 11, COL 1.
AB Sord Computer Systems Inc. (Japan) plans exporting personal computers to US on original equipment manufacturer basis beginning autumn '82. Will sell computers under its own name pending settlement of trademark dispute with US sales agent, Sord, USA (S).
SD INTERNATIONAL TRADE AND WORLD MARKET. DATA PROCESSING EQUIPMENT. PERSONAL COMPUTERS. TRADEMARKS AND TRADE NAMES. SUITS AND LITIGATION.
OD SORD COMPUTER SYSTEMS INC (JAPAN).
GD UNITED STATES

****

ACN
    0707820722
BY DONOVAN, SHARON.
MF N/A
BC HOUSTON CHRONICLE (HC), 1982-06-09, SECTION 3, PAGE 1, COL 1.
BG BIOG.
AB Experts participating in panel discussion on future of personal computer industry at National Computer Conference in Houston (Tex) predict industry is on brink of sales explosion. Note personal computers have absorbed only about 2% of potential market so far. Anticipate stiff competition within industry that will benefit consumers by forcing prices down.
SD DATA PROCESSING AND SYSTEMS. FORECASTS. DATA PROCESSING EQUIPMENT. PERSONAL COMPUTERS. CONVENTIONS AND CONFERENCES. SPEECHES AND STATEMENTS. LABOR. STATISTICS. MARKETING AND MERCHANDISING. SALES (INDUSTRY-WIDE). PRICES.

****

ACN
    0150996013
BY SPENCE, RICHARD D.
MF N/A
BC FINANCIAL TIMES OF CANADA (CFT), 1982-01-04, PAGE 6, COL 1.
IL PHO.
AB Proliferation of data bases and increasing sophistication of software packages are spurring sales of microcomputers to US and Canadian investors. Personal computers

Figure 7.2 continued

allow individual investors access to up-to-the-minute stock quotations and daily closing statistics. Can store reams of information about company finances and securities performance. Can be programmed to calculate capital gains and cash flow. Computer Innovations (Canada) salesman Rob Newmarch reports most sought-after investment feature is access to 'real-time' market quotes and trading information. Photos (L).

SD DATAPROCESSING PROGRAMMING AND INFORMATION STORAGE AND RETRIEVAL. CORPORATIONS. INVESTOR BEHAVIOR. STOCKS (CORPORATE). PERSONAL COMPUTERS. FINANCES. STOCKS AND BONDS (GENERAL). STOCK PRICES AND TRADING VOLUME. DATA PROCESSING EQUIPMENT.

OD COMPUTER INNOVATIONS LTD.

ND NEWMARCH, ROB.

GD UNITED STATES. CANADA.

****

What Does It Cost?

To accommodate its various clients, The New York Times Information Service offers two rate structures, Transactional and Term. The Transactional structure is a pay-as-you-go plan. The only requirement is that you pay for the first hour of use in advance, and that you use that hour sometime within the first 30 days. Under the Transaction plan, you are billed at standard NYTIS rates. The Term plan is designed for volume users. Under this plan, users guarantee to pay NYTIS a certain amount per year. In return, NYTIS offers volume discounts on its databases. In both cases, users are billed directly by NYTIS.

Here are more details on the two plans:

Transactional Plan

• Each NYTIS database priced individually. Hourly charges range from about $75 per hour for The Information Bank to about $165 per hour for Advertising/Marketing Intelligence (AMI). This database access charge entitles you to search for and retrieve bibliographic citations. Abstracts are extra. (See below.)

• Total cost consists of three components:

Database access (see above)

Telecommunications charge. Ranging from $7.00 per hour to $9.00 per hour, depending upon whether you use Uninet, Telenet, or Tymnet.

Units charge. Charge for each abstract you request. Sliding scale. For first 500 in a month, cost is 70¢ per abstract. Next 500, cost is 60¢ per abstract. Cost of 50¢ per abstract for everything over 1000 in a given month.

• Conditions. You sign up to access one or more specific databases and pay for one hour's worth of time on each. Important note: You must use *all* of this prepaid time within 30 days of signup. There is no credit for time that you have paid for but have not used.

Term Plan

• Includes access to *all* NYTIS databases.

• With the exception of Disclosure II, all NYTIS databases are priced at the same hourly rate under a Term Plan. The actual hourly rate depends upon the number of hours the client agrees to buy over the course of a year.

   The greater the number of hours committed to, the lower the hourly rate.

   Term Plan hourly rates range from $140 per hour for a contract committing to $3500 per year, to $85 per hour for a contract committing to $160,000 per year.

• Actual charges are paid monthly as databases are used. Reconciliation at year's end.

• Important note: If it appears that actual usage will exceed the time you have contracted for, you may cancel your original contract and sign a new one involving a greater number of hours per year and a higher hourly discount.

Unique or Outstanding Features

• Uniform NYTIS protocol. "Protocol" in this sense is information industry jargon for the procedures you use and the commands you enter to search a particular database. Until relatively recently, at least two different protocols were required to search different New York Times

Information Service databases. In January of 1981, the company began to convert all of its databases for use with a uniform NYTIS protocol. This makes the service much easier to use than in the past.

- Many publications not online anywhere else. The New York Times Information Bank is the only widely available service that offers you electronic access to magazines like *Time, Newsweek, U.S. News & World Report, Sports Illustrated,* the *Atlantic Monthly,* and *The New Yorker.* As with all NYTIS offerings, the primary criterion for deciding whether a particular article will be included in the database is newsworthiness. Consequently, you will find few if any references to the fiction published in the literary magazines. But you will find citations for book and film reviews, interviews, and similar articles.

- Special schools program. NYTIS has made its services available to students and professors in schools of journalism, law, business, and library science for a very nominal fee. Several restrictions apply. The service is available only on Saturdays and each institution is limited to a maximum of 10 hours of use per month under this program.

Support Services, Training, and Publications

- Offline printing or "deferred print." As with many other databases, you can ask NYTIS to generate a high speed printout of your search results. The hard copy will be mailed to you the same day.

- Stored searches. Once you've developed a list of search words that successfully retrieve information on particular subjects, you can store your "strategy" on the system and run it automatically any time you like.

- SDI (Selective Dissemination of Information). Customers who want to automatically receive printouts of new material on particular subjects can opt for this service. A successful search strategy is stored on the system and run automatically after each update. Any resulting material is then printed out and mailed to the customer.

- NYTIS *Thesaurus* and User Guides. The New York Times Information Service provides its *Thesaurus* for use in controlled-vocabulary searches. There is a separate *User Guide* for each database.

- Online System Monitors. Customer support personnel are available from 8:00 AM through 10:30 PM (EST) each business day. You can reach them either by sending an online message or by dialing toll-free (800) 631-8056. In New York, call (212) 594-6663; in New Jersey, (201) 539-5911.

• Training. At least two training options are available. One involves either a day or a day and half of training at your location, plus a certain amount of free online practice time good for the first 30 days of use. The other involves a one-day session at the nearest Information Bank office and somewhat less free online time.

For More Information . . .
NYTIS maintains sales offices at the following locations:

New York, New York, (212) 683-2208
Washington, D.C., (703) 243-7220
Chicago, Illinois, (312) 236-6800
San Francisco, California, (415) 522-2600
Los Angeles, California, (213) 852-7003
Houston, Texas, (713) 965-9371
Toronto, Ontario—Represented by INFO GLOBE, (416) 598-5250

London, England
Suite 408
International Press Centre
76 Shoe Lane
London EC4A 3JB
01-353-2174

Tokyo, Japan
The Nihon Keizai Shimbun
9-5 Ohtemachi, 1 Chome, Chiyoda-Ku
Tokyo, 100, Japan
(03) 270-0251

The address of the corporate headquarters is:
New York Times Information Service
1719A—Route 10
Parsippany, NJ 07054
(201) 539-5850
Telex: 136-390

NewsNet

What's a newsletter? Would you pay $25 an issue for eight typewritten pages delivered once a month? It would depend on what was *on* those pages, of course. If each page were packed with timely, expert, and possibly even "inside" information on your industry—information that nonsubscribers might not discover until several weeks later—you would gladly pay the $300 or more a year. And many business people and professionals do just that. A single day of advance warning alone can more than pay for your subscription.

Many newsletters are produced by as few as one or two experts in a particular industry, supported by a small staff of clerical workers and assistants. Each focuses intensely on a single industry or other area, conducting research, interviewing key figures, and gathering and analyzing information.

Obviously with a product as perishable as this, speedy delivery is a major concern. And that's where NewsNet comes in. A subsidiary of Independent Publications, Inc., of Bryn Mawr, Pennsylvania, NewsNet offers newsletter publishers and subscribers *instant* delivery of their information. In some cases, the newsletters must be entered into the database manually. But they are the minority. More than 60 percent of all newsletters on NewsNet are transmitted directly from the communicating word processors and computers of their creators to the firm's central computer facility.

Subscribers have only to dial a local network number, sign on, and read the latest edition. In some cases, the newsletter is available online only a few hours after leaving the authors' keyboard. In the meantime, its print version is slowly wending its way through the mails to your door.

That is one way it can work. But this is only the beginning of News-Net's services. Perhaps most important of all is the fact that *you do not have to be a subscriber to the print version of a newsletter to read its online edition.* There are some exceptions, but NewsNet has a royalty arrangement with most newsletter producers that permits its members to read those publications, even if the members do not subscribe to the newsletter. Prices are set by the publisher, and of course print-version subscribers get preferred rates.

What's more, the entire database—all the newsletters together—can be keyword-searched. Newsletters are classified by industry group. You can elect to search every group, every back issue of every newsletter in a specific group, or every individual newsletter—and there are approximately 150 newsletters to choose from. You can also send letters to the newsletter authors or to NewsNet staff, order print subscriptions, and sign up for "NewsFlash," the firm's name for its selective dissemination of information (SDI) service.

What's Available on the System?

NewsNet offers newsletters in nearly 30 different industry groups or categories, and the firm is constantly adding new publications to the list (see Figure 7.3). Many newsletter publishers offer *daily* updates on such time-sensitive information as pricing, legislation, tax information and rulings, and contract awards.

——— **Figure 7.3. Newsletters Available on NewsNet.** ———

Advanced Office Concepts
Agricultural Research Review
Air/Water Pollution Report
Altman & Weil Report to Legal Management
Bank Network News
Banking Regulator
CableNews
Cellular Radio News
Church and Society
Coal Outlook Marketline
Communications Daily
Computer Farming Newsletter
Computer Market Observer
Consumer Electronics
Corporate Acquisitions and Dispositions
Data Channels
DBS News
Distributed Processing Newsletter
Electric Vehicle Progress
Employee Retirement Plans
Energy & Mineral Resources
Entrepreneurial Manager's Newsletter
Executive Productivity
F&S Political Risk Letter
Farm Software Developments
Federal Research Report
Fiber/Laser News
Fiber Optics & Communications
Financial Management Weekly
Grants & Contracts Alert
Grants & Contracts Weekly
Hazardous Waste News

Health Benefit Cost Containment
International Intertrade Index
IRS Practices & Procedures
ISDN News
Land Use Planning Report
Legislative Intelligence Week
Link News Briefs
Media Science Newsletter
Mini/Micro Bulletin
NAA Hotline
NewsNet's OnLine Bulletin
Office Technology Management
Online Database Report
PACs & Lobbies
Public Broadcasting Report
RFC News Service
RadioNews
RadioNews Bulletin Service
Real Estate Intelligence Report
Regulatory News Release
Research Monitor News
Runzheimer on Automotive Alternatives
Runzheimer on Preretirement Counseling
S. Klein Newsletter on Computer Graphics
Satellite News
Satellite News Bulletin Service
Satellite Week
Solar Energy Intelligence Report
Source
Tax Notes Bulletin Service
Tax Notes Today
Tax Shelter Insider
Taxes Interpreted

Figure 7.3 continued

Telephone Angles	The Seybold Report on Office
Telephone News	Systems
Telephone News Bulletin Service	Toxic Materials News
Television Digest	Travelwriter Marketletter
The American Sentinel	Update/The American States
The Computer Consultant	VideoGames Today
The Corporate Shareholder	VideoNews
The Fearless Taster	Video Week
The Gold Sheet	Viewdata/Videotex Report
The Photoletter	Washington Farmletter
	World Environment Report

Note: NewsNet is constantly adding publications to its database, and by the end of 1983, it expects to have between 300 to 400 newsletters on the system. The firm ultimately plans to offer nearly 2000 of the 10,000 newsletters currently available. Thus, even though the newsletters you are interested in are not on this particular list, they may very well now be on the system.

Sample Output

You can reach NewsNet through your local Telenet or Tymnet access number (300 or 1200 baud), and when you sign on, you will be notified of any letters from the NewsNet staff or replies from newsletter publishers that may be waiting for you. System bulletins and announcements of newly added newsletters follow. If you are familiar with the system, at that point you may enter the command and publication code that will take you directly to the newsletter you want to read. Or you may ask the system to display its Main Menu:

```
****************************************************
                   COMMAND MENU
****************************************************


     READ     ***   Read full text
     SCAN     ***   Scan headlines
     SEARCH   ***   Search for keywords
     PAGING   ***   Set terminal to page-at-a-time display
     NOPAGE   ***   Set terminal to continuous display
     FLASH    ***   NewsFlash service
     INDEX    ***   Index, cross-referenced by industry
     PRICES   ***   Price list
```

```
INFO       ***   Information on services
LIBRARY    ***   Library of sample issues
MAIL       ***   Feedback to publishers/NewsNet
ORDER      ***   Order services or products
USER       ***   User services
HELP       ***   General Instructions
BACK       ***   Return to previous prompt
STOP       ***   Return to top of a function
QUIT       ***   Return to top level prompt
OFF        ***   Exit NewsNet, sign off

Enter command or RETURN
-->
```

Most of these commands produce sub-menus to step you through the task you wish to accomplish. However, once you become familiar with the system, you can skip the intermediate menus through the process of "command stringing." (*Note:* READ, SCAN, SEARCH, MAIL, PAGE, NOPAGE, and HELP must be spelled out. For the other commands, you may use just the first three letters.) Typing INFO TX01 at the command level (-->), for example, will take you directly to the information module on publication TX01 ("IRS Practices and Procedures").

Typing QUIT will always return you to the Command Menu and command level prompt. You may also type any Main Menu command at virtually any time, regardless of where you are in the system. And typing any command, followed by HELP will display information on how to use that command. The system, in short, is very user-friendly.

If you know what newsletter(s) you want to READ, SCAN, or SEARCH, you may type the command followed by the publication's code number. The LIBRARY command gives you access to the NewsNet online library of sample issues of each newsletter. In the library you may read a newsletter and get a feeling for its coverage before deciding whether to pay the extra charges to read its current issues. MAIL allows you to send electronic mail to newsletter publishers or NewsNet staff. INDEX displays an index of newsletters and can be used to generate a customized list of the actual publications in the database that deal with subjects of interest to you.

The ORDER command can be used to order a subscription to any newsletter or to request more information about it. USER displays a list of all the newsletters you may access, shows you how to change your password, and displays the connect time used to-date in the current month. INFO will present one to two paragraphs describing each newsletter, its areas of coverage, its publication schedule, etc. PRICES will display an up-to-the-minute list of the newsletters available on the system and what it will cost to READ each one. And FLASH will allow you to create a customized automatic-update profile (see "Unique or Outstanding Features," below).

There are a number of ways to search for information and a number of ways to make your search more specific. But as a simple example, consider what happened when *Link News Briefs,* a publication of the authoritative high-tech market research and consulting firm, was searched first for references to "Visicorp" and then for references to "CompuServe."

-->Visicorp
     1 Occurrences . . .

-->READ

Copyright
LINK NEWS BRIEFS
Thursday July 15, 1982
DRI AND VISICORP DEVELOP P.C.-ORIENTED SERVICE
MCGRAW-HILL subsidiary, Data Resources Inc., and VisiCorp, maker of VisiCalc have announced an agreement that will enable personal computer uusers to use VisiCalc to access DRI's "database of more than 10 million business and economic indicators." This means that for the first time personal computer users . . .

-->CompuServe
     3 Occurrences . . .

     -->READ 2   [We have selected the second of the three items.]

Copyright
LINK NEWS BRIEFS
Thursday July 15, 1982

H&R BLOCK REPORTS ONLY MODEST INCREASES, BUT COMPUSERVE SUBSIDIARY DOES WELL

H&R Block Company reported, "net earning for fiscal year ended April 30, 1982 reached $38,262,000, an increase of 1.6 percent over $37,657,000 earned the previous year." These figures are interesting when considered with the fact that H&R Block subsidiary CompuServe Incorporated contributed $33,170,000 in revenues during the first fiscal year 1982, up 20.1 percent from $27,618,000 in the prior year. A significant increase when compared with its parent company. (Company Press Release)

Some newsletters even contain charts to help you see at a glance the latest figures on cost, sales, and projected trends. For example, consider this online output from the newsletter *Advanced Office Concepts.*

Copyright
ADVANCED OFFICE CONCEPTS
     June 12, 1982

TABLE: COST PER OA SYSTEM WORKSTATION/USER

TABLE III COST PER OA SYSTEM WORKSTATION/USER		
CONFIGURATION	LOWEST COST	AVERAGE COST	HIGHEST COST
---	---	---	---
SMALL SYSTEMS 3 Workstations & 1 Printer	$17,500/ws	$49,000/ws	$98,500/ws
MEDIUM SYSTEMS 12 Workstations & 4 Printers	$11,900/ws	$20,200/ws	$27,700/ws
LARGE SYSTEMS 32 Workstations & 10 Printers	$ 9,000/ws	$12,500/ws	$19,900/ws

Cost per workstation figures for "typical" Office Automation systems now on the market, calculated considering system overhead of central computer (where applicable), disk storage and communications facilities, and software as well as workstation and printer costs.

The same newsletter contains similar charts comparing the features of the major portable personal business computers, from the Dynalogic Hyperion to the Teleram "Small Wonder." Plus pages of fact-filled text and analysis on every aspect of the office of the future.

We have given only a few brief samples. The only way to experience the real power and versatility of NewsNet is to try your hand at the system.

What Does It Cost?

The minimum monthly charge for a NewsNet subscription is $15. But that is applied against usage, so you receive more than just access to the system for your money. There is no sign-up or initiation fee in North America.

Standard NewsNet "connect" charges at 300 baud are $24 an hour (40¢ a minute), relatively low by information industry standards. This entitles you to scan headlines of various newsletters, conduct free text searches, and use NewsNet services like the Library and Feedback. Weekend, holiday, and "off peak" (8:00 PM to 8:00 AM) rates are $6.00 per hour less. Telenet, Tymnet, and Uninet network access charges are built into the NewsNet rates.

The cost of actually reading a newsletter is set by its publisher, and consequently, charges vary. "Validated" subscribers—people who subscribe to the print version—typically pay $24 an hour to read their newsletters online at 300 baud. Nonsubscribers may be charged anywhere from $24 to $120 an hour, depending upon the publication. Reading rates at 1200 baud are double in all cases. But since the information comes to you four times faster, this may be the more cost-effective alternative.

In some cases, the online edition of a newsletter may not be available to you if you are not a subscriber to the print version. But this restriction applies to fewer than 10 percent of the publications.

Unique or Outstanding Features

• NewsFlash. This special NewsNet feature is designed to automatically keep you up-to-date on the latest information pertaining to the topics you specify. For an additional fee, you may store up to 10 separate keywords or phrases on the system in what is called an interest "profile." Then, every time new information is added to the database, the system will automatically check for any matches with your keywords. When a match is found, the article headline and related information will be placed in your "in" basket.

The next time you sign on, the system will automatically notify you of your "in" basket contents. You may then choose to read the articles cited or to move on to something else.

The search criteria offered are quite powerful. For example, you may opt to have the entire database of all newsletters automatically searched, or you may specify one particular newsletter or a particular industry group. In addition, the system automatically searches stories carried on the UPI newswire in all cases.

There is even a "wildcard" option that enables you to specify the most crucial letters of a word without limiting yourself to one specific word. The wildcard symbol is an asterisk (*). If you specify COM*, the system will produce matches for "communications," "intercom," "telecommunications," and other words containing those crucial characters.

The cost is $5.00 per month for each keyword or phrase you specify. You may specify up to 10 keywords or phrases. And, in addition to online "in" basket notification, you may also opt for NewsNet's "outcall" service. This option requires that you have a NewsNet Teleprinter (see below). The printer must be on 24 hours a day. When an update including a match of one of your keywords comes into News-

Net, the system will automatically transmit the item to your printer. As the firm's sales literature points out, this provides you with what amounts to a customized newswire service.

• Equipment Rental. If you don't have a personal computer or communicating word processor, Scanset 415 Video Terminals equipped with built-in automatic dialers for one-buttom dial and sign-on are available from NewsNet at a cost of $39/month. You may also rent a 3M Whisper Writer teleprinter/keyboard unit customized to support auto-dial auto log-in ($59/month), or a Scanset/printer configuration ($78/ month).

Support Services, Training, and Publications

Each subscriber receives a User's Manual. And there is a toll-free Customer Support number to call if you experience problems. There is no formal training program.

For more information, contact:

NewsNet
945 Haverford Road
Bryn Mawr, PA 19010
(215) 527-8030
(800) 345-1301

Should You Sign Up?

If you find information exciting, you will be sorely tempted by both the NYTIS Information Bank and by NewsNet. But as with any database, a sensible decision on whether to subscribe or not must be based on your *need* for that information it provides. And here you should remember that both of these databases are designed to be used as business tools. As such, neither is really appropriate for most *individual* computer owners.

For corporations, small businesses, professionals, and others, however, it will be very hard *not* to subscribe to one or both services. When you consider the value of the information they provide, the time they can save you, and how their cost compares with other business expenses, a subscription to NewsNet or NYTIS can easily become a necessity.

...8...

Computer Bulletin Board Systems
Free for the ASCII-ing

I t's nine o'clock on a Saturday. The regular occupants of the comfortably furnished den in the house on Maple Street have gone off to their evening activities. The room itself is dark, except for the pale luminescent glow of a computer screen in the corner. In the upper left corner of the screen a cursor silently blinks, and on the modem sitting next to the computer console three red LEDs stare in clear-eyed anticipation.

Suddenly, a fourth modem light comes on and begins to blink rapidly: Someone has called! Moments later, one of the computer's disk drives begins to click and whirr and the following text appears on the screen:

WELCOME TO "THE MAPLE STREET MESSENGER"!

This system operated and maintained by:
The Smith Family—Voice Line: (123) 456-7891

YOU ARE NOW THE CONSOLE

To learn more about this system, type "HELP."

You are caller # : 10,758

>> .... **BULLETINS** .... <<

MM/DD/YY   New file WHATSNEW lists all additions and deletions on the system. Experimental, but it seems to be working OK. Starting MM/DD/YY.

This program has a menu of options. Your messages are automatically saved on disk. Please kill messages addressed to you after you have read them.

Have fun! When you are done, type this:

>BYE

Five or 500 miles away, a young woman sits at her computer and watches as this message simultaneously appears on her own screen. She taps the keys necessary to sign on and then enters a command to SCAN the most recent messages and bulletins posted on the system by other callers. Subject lines or "headers" describing each message begin to scroll up her screen:

Nr. 1176 = 12 lines, dated MM/16/YY From: ROBERTA ROE To: ALL Re: CBBS LISTS
Nr. 1225 = 9 lines, dated MM/28/YY From: DAVE DOE To: ALL Re: ATARI BBS
Nr. 1228 = 5 lines, dated MM/30/YY From: JERRY JONES To: ALL Re: IBM PC OWNERS

The headers give the number of messages referred to, the number of lines it contains, the date it was posted, the name of the person who did the deed, the person or group it is addressed to, and the subject covered. Whenever the woman wants to read a particular message, she can stop the scroll and enter the message number. Or she can make a note of all the messages she wants to read and enter them after all the headers have been displayed.

Let's assume that the scroll has run its course and that she now wants to read messages 1176 and 1228. She enters the command to READ the specified messages and the following appears on her screen:

>>Msg Nr. 1176 Date entered: MM/16/YY From: ROBERTA ROE To: ALL Re: CBBS Lists
NATIONAL CBBS LIST
Send $1.00 and a large SASE for a copy of this list of over 300 CBDO across the U.S. to:
Other Networks Newsletter
P.O. Box 14066
Philadelphia, PA 19123
P.S.:
This list has some great stuff!! Novation, McGraw-Hill and more!

>>Msg Nr. 1228 Date entered: MM/30/YY From: JERRY JONES To: ALL Re: IBM PC
OWNERS
HEAR YE, HEAR YE!
TECHNICAL EXPERTISE AVAILABLE TO ALL MEMBERS FOR THE
ASKING. MONTHLY MAGAZINES SOFTWARE AND TECHNICAL
LIBRARIES AND MUCH MORE. CALL 1-800-331-2347 FOR MORE
DETAILS.

The *Other Networks Newsletter* is a real publication. It focuses on networking—both in the electronic sense and in the sense of making contact with others sharing your particular interest. The IBM/PC "800" number is real, too (for best results, call during the week, not on weekends).

Next she might leave a message of her own. Or, depending upon the other features offered by the Maple Street Messenger computer bulletin board system, she might play a computer game, download a computer program into her own machine, upload one that she would like to contribute to the system library, order a product that the Smith family might offer for sale through the system, leave a private message for the SYSOP or "system operator," or simply sign off.

When she does indeed sign off, the system may respond with the message:

Good-bye. Call again soon . . .

When it receives a sign-off signal, the Smith family's computer will perform an automatic reset routine. The blinking cursor will appear again in the upper left corner of the screen, the modem will continue to stare expectantly, and everything will be as it was—until the next time someone calls.

The CBBS Revolution

Welcome to the exciting world of computer bulletin board systems, or "CBBSs" or "BBSs" as they are often called. There are at least 450 such systems operating in the United States and Canada, but no one knows for sure how many more there may be. Most are privately run. All of them are free. And whatever their total numbers, taken together they form a thriving computer "underground" that has the potential to revolutionize personal communications.

Computer bulletin boards already serve as a meeting ground for diverse groups of people scattered across the continent—a place where they can exchange comments, ideas, computer programs, tips, announcements, and other information. The phenomenon is just beginning. But the potential impact is staggering. As computer and modem prices continue to fall, as "discount" long-distance services like those offered by MCI, ITT, and other firms continue to spread, more CBBSs will come online. In the future, when everyone in the nation knows and converses with several hundred citizens on a regular basis, CBBSs may be seen as *the most significant* result of the personal computer revolution. At the very least, the existence of computer bulletin board systems means that no one need ever be alone again.

What *Is* a Computer Bulletin Board System?

A basic computer bulletin board system or "board" requires just three components:

- A standard personal computer equipped with a communications card. At least one floppy disk drive and 48K of RAM (random access memory) are usually, but not always, required.

• A modem capable of automatically answering the phone.

• CBBS software.

That's all there is to it. The only additional requirement is a person to manage things by serving as the "system operator" or SYSOP.

It is worth noting that the only "special" component an individual must buy is the CBBS software. The cost may be as low as $75 for a basic package. But even that may not be necessary. Some communications packages, like MicroCorp's Intelliterm™ for the TRS-80 Model III and IBM/PC and Southwestern Data System's Z-Term™ Professional for the Apple II, provide a computer bulletin board module as well as all of the standard communications features. The cost for such full-featured packages is typically around $150. Thus, for a rather small additional investment, anyone who already owns a communicating personal computer and an auto-answer modem can set up a computer bulletin board.

As you might expect, however, many CBBSs are much more elaborate than this. Some systems have as many as six floppy disk drives. Some use hard disk drives for truly massive storage. And some use highly developed software that makes them seem for all the world like mini-information utilities.

Endless Variety

The first computer bulletin board system was created by Chicagoans Ward Christensen and Randy Suess in 1978 to enable local computer club members to call in and leave simple messages for one another. This "granddaddy" of all CBBSs is still in operation, and you can call it by dialing (312) 546-8086 any time of day.

Once the basic concept and the software to support it had been established, it was not long before individuals skilled in computer programming began to create software that went far beyond simple message posting. Many of these advanced systems present a caller with an extensive menu of features to choose from.

For example, you may be able to enter a command that will ring a bell to summon the SYSOP to the machine for direct communication. If the SYSOP is not available, you can leave a private message (as opposed to a publicly available bulletin). You may be able to order products offered by the SYSOP, enter a special password to access an "X-rated" part of the board, play a computer game, or read any number of articles on file in the CBBS's "library."

Tons of Free Software

And then there's the free software—tons of free, public-domain or user-contributed software are available from CBBSs across the continent. And all of it can be downloaded directly into your own computer. Only two caveats apply. First, although *any* communicating personal computer can access *any* CBBS, in order to be useful to you the software you download must be written for your particular computer. Second, you may be required to upload a program of your own before the system will permit you to download from its library. This is not always the case, and often a simple typed message will do. But understandably, bulletin board operators want to promote exchange for the benefit of all.

Online Tip: Attention CP/M users. An article by Tony Bove and Kelly Smith in *DataCast* magazine will show you how to access Remote CP/M (RCPM) systems to download over 2400 free CP/M programs. Fifteen pages long, the article provides step-by-step instructions on how to accomplish this feat and includes a directory of RCPM systems to call in every region of the United States and Canada. (You must be running MODEM 4 or MODEM 7 communications software to download.) Contact:

> *DataCast*
> Wireless Digital, Inc.
> 345 Swett Road
> Woodside, CA 94062

Annual subscription (6 issues), $18.00. (Ask for issue 004.)

Bulletin Board "Families" and How to Sign On

As mentioned above, it makes no difference what kind of computer you use—as long as your machine can communicate, you can access any bulletin board in existence. However, as you enter this world, you will discover that bulletin boards fall into certain classifications like "ABBS," "Forum 80," or "North Star Remote." These names refer only to the type of bulletin board software that CBBS is running. They have nothing to do with compatibility or the quality of what you will find.

"ABBS," for example, stands for "Apple bulletin board system." It is a software package offered by Software Sorcery, Inc., of McLean, Virginia. "Forum 80" is designed for TRS-80 Model III computers and is available either from its author, Bill Abney, of Kansas City, or from the Small Business Systems Group of Westford, Massachusetts. "North Star Remote" is a CBBS package for North Star computers. And so on.

The names are important only because each "family" uses the same commands to accomplish the same thing. Thus, if you are familiar with the commands required by an ABBS (pronounced "Abbies") system, you can call up any bulletin board identified as an ABBS and know exactly what to do to scan and read bulletins, download software, and access files. The content of the board itself is strictly a function of the individual SYSOP and the people who post messages on the system.

Online Tip: If you don't know what to do, every bulletin board system in operation will tell you. All have a "help" feature that will present the required commands and explanations of each. If you plan to regularly use a number of boards belonging to different "families," be sure to download and print out the instructions for each one. This will eliminate the need to spend time reviewing them online and, not incidentally, increase the time the CBBS is available to other users.

Signing on to a CBBS is usually even simpler than signing on to an information utility or other database. Normally you will be asked to enter your name, city, and state. Many systems collect this information for statistical purposes. But it can also be important if you want responses from other users.

The system will "go away" for a moment while it checks its files to see if you've ever been on the board before. If you have, it may respond with a "Welcome back!" or with a message sent to you by the SYSOP. If not, you will be invited to proceed. Next you may see the following series of questions:

```
WILL YOUR TERMINAL HANDLE LOWERCASE (Y/N) ? Y
Do you need line feeds (Y/N) ? n
No. of nulls (0 - 50) ? 0
```

These questions allow the CBBS system to accommodate your requirements. For example, some personal computers can only transmit capital letters, and some can use both upper- and lowercase. (Notice how the case changed in the second question after a "Y" for "yes" answer to the first question.) The line feeds question refers to the software *you* are using. Line feeds are a relic from pre-microcomputer days, when most communications equipment consisted of line printers so stupid that they did not know enough to advance the paper one line each time they received a carriage return or "enter" from the system they were communicating with. If the other system did not send a "line feed" signal with each carriage return signal, the printers would type one line on top of the other.

If you answer "yes" to the line feed question, the CBBS computer will send your system a line feed on carriage return. However, since most personal computer communications software is "smart" enough to automatically add a line feed signal whenever it receives a carriage return from the CBBS system, you will probably want to answer "no." If you're in doubt, check your software documentation.

The "nulls" question also refers to printer-based systems. Basically, a null is a time-waster. It is a no-count signal that the CBBS computer can add after sending each carriage return, to allow a pause designed to give the printing element on your printer time to make its way back to the far left before it is ordered to print another line. Each null is a fraction of a second. Again, consult your printer manual if you are in doubt. Otherwise, you can probably enter "no" for this question.

When you have answered all of these questions, the system may file them away under your name. Then the next time you sign on, it will know how to treat your system. Or you may have to go through the whole thing again. It all depends upon the CBBS software.

In any case, the next thing you will see is a "greeting" or "welcome" message giving you the name of the system, the location, and any other information the SYSOP chooses to include. You will also be told what to do to get a list of commands for using the system and how to ask for online help.

Online Tip: The baud rate you should use to access any CBBS will always be specified in any listing of available phone numbers. But you may also see a symbol signifying "ring back." This refers to the procedure that lets the computer share the phone line with human beings. Whenever you are accessing a CBBS in which "ring back" is specified, call the number, let it ring once, and then call again and get set to go online.

How to Locate Hundreds of CBBS Numbers

There are at least four ways to assemble a list of the CBBS numbers available to you. But there is one thing you should keep in mind about all of the numbers you uncover: Because virtually all CBBSs are run as a noncommercial undertaking by individuals, you should expect a certain amount of irregularity. Some of the CBBS phone numbers you find may have changed, some systems may have ceased operation, and some may not always be available.

Online Tip: Most people start by sampling a number of CBBSs and finally settle on two or three systems that they like and access regularly. They get to know the system and the other people who use it. Consequently, after the first exploratory stage, changeability of CBBS systems is not usually a factor.

The first thing you should do is to send for *The On-Line Computer Telephone Directory*. Created and published by Jim Cambron of Kansas City, Missouri, this is *the* directory of available CBBSs. Cambron takes great care to verify each and every one of the 450 or more numbers he publishes. He has written special software that enables his TRS-80 to automatically dial each number on the list. If the system does not receive an appropriate answer, the number is removed from the directory. To subscribe, contact:

J. A. Cambron Company, Inc.
P.O. Box 10005
Kansas City, MO 64111
(816) 756-1847
CompuServe: 70040,414

Published and mailed quarterly. Teletypeset.
1 yr. subscription: $19.95
2 yrs.: $28.95

The second thing you should do, while you are waiting for your online directory to arrive, is to call the CBBS owned and operated by Novation, Inc. The number is (213) 881-6880, and you should type CAT at the LOGON PLEASE prompt. (See the Introduction of this book for more details.) The Novation number will give you several hundred CBBSs, but the list is not updated on any regular basis.

The third thing to do, if you belong to The Source or CompuServe, is to sign on and check *their* bulletin boards for references to CBBS, Bulletin Boards, BBS, Networking, and related topics. If you are a member of The Source, you should also check the PARTICIPATE portion of the system (type PARTI at the Command Level prompt –>) for Conferences dealing with bulletin boards. You might also try the user publishing portions of both information utilities.

Finally, one of the best sources of CBBS numbers are other CBBSs. Many of the systems you turn up in the first three steps will offer a feature to download lists of other CBBS numbers.

Special Interest Boards

On your journeys through CBBS-land you will discover many boards devoted to single subjects. The following list includes a number of these "special" CBBSs that you may want to try:

Satire and Humor
(212) 245-4363

PASCAL and SF
(703) 255-2192
ABBS operated by Craig Vaughn

Berkley Conference Tree
(415) 538-3580
(Hit <ENTER> twice for
   instructions)

CommuniTree
(415) 928-0641

People's Message System
(714) 449-5689
Creator Bill Blue's home base

AMRAD   *Good*
(703) 734-1387
Good list of CBBSs

Computer-Dial-a-Joke
(213) 773-6591

Genealogy Interest Group
(703) 978-7561

Commodities Interest Group
(816) 931-3135

Avionics Interest Group
(913) 782-5115

Kinky Kumputer
(415) 647-9524
S-E-X!

Astronomy
(212) 787-5520

International Apple Corps
(415) 585-6334

Adventure Board
(201) 376-8055
Adventure fantasy game

ABBS Gamesmaster
(312) 475-4884 (24 hours)
A 35-room "house" with each room
   devoted to a different game

Forum-80
(816) 861-7040
Creator Bill Abney's home base

NASA
(301) 344-9156
Check Space Shuttle schedule
   and read news about shuttle
   missions

Pacific Medical Bulletin Board
   (PMBB)
(805) 522-1789 (9AM to midnight,
   and all day weekends, EST)
For medical and related
   professions

Write for list of PMBB features:
1018 N. Currier Ave.
Simi Valley, CA 93065

IBM/PC
(703) 560-0979
The Washington, D.C., PC club

Starbase 12
(617) 876-4885 (5 PM to midnight
  Mon.–Sat., 2 PM to midnight
  Sun., EST)
Operated by "Sith Lord." Science
  Fiction par excellence

Online Tip: One interesting area of the CBBS phenomenon is the possibility of linking personal computers to a ham radio network. Joe Kasser, president of the Chesapeake Microcomputer Club, is an expert. If this interests you, read his article ("The Club Computer Network") in the May 1980 issue of *Byte* or contact him directly at:

> 11532 Stewart Lane
> Silver Spring, MD 20904
> HAM Call Sign: G3ZCZ

Online Tip: If you are interested in the potential of CBBSs for community and social interaction, there are at least two areas to investigate. First is the *Other Networks* quarterly newsletter. An excellent resource for "networking" numbers and related information. Subscriptions are "$15.00/year, or $5.00 for those living lightly." Contact:

> Other Networks
> P.O. Box 14066
> Philadelphia, PA 19123

Second, there is the Microcomputer Information Support Tools (MIST) package from Peter and Trudy Johnson-Lenz for "networking as a social activity that connects people and allows them to access resources." Their address is:

> Peter and Trudy Johnson-Lenz
> 695 Fifth Sttreet
> Lake Oswego, OR 97034
> (503) 635-2615 message phone
> EIES Network ID# 118 (P&T)

How to Start Your Own Computer Bulletin Board

To set up your own CBBS, you'll need your computer, an auto-answer modem, and bulletin board software. It may be possible to get by with a single disk drive, but for all practical purposes, two drives is really the minimum requirement. You should also be aware that bulletin board software is usually written to be used with a particular brand of modem. If you really get involved in the CBBS world, you will also want to consider ordering a separate telephone line for your system. If you don't plan to install a separate phone line in the near future, make sure that the bulletin board software you buy supports a ring-back feature to allow you to share the phone with your computer.

Before establishing your own system, you will undoubtedly want to sample lots of different bulletin boards. And, you'll want to thoroughly investigate the various types of bulletin board software that may be available for your system. You may be able to get the information you need from your computer store. But if you can't, you can write to the addresses listed below for more information on specific packages. The prices of these products range from about $40 for a basic program features to about $350 for full-featured package.

Bulletin Board Software for Apple II Computers

ABBS Version 4.0
Software Sorcery
7927 Jones Branch Drive,
   Suite 400
McLean, VA 22102

Conference Tree
Communitree Group
470 Castro Street, Suite 207-3002
San Francisco, CA 94114

Peoples Message System (PMS)
Bill Blue
P.O. Box 1318
Lakeside, CA 92040

Net-Works
Advanced Data Systems
7468 Maple Ave.
St. Louis, MO 63143

Bulletin Board Software for Radio Shack TRS-80 Models I and III

Bullet-80 (for Model I)
Computer Services of Danbury
P.O. Box 993
Danbury, CT 06810

Connection-80 (for Model I)
B. T. Enterprises
171 Hawkins Road
Centereach, NY 11720

ST80-X10
ST80-PB
ST80-CC
MOUSE-NET
(all for Models I and III)
Small Business Systems Group
6 Carlisle Road
Westford, MA 01866

FORUM-80 (for Models I and III)
Small Business Systems Group
6 Carlisle Road
Westford, MA 01866

Message-80 (Models I and III)
Microperipheral Corporation
P.O. Box 529
Mercer Island, WA 98040

Commodore PET and CBM Computers

PET Bulletin Board System (PBBS)
TNW Corporation
3351 Hancock Street
San Diego, CA 92110

North Star Computers

North Star Remote Bulletin Board
The MicroStuf Company
P.O. Box 33337
Decatur, GA 30033

CP/M-based Systems

CBBS
Randy Suess
5219 West Warwick
Chicago, IL 60641

Conclusion

If you do nothing else with your communicating personal computer and modem, access a computer bulletin board system. In addition to providing an inexpensive (or cost-free) introduction to life online, CBBSs offer you a front row seat at the "Revolution." The impact of the CBBS phenomenon has yet to be felt, but it's coming. When it arrives, it will sweep the nation.

But there's no need to wait for the number of personal computers to reach the critical mass necessary for this to happen. You can sign on to a CBBS right now and begin enjoying the fruits of the Revolution before it actually takes place.

...9...

Keyboard Commerce
Electronic Shopping, Banking, and Barter

How would you like to save over $300 on a brand name dishwasher and $300 more on a brand name microwave oven? A couple in Illinois did just that by ordering the items from their personal computer terminal. The items arrived in factory-sealed cartons, with full manufacturer warranties, approximately two and a half weeks after they entered their order. Their only cost was $25 for an annual membership in a shopping service called Comp-U-Store, and about $50 connect time charges, for a net savings of $525.

This is only one real-life example of how personal computers can and are being used in the world of commerce. Other individuals routinely sign on to CompuServe to pay their bills, transfer money from one account to another, and check their current balances through CompuServe's electronic banking feature. Still others frequently take advantage of the opportunity to "cut a deal" on Tradenet, a service offered through The Source by Barter Worldwide, Inc.

"Keyboard commerce," in short, is booming. In years to come, many different shopping, buying, trading, banking, and financial services will be available to anyone with a communicating personal computer. In this chapter, we will look at three services that were among the first in the fields of electronic shopping, electronic banking, and electronic barter.

Comp-U-Store: Products and Price Quotes

Comp-U-Store (formerly "Comp*U*Star"), is a unit of Comp-U-Card of America, Inc., of Stamford, Connecticut, the original shop-at-home service. Comp-U-Card was founded in 1973 to offer its customers computerized price quotes and the opportunity to purchase items over the phone.

The firm solicits price quotes from over 200 manufacturers, wholesalers, and retailers on some 50,000 brand name products. The information is entered into a computer. Whenever a member calls to ask the price of an item, the computer scans its memory for all available quotes and displays the lowest quote on the terminal of the customer service representative handling the member's call.

Prices typically range from 10 to 40 percent—and occasionally 50 percent—off the manufacturer's suggested retail price. In addition to receiving a price quote, members also have the option of ordering the product at the price given and charging their purchase on a major credit card. Checks are also accepted, but no merchandise is shipped until the check clears. This typically adds two weeks to the delivery time.

With over two million members, the Comp-U-Card "phone-in" service is still the largest portion of the firm's business. But it is obviously perfectly suited for access by personal computer. Just replace the customer service representative's terminal with a personal computer linked to the Comp-U-Card by telephone, and—Presto!—instant online shopping service.

This is precisely what Comp-U-Card has done by offering Comp-U-Store. Available on The Source, on CompuServe, and by direct subscription, the service provides the information identical to the phone-in version described above, but it offers a number of additional advantages as well.

The phone-in service is open from 9:00 AM to 9:00 PM Monday through Friday, and from 9:00 AM to 5:00 PM Saturday, and is closed all day Sunday and on major holidays. The online version is available 24 hours a day, 365 days a year. The online version also features a program that will ask you questions to help narrow your choices. And it will present descriptions and model numbers for all of the items in the database that meet those criteria. To use the phone-in service, you must know the exact model number of the item you want before you place the call.

What's Available?

- More than 50,000 products, including major appliances, cameras, flatware, luggage, musical instruments, sporting goods, stereo equipment, TVs and VCRs, watches, and more.

- Over 200 brand names represented, including Admiral, Canon, GE,

Gorham, Litton, Maytag, Nikon, Omega, Pioneer, Seiko, Singer, Sony, Westinghouse, and Zenith.

- Typical prices are 10 to 40 percent off suggested manufacturer's retail. But the service offers many monthly "specials" with potentially even larger savings.

- "Comp-U-Stakes." Weekly online auctions of TVs, stereo equipment, and other products. Items go to the highest bidder(s). But no obligation to buy if you later decide you don't want the item.

What Does It Cost?

A direct subscription to Comp-U-Store costs $25 a year ($40 for a two-year membership) and entitles you to dial the service toll-free to search for and order products at any time. The membership fee is fully refundable if you are not completely satisfied. Additional "bonus" months may or may not be available.

Rates for direct access to Comp-U-Store are $18 per hour Monday through Friday between the hours of 9:00 AM and 5:00 PM (EST), and $5 per hour at all other times. Comp-U-Store is available for direct access 24 hours a day.

Your membership also includes a no-fee Visa card offered through Bank One of Columbus, Ohio—the same institution that handles both Merrill Lynch Cash Management Accounts and CompuServe VIP accounts. Visa credit lines range from $1000 to $5000, subject to approval.

Online Tip: For many years, firms such as IBM, DEC, General Foods, and others have offered Comp-U-*Card* memberships to their employees for free or at reduced rates. Check with your employer, labor union, or other organization to see if a similar deal is offered for Comp-U-*Store* memberships.

Means of Access

In addition to direct subscriptions, Comp-U-Store is also available on The Source and CompuServe. (The two information utilities actually connect you to the Comp-U-Store computer.) In both cases, you are free to search the entire Comp-U-Store database for products and price quotes without actually becoming a member of the service. Standard Source and CompuServe connect time rates apply, but that is your only cost. (A premium used to be charged when the service was known as

"Comp*U*Star," but this policy was changed when the service changed its name to Comp-U-Store.)

If you decide to order a product, however, you will have to take out a Comp-U-Store membership. And, of course, you can sign up by keying in your membership information online.

Other Features and Notes

• Comp-U-Store prices can be searched by any member, regardless of location. But product ordering and delivery is limited to the 48 contiguous states of the U.S.A. Products are shipped in factory-sealed cartons and delivered directly to your door.

> **Online Tip:** You can arrange to have the merchandise you order shipped to any address, making it possible to use Comp-U-Store to send gifts the way you might use an FTD florist to send flowers. The difference is that delivery is not "instantaneous."

• All prices quoted *include* shipping and handling and any applicable taxes.

• One hundred percent guarantee. All merchandise ordered through the service carries full manufacturer warranties and guarantees.

• Payment can be made by check or major credit card.

• Delivery times are usually quoted as "four to six weeks," but many customers report receiving their orders in two to two and a half weeks.

• Comp-U-Store members receive a monthly newsletter, free of charge. The publication is designed to keep members up-to-date on "monthly specials," new product offerings, special discounts, and the like.

• Your Comp-U-Store membership fee is fully refundable should you be dissatisfied with the service. Membership renewal is automatically charged to your credit card, however, so be sure to give the service plenty of warning if you decide against renewing.

Online Tip: Since different product models are usually identified by serial number, it's a good idea to do a little research before using the service. This will give you an idea of what the products are like and what you would have to pay for them locally. But since you may discover models in Comp-U-Store's files that you have *not* seen locally, you should probably count on accessing the database at least once to survey the field and once more to actually place your order.

For More Information . . .

You will find complete descriptions of the Comp-U-Store service on both The Source and on CompuServe. But you can also contact the firm directly at:

    Comp-U-Store
    777 Summer Street
    Stamford, CT 06901
    (800) 243-9000

Online Banking: Checking Your Checking Account (and More)

Electronic banking "tests," "trials," and "programs" are sprouting like loan offers after a fall in interest rates. They're everywhere. And they're spreading rapidly, as normally sedate bankers scramble to avoid being left in the electronic dust of the videotex/teletext/personal computer revolution. Indeed, the whole industry is in a state of flux and is likely to remain so for some time to come. Outdated rules and prohibitions are being replaced with new regulations that tacitly acknowledge the twentieth century and the existence of an electronic age. And there are more changes to come.

In the meantime, online personal computer-based electronic banking has begun. It will be years before the concept fulfills its potential, but it is here now for subscribers to the CompuServe Information Service.

CompuServe offers you access to the services provided by at least three banks. These are:

The United American Bank of Knoxville, Tennessee
(615) 971-2265

Shawmut Bank of Boston
(617) 292-2317

The Huntington National Bank of Columbus, Ohio
(614) 476-8330

To use the online services of any of these banks, you must first open an account, and that can only be done by contacting the bank directly. The different institutions have different requirements. For example, if you want to sit at your keyboard and order the Huntington National Bank to pay certain bills on certain dates, you must first have a "pay-by-phone" account, regardless of whether you plan to ever use it in that way. Be sure to ask about requirements like this when you contact the bank of your choice.

It's important to emphasize that electronic banking is still "under development" on CompuServe, as it is everywhere else. Electronic banking is available. It works. And it is accessible to any CIS subscriber. But some of the features are bound to be expanded or changed. Nevertheless, it *is* possible to present an overview of the system, which is what we will do here.

Your first step is to select the bank that you have your account with. The system will "go away" for a moment as it performs the necessary switching to connect you directly to the particular bank's computers. Then a menu similar to the following will appear:

```
CompuServe        Page UAB-1

1 Bank Information
2 Tel-A-Pay bill paying
3 Current statements
4 CD rates
5 User information
0 All banking completed

. Enter your choice,
or H for more information.. =!
```

Selection 1 will give you general information on the bank. And selection 2 will generate the following menu:

```
                  Welcome to Tel-A-Pay

1 Payment instructions
2 Add or delete merchants
3 Cancel or change payment
4 Pay bills

. Last menu page. Key choice
or M for previous menu.. =!
```

202 . . .

The selections on this menu will allow you to tell the bank which creditors you want to pay, how much, and when you want the payments to be made. You can, if you like, enter your bill-paying instructions a month or more ahead of time. On the first of the month, you can effectively say, "Pay MasterCard $25 on the 17th of the month, pay Visa $30 on the 23rd, pay Nassau Liquors the full amount on the 30th," and so forth. You may even be able to make these "standing orders"—to be executed automatically each month until you say otherwise.

The "current statements" option from the main banking menu will allow you to look at your present checking and savings account balances and at all of the checks that have cleared to date:

Current Statements

1 Checking account 0877440
  (Household)

2 Checking account 0742426
  (Investment)

3 Savings account 120044668
. Last menu page. Key choice
or M for previous menu.. =!1

CompuServe   Page UAB-14

Checking account 0877440

	Current Balance		997.20
Date	Item	Amount	Balance
0322	Last Statement		640.28
0323	Check	50.00	590.28
0323	Check	10.00	580.28
0329	Check	140.22	440.06
0330	Deposit	630.00	1,070.06
0407	Check	72.86	997.20

. Last page.
Key M for menu.. =!

Bill paying and checking the status of your accounts are basic to electronic banking. However, other features may be available as well. For example, you may be able to get the latest interest rates on Certificates of Deposit (CDs) or other financial products offered by the bank. Here's a short sample:

```
                    CD Rates
            1 Under $100,000
            2 $100,000 or more
            . Last menu page. Key choice
            or M for previous menu.. =!1


        CompuServe              Page UAB-17

        **** CD rates under $100,000 ***
        MM/DD/YY
        30 - 89 Days ............... 5.25 %
        90 Days - 1 Year ........... 5.75 %
        1 - 2.5 Years ............... 6.00 %
        2.5 - 4 Years ............... 6.50 %
        4    - 6 Years ............... 7.25 %
        6    - 8 Years ............... 7.50 %
             8 Years ............... 7.75 %
        Diamond CD $10,000 min .. 15.925%
        2.5 Year money market .... 11.75 %
        . Last page.
        Key M for menu.. =!
```

In the future, you may even be able to *buy* CDs, travelers checks, money orders—even stocks and bonds—with your personal computer. Other features being tested by banks across the nation include the transferring of funds from savings to checking accounts and vice versa, the option of using bank-supplied computer programs to balance your checkbook or manage your household budget, online loan applications, and the opportunity to monitor bank credit card use by calling up a current statement whenever you like.

The CompuServe offering is the first personal computer-accessible banking system to "go public." And while it is far from being a completely developed system, it is certainly worth looking into for those who want to start doing their banking online.

Make Me an Offer!—Online Barter

Before there were banks, or money, or credit cards, there was barter. It is a practice as ancient as civilization itself. But now it has been updated and refined with the aid of computers. And it is accessible to anyone with a Source subscription and something to trade.

"Tradenet," a service of Barter Worldwide, Inc., on The Source allows you to run a keyword search on an extensive list of individuals and companies interested in trading skills, products, collectibles, software, services, and hundreds of other valuables. Please see Figure 9.1 for a sample listing of the kinds of products and services bartered on Tradenet.

——————— **Figure 9.1. Typical Products and Services** ———————
Bartered on The Source.

ACCOUNTING SERVICES
ACCOUNTING SOFTWARE
ACTORS/ACTRESSES/
  CASTING
ADVERTISING/CUSTOM
  T-SHIRTS
ADVERTISING-MEDIA/
  MAGAZINES
ADVERTISING-MEDIA/RADIO
AIR CHARTER/PILOT
  TRAINING
AIR TRAVEL/CORPORATE/
  TIMESHARE
ANSWERING SERVICE/TOLL-
  FREE/800
ATTORNEYS
AUTOMOBILES
BEVELED GLASS
CASTING SERVICES
COLLECTIBLES (RARE
  COINS)
COMMERCIALS/TELEVISION/
  CASTING
COMPUTER/PRINTERS/
  CENTRONICS
COMPUTER PROGRAMMING
COMPUTER/SYSTEMS/
  MICROMATION
COMPUTER/SYSTEMS/TI
COMPUTER/TERMINALS/TI
CONSULTING/COMPUTER/
  APPLE
CONSULTING/RARE COINS/
  INVESTMENT

CONSULTING/
  ENVIRONMENTAL/
  MEDICAL
CONSULTING/PENSIONS
CONSULTING/SOFTWARE
  PACKAGING
CONSULTING/VIDEOTEX
CP/M (TM) COMPUTER
  SOFTWARE
CUSTOM TOURS
DENTAL OFFICE SOFTWARE
DENTIST
DISKETTES/HARD DISKS
DRAPERY & UPHOLSTERY
  FABRIC
ENVELOPE STUFFING/
  MAILING
EXECUTIVE SEARCH
FILMS CASTING/LOCATIONS
FLIGHT INSTRUCTION/
  MINNEAPOLIS
FORM LETTER ASSEMBLY/
  STUFFING
FRAMING
FURNITURE/OFFICE
GEMS
HEADHUNTERS
  (EXECUTIVE SEARCH)
HOTEL ACCOMMODATIONS
INCENTIVE PREMIUMS
INDUSTRIAL FILMS
  CASTING
INVENTORY SOFTWARE
INVESTIGATIONS

LOTS/REAL ESTATE
MICROSOFT (TM) BASIC
MOBILE TELEPHONES
MOTORCYCLES
ONLINE TYPOGRAPHIC
  SERVICES
PERSONAL IMPROVEMENT
  TAPES
PHOTOGRAPHY/
  COMMERCIAL
PHOTOJOURNALIST
  FREELANCE TRADE
  TRAVEL
PICTURE FRAMING
RESORTS/SKI/VACATION
RESTAURANT/DELAWARE/
  WILMINGTON
RESTAURANT/
  MASSACHUSETTS/BOSTON

TALENT SCOUT/CASTING
  SERVICES
TYPOGRAPHIC/
  TYPESETTING (ONLINE)
VACATIONS>CALIFORNIA/
  SKI
VACATIONS>FLORIDA
VACATIONS>HAWAII
  HOTELS
VACATIONS>WHITEWATER
  RIVER RAFT
VIDEOTEX CONSULTING
WAREHOUSING
WATS SERVICE/INCOMING
WRITING/TELEVISION/
  SCREENPLAYS

Tradenet is designed to make it easy for the parties in a barter deal to find each other. Here's how it works. Any Source subscriber may enter a listing on the Tradenet by filling out a form like this one:

RETAIL PRICE UNIT:	TELEX MACHINE
BRAND(S):	TRANS-LUX
MINIMUM:	ONE (USED)
MAXIMUM:	
DIMENSIONS:	18″ × 16″ × 5″
WEIGHT/UNIT/ CASE:	
RETAIL PRICE UNIT:	$2,700 (NEW)
TOTAL RETAIL VALUE:	
WANT ITEM(S):	COMPUTER EQUIP-MAKE ME AN OFFER

Notice that both "have" items and "want" items are listed. The barter process is very fluid and flexible, and you are not required to fill in all of the blanks. In fact, although you obviously have to fill in either a "have" or a "want," you are not required to fill in both.

This form gets sent to the folks at Barter Worldwide, and they write up a listing, assign a client number, and place it in the proper category on the system. Once your listing is on the system, anyone can search for it by keyword or by entering a category number. Here, for example, is a listing that might appear if you searched the system for the keywords "legal services" or for the keywords "computer equipment."

CLIENT #025

ATTORNEY

HAS: LEGAL SERVICES

THIS IS AN ATTORNEY PRACTICING IN NEW YORK WHOSE PRACTICE IS LIMITED TO APPEALS AND MOTIONS, FOR NEW YORK AND FEDERAL CASES.

FEE: $60/HR FOR LEGAL SERVICES RENDERED, PLUS COSTS AND ANY DISBURSEMENTS

WANTS: TERMINALS & HARD DISK STORAGE FOR AN ALPHA MICRO.

ALSO WANTS: FURNISHINGS FOR A HOME HE IS BUILDING.

If this proposal sounded interesting to you, the next step would be to contact Barter Worldwide via SourceMail. The firm would then do its best to arrange a trade between you and Client #025. There is no charge for placing a listing on the system. Only when a trade is actually arranged do the participants pay a commission to Barter Worldwide.

Barter Worldwide charges a commission of 10 percent of the cash value of all trades, and the minimum retail value of the trade must be at least $500. For real estate trades, there is a finder's fee of 1 percent of the market value of the property. But that's about it. The whole process is really a simple, effective use of computer power to bring together two interested parties.

Online Tip: To access the Tradenet on The Source, type BARTER at the command level (–>) prompt. Or use the menu approach. If you decide to place a listing, try to be as specific as possible about what you want or what you are willing to trade. And a little salesmanship isn't out of order. If you have a degree in fluid mechanics and are offering services as a fluid mechanic, by all means say so.

Conclusion

Perhaps the most important thing to remember about "keyboard commerce" is that things are just getting started. The opportunities available are significant, but they are relatively limited compared with what will be available in the future. The banking industry in particular sees keyboard commerce as the wave of the future, and in the years to come you can count on many more banks making their services available online.

As the number of personal computer users expands, new online shopping services are also a possibility. Though the future is less clear in this area, it is more than likely that many of today's mail-order catalog houses will ultimately offer customers an opportunity to search for and order products online. A "super catalog" service providing you with access to many individual mail-order catalogs is also a distinct possibility, as is a dedicated "barter only" service.

All of these things will take years to develop. In the meantime, if you sample the services described in this chapter, you will be pleasantly surprised at what is *already* available online.

...**10**...

Computerized Conferencing
EIES and PARTICIPATE

Computerized conferencing is one of those elegantly simple concepts that seems so right and so obvious—after someone else has thought of it. It is also one of those ideas that, once it is fully developed and widely implemented, has the potential to fundamentally change the way we as members of a society meet, exchange information, and work together to achieve a common goal. Besides, it's a lot of fun.

Also known as "teleconferencing," "computerized conferencing," or just "CC," the concept is based on the ability of a central computer to store, retrieve, and display information. As long as the computer is up and running, it can send information to and accept information from any individual, at any time, from any location on the globe. That is the fundamental truth that defines this corner of the electronic universe.

In an age of information utilities, $100 microcomputers, and hundreds of free computer bulletin boards, none of this sounds too amazing. But in 1971, before the first "Apple" seeds had been sewn, the idea represented a conceptual breakthrough. That was the year that Murray Turoff, professor of computer science at the New Jersey Institute of Technology, publicly introduced the system he had been developing for a number of years under the aegis of the Office of Emergency Preparedness (OEP) in the White House. Known as the Emergency Conferencing System and Reference Index, it played a crucial role in administering the wage/price freeze imposed by the President that year.

The freeze created a huge nationwide demand for information, guidelines, rulings, official statements, and policy clarifications. The 10 OEP regional offices were flooded with requests from businesses, labor unions, and administrators. It quickly became obvious that conventional mail and telephone communications were completely inadequate for dealing with the situation. The first week the freeze went into effect, the New York office alone received over 10,000 calls—an average of nearly 5 a minute.

What was needed was some form of centralized information exchange that could be accessed by many individuals, regardless of time of day or physical location. Dr. Turoff's system provided the answer. Officials at the main OEP office in Washington could place policy statements on the system for regional offices to read at their convenience. Questions could be entered and answered, and both could be displayed for all to read.

Most important of all, groups of people—many of whom could never be brought together in the same place at the same time—could easily use this centralized information exchange to "discuss" proposals and ideas. At any time of the day or night, discussion-group members could use a computer terminal to contact the system. Once online, they could read all of the comments made by all other members and add comments of their own. The system worked well, and versions of it are still used by several government agencies today.

Building Upward from a Bulletin Board

This was the historical beginning, and Dr. Turoff is widely acknowledged as the "father of teleconferencing." *The Network Nation: Human Communication via Computer* (Addison-Wesley, 1978), a joint work by Murry Turoff and Starr Roxanne Hiltz, professor and chairperson of the sociology department at Upsala College, is the bible of the field.

But for a clearer idea of how computerized teleconferencing works, it can be helpful to have a basic understanding of its technological beginnings as well. Let's start with the basic fact that a computer can store and retrieve information and quickly build upward from there.

Because of this basic capability, any computer can be used as a simple bulletin board. A person can sit down at a terminal attached directly to a computer and create a file on the system. Let's assume that a fellow named Joe has created a file he has called "Announcements" and that he has typed in the following message: "Party at Joe's place Friday night. 8:00." As far as the computer is concerned, files are very much like manila folders—this one, "tabbed" with the word "Announcements." The computer stores it away in its "file drawer" where it will be available to anyone who wants to pull it out and read its contents.

Now let's suppose that Susan comes along, sits down at the same terminal, and tells the computer to display the Announcements file. She plans to go to the party but she needs directions and she knows Joe will be out of town for the next few days. So she types "Help—I need driving directions to Joe's party. Does anybody know if you turn left after the Slausson cutoff? Or turn right at the fork in the road?" Like an additional piece of paper being added to a manila file, this message will be added to the Announcements file in the computer's memory and it will be displayed along with the first message the next time someone asks to read the file.

The next person to sit down at the terminal is Bob. He has been to Joe's place many times and even knows a shortcut that can clip 10 minutes off the travel time. So he types "Susan—Here's how to get to Joe's place . . ." and gives his directions. This, too, will be added to the file and be available for everyone to read.

This crude bulletin board system represents the simplest use of a computer's information storage and retrieval abilities for human communication. In fact, that is *all* the computer has done so far. It has accepted information from one of its attached terminals, filed it away, and displayed it on command.

Now let's compress several decades of technological development into just a few paragraphs and expand things radically. First, instead of a simple attached terminal, we decree that people will now be able to use their personal computers to "talk" to the central computer over the phone, regardless of where they are in the world.

Ramon Patel in Madras, India; Anthony Polizano in Milan, Italy; and Monique Musset in Paris have all read about Joe's party in the Announcements file, and each is planning to catch the next plane out. Each has also put a message in the file notifying Joe—and anyone else who reads the file—that they are on the way.

Things are getting out of hand. A simple little white wine affair has turned into an international convocation. Nothing can be done this time, but in the future Joe will realize that he has two choices. He can either decline to place his announcement on the bulletin board, in which case Susan would not hear about it and Bob would not be able to give Susan directions. Or he can post his message and take his chances.

Now let's upgrade the software. Let's make it possible for the computer to do much *more* than simply store and retrieve information. From now on, only those people with a special password will be able to "get into" the Announcements file—and Joe alone controls who receives the password.

Adding this "controlled access" feature transforms our crude computer bulletin board into a crude computerized conferencing system. It makes it possible for a specific group of people to exchange messages among themselves with the privacy and mutual trust that are essential to any *real* human communication, regardless of where it takes place.

The Secret's in the Software

It is important to notice that this transformation was brought about by the software—the specific instructions fed into the computer—that enabled it to offer the limited or controlled access feature. This is a crucial point, since unlike information utilities and databases, computerized teleconferencing systems have no products or information to sell. The system itself *is* the product, and the software *is* the system.

Computer software is always the realization of a vision. Whether it is a conventional accounts receivable package or a phenomenally successful spreadsheet program like VisiCalc®, someone somewhere must sit down and visualize the way it will work and what it will do before a single line of computer programming can be written.

That is always a challenge, even for the routine "number crunching" programs in which everything is relatively cut and dried. Designing a program to handle human communications, however, with all of its unpredictable variables and needs, raises the difficulty by several orders of magnitude. Given the complexity of the task, it is not surprising that CC systems have taken years to develop.

There's also the fact that until 1982 the equipment needed to take advantage of such systems was too expensive for most people to afford. But now, with prices rapidly falling and widespread personal computer ownership a reality, computerized teleconferencing is ready to fulfill its true potential.

Getting into Computerized Conferencing

A number of organizations offer CC services by providing access to a computer that has been equipped with the proper software. Tymshare, the parent company of the Tymnet packet-switching network, offers "Augment," for example. This is a full-featured system designed primarily for corporate customers. Other firms offer CC software designed to run on corporate computers. Cross Communications of Boulder, Colorado, for example, offers a complete conferencing package called "Matrix" designed to run on DEC minicomputers.

For the personal computer owner, however, the two most important names to know in the teleconferencing field are the Electronic Information Exchange System (EIES, pronounced "eyes") and PARTICIPATE. EIES is an independent system accessible by Telenet and Uninet. It was developed in 1975 by Murray Turoff under a grant by the National Science Foundation, and is considered the original public computerized conferencing system. PARTICIPATE was developed by Chandler Harrison Stevens and is a service of Participation Systems, Inc., of Boston. PARTICIPATE is available only on The Source.

These are the two systems we will present here. You will find specific information on each later in this chapter. But since they are quite similar—PARTICIPATE was actually developed on the EIES system—no distinction will be made between the two in the following sections.

The Conferencing Concept

A computer conference on EIES or PARTICIPATE can be started for any purpose by anyone who is on the system. Specific individuals can agree to form a conference on a given date to discuss a given topic, of course. But it is also possible to establish a conference that's open to anyone with an interest in the topic. The procedure usually involves giving your conference a name and then entering a one-page writeup of what you want to discuss, suggestions on who might be especially interested, how you think the conference will develop, and so on.

The system will automatically place your title on its Directory of Current Conferences, where it will be visible to anyone who looks at the directory. If someone signs on and thinks your title looks intriguing, he or she can enter a command to read your introductory page. The individual may then decide to "join" your conference and possibly enter a comment, or move to some other conference to see what's happening there.

Most conferences are formed to discuss and share information, opinions, and ideas on a single topic. The topic can be as broad as "television," or as focused as "television and its effects on children under six years of age." A conference can include any number of members from 2 to 200 or more, though for practical purposes, the maximum number is probably around 30 or 40 individuals.

For example, let's assume that someone has started a conference on fiber optics and given it the title "FIBOP." Suppose that at some point John, one of the members of FIBOP, types in a message citing a problem he is having with a particular application. For some reason, there is plenty of light going into the fiber but very little coming out the other end. A Canadian scientist signs on the next day and sees the message. As it happens, she and her colleagues have previously encountered the identical problem and developed a solution. She sits at her keyboard and enters a message responding to the original inquiry: "John, we've had the same problem and we've found that if you . . ."

That response, like the query that preceded it, will be given a number and will become part of the permanent record of the "conference proceedings." Both will be available for any conference member to read and/or comment upon. The complete record can be read by any conference member at any time, and most new conference members do just that.

Some conferences have been going on for years, accumulating a backlog of several hundred messages and contributions. Once you've brought yourself "up to speed," it could be very inconvenient to have to keep track of the last message you read the last time you were online, particularly if you are a member of a number of conferences.

But, thanks to well-developed conferencing software, that won't be a problem. If you have joined one or more conferences on PARTICIPATE, the system will automatically notify you of any comments that have been added to any of your conferences since you last signed on. You can then choose to read just those contributions.

Computerized Conferencing—Refinements

The conferencing technique described so far applies to a "public" conference open to all individuals on the system. But there are also closed conferences; these may be completely private or offer a "read only" option that allows nonmembers to read the proceedings but does not permit them to add comments of their own. Access is normally controlled by the conference moderator—usually the person who organized the conference in the first place.

EIES and PARTICIPATE include a number of other features that reflect the thought and care that has gone into creating systems and software designed for human communication. The following, for example, can be found on one or both systems:

• Ability to search for conferences by keywords contained in their descriptive subject lines.

• Electronic mail options. Automatic notification of pending letters sent to you by other users.

• A "text editor" or online word processor for use in preparing reports and other items you might want to contribute to a conference.

• A voting option designed to let you register your vote on questions being considered by the conference.

• "User status." Get a list of who is online at the moment, what conference they belong to, and so on. Also an option to place a brief biography of yourself on file with the system for anyone to read. A good way to meet others with similar interests.

• Instantaneous message delivery. If you want to send a message to someone who is currently online, you can enter a command that will make the message appear on the person's screen the next time he or she hits the <ENTER> key.

• Monitors and helpers to aid you in using the system. Immediate help may be available online. If not, you can enter a question and be certain that a designated helper will respond by electronic mail.

These and other features make it easy to communicate on an EIES or a PARTICIPATE conference. But perhaps the most significant feature offered by both systems is not so much a feature as an *atmosphere*. In both cases there is a tremendous camaraderie among members, most of whom will never hear each other's voices or meet face-to-face. There's the healthy pioneering spirit of individuals united in a common exploration. And in a medium free from the distractions of physical appearance, social status, and other barriers, there is true communication.

What Topics Are Discussed?

The topics under discussion at any one time are limited only by human curiosity. Figure 10.1, for example, gives a partial listing of the conferences taking place on EIES during one particular month. Figure 10.2 shows the subject lines of a number of PARTICIPATE conferences.

———————— **Figure 10.1. EIES Conference Topics.** ————————

The following list contains the titles of many of the conferences in progress on the Electronic Information Exchange System (EIES) during a single month. The numbers in parentheses are code numbers that can be used to access each conference. Since conferences are constantly being concluded, added, or changed, it is important to think of this list as an illustrative snapshot and not a permanent directory.

CCBS REVIEW (1012)
CC FOR DEVELOPING COUNTRIES (1015)
COMPUTERS IN EDUCATION (1021)
CONFERENCE AND NOTEBOOK NOTICES (1008)
DREAMS (1019)
EIES FEATURES PROCEDURES (1045)
EIES NEWS NETWORK (1020)
EIES POETRY CORNER (1001)
EMERGING TRENDS: FOOD AND POPULATION (1018)
ESSAYS AND LETTERS (1072)
EXPLANATIONS (1007)
FRENCH (1047)

FUTURE SCENARIOS (1016)
GENERAL TECHNOLOGY TRANSFER CONF (1071)
GRAFFITI (1005)
IMPACTS (1003)
INFORMATION SCIENCE (1010)
LIBRARY FUTURES (1022)
MARINE EDUCATION (1073)
MISCELLANEOUS ADVERTISEMENTS (1080)
NOTICES (1004)
OPPORTUNITIES (1009)
OSOL (1013)
PAPER FAIR (1017)
PERSONAL COMPUTERS (1014)
PRACTICE (1000)
PRIVACY (1025)
PROBLEMS AND SUGGESTIONS (1002)
PUBLIC PROCEDURES (1040)
PUBLICTECH AS EIES-WIDE EXPERIMENT (1070)
RELIGION AND TECHNOLOGY (1029)
TELENET EXPERIENCES (1011)
TERMINALS (1006)
TOWN MEETING (1030)
TOXIC WASTE MANAGEMENT (1031)
UNINET EXPERIENCES (1023)
WFS 82 (1050)

Joining the "PARTI"—How PARTICIPATE Works
The only way to really get a feeling for teleconferencing is to actually take part in one. But it is possible to get a general idea of how computerized conferencing works and what to expect when you go online.

> **Online Tip:** You may find that computerized conferencing is unlike anything you have ever done before. And you may find it's highly addictive. Many users report experiencing withdrawal symptoms when—for one reason or another—they are unable to sign on each day. It's important not to make more of this than it deserves. Still, forewarned is forearmed!

In this section we will concentrate on PARTICIPATE, since it is the system most people will use. EIES has many real-life applications, but the system considers itself more of a "laboratory" for developing and studying the computerized conferencing concept. It can accommodate only a limited number of people, and with fewer than 1000 members it is considerably smaller than PARTI.

Initial Sign-on

Any subscriber to The Source is free to use PARTICIPATE at any time; there is no extra cost. (See Chapter 3 for more information on The Source, rates, and sign-up procedure.) You have only to type PARTI at the Command Level prompt. This will take you directly to PARTICI-PATE, and PARTICIPATE will take you through its introduction.

The only requirement is that you officially "sign up" by entering the name or "handle" by which you or your organization would like to be known on the system. This is the "signature" that will automatically be added to any notes or messages you create on the system. You will also be asked to select a password. This feature is designed to provide each user of a multi-user account with a separate identity.

Next, you will be asked to specify the SCAN line limit you wish to use. There will be many times when you will see the title of a conference or a note and wish to know more about it, but you may not want to spend time reading all of the information. If you specify a SCAN line limit of five lines, each time you enter the SCAN command the system will show you just the first five lines of information. You may specify any number you like, though five really is sufficient in most cases.

You will also be asked if you want the system to automatically print the command choices open to you at appropriate times when you use the system. This is an optional setting, but until you become familiar with the commands, you should definitely opt for this feature.

Finally, you may enter your address and a brief description of yourself, your interests, your organization, your SourceMail address, and so on. This is completely optional. The information is filed under your name and is available to anyone on the system with the command PRO-FILE YOURNAME. It's a very valuable feature. Since individuals using PARTI are known only by their "handles," there is no way to know who the various people are in the normal course of things. The address-and-description file solves this problem.

Online Tip: The online documentation for PARTI makes this clear, but it doesn't hurt to emphasize it: You can MODIFY any of the information you entered during the sign-up phase at any time. Change your password, change your description, change your SCAN line specs, etc.

Overview

The PARTICIPATE system required more than a dozen years to develop, and every attempt has been made to incorporate the best features of previous conferencing systems while eliminating the less convenient aspects. The result is a system that is incredibly flexible and quite "user-friendly." It is fair to say that PARTICIPATE is designed to make the "many-to-many" communication that is at the heart of computerized conferencing as effortless as possible. As with any full-featured system, however, you should expect to spend a little time mastering the commands necessary to take full advantage of all that it offers.

Online Tip: PARTICIPATE has foreseen this need, and the firm has created a special conference newcomers can use to experiment and get to know the system. Indeed, once you have completed the initial sign-on questionnaire, you will automatically be invited to join the "PRACTICE" conference. The system will tell you what to do to join. You should definitely do so.

You will find that all of the documentation and instructions you need are available online. And the first time you enter PARTICIPATE, you should plan to download and print out all of them.

Anyone can propose to open a discussion on a particular topic. The proposal or note will contain a description of the topic, what particular aspects might be discussed, and possibly a little sales copy to encourage people to join. Here are two typical proposals:

"ADVENTURE ON PARTI!" Conference 82.2172, about "D&D OVER PARTI?" (answers: 15)

Hey all you adventure lovers out there! Now is your chance to voice your opinions! How many of you would actively participate in a game over PARTI? Let's hear from you! It doesn't cost anything, and it's easy to do! One person with a DM or GM dungeon, and the rest answer! Directions and answers could be sent weekly! C'mon all you adventure lovers, let's get together and play over PARTI!

"BOOKS" Conference 82.2155 EMACS MANIAC, about "USER CONTRIBUTED REVIEWS" (answers: 28)

In the information age, there are still those lone souls who rely on books as a prime reference source. As the price of mass storage drops, the price of paper rises, and the consumer pays! For all those individuals looking for a little more background on a book than its back cover, this is your conference.

To get things started, the creator of the note might invite specific individuals to join, in which case they would be automatically notified the next time they signed on to the system. Others might come across the subject line, request a SCAN or the note, and decide to join at that time.

Online Tip: In most cases you will be able to read all of the comments entered by others in a given conference. And if you are not already a member, you will be given an opportunity to JOIN the conference. When you JOIN a conference, you will automatically be notified of any comments that have been added since your last sign-on. This can be very convenient for conferences that you want to follow closely.

However, if at some point you decide that you are no longer interested in receiving comments from a conference, you may use the LEAVE command to remove your name from the automatic address list. You may JOIN and LEAVE any conference at any time.

All of this is quite informal. There are no restrictions and no moderator to decide which comments should be deleted or retained or to keep the discussion on track. If at a later time it seems appropriate to *organize* the conference more formally—or if someone wants to start with an *organized* conference—this can be done, too.

Perhaps even more important, any individual or group of individuals can start a subconference at any time. For example, a number of people might join a conference on "television." But one or two of them might decide that they wanted a conference to discuss just videotape recorders, or just VHS videotape recorders, or just television commercials, or any other aspect of the main topic. The "television" conference would continue as before, but other conferences on more specific topics would branch out from it. And still more conferences could branch out from these subconferences.

Branching is a key concept in PARTICIPATE. Among other things, it makes it possible to "meet" with a large group to discuss a general topic (in the main conference) and then "meet" with smaller groups to discuss specific aspects of that topic. This makes it easy to locate information on the topics you are most interested in—without having to search through all of the comments contained in the main conference.

How to Locate the Conferences You Want to Join
PARTICIPATE will eventually have a unified table of contents. But

until this feature is added, here's how to find the conferences you might want to join:

- Step 1

  Set your computer to download the list you are about to generate. Then at the system's action prompt (ACTION-> Read, Write, Other?) type PROFILE CONFERENCES and hit <ENTER>. (The command READ ABOUT will also work.) This will generate a list of all of the organized (as opposed to informal) public conferences that are open to everyone (see Figure 10.2).

—— **Figure 10.2. Organized Conferences on PARTICIPATE.** ——

When you type PROFILE CONFERENCES at the action prompt you will receive the current list of organized public conferences on PARTICIPATE to which everyone has access. These are the more formal conferences. They have a moderator to oversee things and to keep the discussion on track. (For a sample list of the *informal* conferences and branches, see Figure 10.3.)

The name in quotation marks is the quick-reference name of the conference. You may use either the quick-reference or the actual number that follows it to go to a particular conference. This is followed by the name of the conference organizer and information designed to give you a general idea of what the conference is all about. The "answers" indicate the number of comments or messages that are available for you to SCAN or READ in each conference.

ACTION-> Read, Write, Other? PROFILE CONFERENCES
You have access to these organized Conferences:
"PARTI" Conference 82.1. PARTICIPATION SYSTEMS, organizer, about "NEW
CONFERENCE OPENERS TARGETING THE BROADEST AUDIENCE: JOIN HERE FOR
ANNOUNCEMENTS ABOUT PUBLIC CONFERENCES" (answers: 358) FRI, 01/01 00:00 (0
characters)

"SUGGESTIONS" Conference 82.1767 PARTICIPATION SYSTEMS, organizer, about "WHAT
    WOULD YOU LIKE TO SEE CHANGED IN/ADDED TO PARTI?" (answers: 108)

"PARTI USES" Conference 82.3337 PARTICIPATION SYSTEMS, organizer, about
    "QUESTIONNAIRE ON USES YOU MIGHT MAKE OF PARTI" (answers: 26)

"INQUIRIES" Conference 82.3336 PARTICIPATION SYSTEMS, organizer, about
    "QUESTIONS YOU MIGHT HAVE ABOUT PARTI AND ITS APPLICATIONS" (answers: 5)

"FACILITATORS" Conference 82.2 HELPER, organizer, about "HELPING OTHERS TO
    PARTICIPATE" (answers: 53)

"PRACTICE" Conference 82.3910 HELPER, organizer, about "A PLACE TO LEARN THE
    SYSTEM, AND TO MAKE MISTAKES" (answers: 12)

"SYSTEMS" Conference 82.245 MIT/CISR, organizer, about "MANAGEMENT
    INFORMATION, EXECUTIVES ONLINE, OFFICE AUTOMATION, DECISION SUPPORT &
    TELECOMMUNICATIONS SYSTEMS" (answers: 34)

Figure 10.2 continued

"SOFTWARE" Conference 82.1922 STC-EDIT, organizer, about "KEEPING UP WITH THE FIELD" (answers: 5)

"PERSONAL COMPUTERS" Conference 82.1924 STC-EDIT, organizer, (answers: 17)

"SOFTWARE" Conference 82.1922 STC-EDIT, organizer, about "KEEPING UP WITH THE FIELD" (answers: 5)

"TRAVEL" Conference 82.2015 STC-EDIT, organizer, (answers: 5)

"ELECTRONIC MAIL" Conference 82.2016 STC-EDIT, organizer, (answers: 1)

"USER GROUPS" Conference 82.2017 STC-EDIT, organizer, (answers: 5)

"EIES" Conference 82.2058 MCKENDREE, organizer, about "FEATURES AND FUNCTIONS OF ADVANCED COMPUTERIZED CONFERENCES" (answers: 16)

"SIMPLIFIED SCAN" Conference 82.1658 LLOYD, organizer, about "VOTE FOR OR AGAINST A SIMPLIFIED SYSTEM OF SCANNING THE TREES." (answers: 14)

"GLIDE FORMATION" Conference 82.2215 MICHAEL PHILLIPS, organizer, about "AN INTERACTIVE NEWSLETTER" (answers: 20)

"UCSD" Conference 82.2101 CMC MICROPRODUCTS, organizer, about "A PLACE FOR UCSD NOTES TO BE TRADED AND EXPANDED UPON . . ." (answers: 11)

"NETWITS II" Conference 82.2095 FORD AND ZAPHOD, organizer, about "MUTANTS MATING CALL . . . (AND TREKKIES, AND D&D'ERS . . ., JUST BE WARPED!)" (answers: 10)

"THE GUIDE . . ." Conference 82.2340 FORD AND ZAPHOD, organizer, about "THE HITCHIKERS GUIDE AND THE RESTAURANT AT THE END OF THE UNIVERSE . . ." (answers: 8)

"DOCTOR WHO" conference 82.2341 FORD AND ZAPHOD, organizer, about "THE GOOD DOCTOR . . ." (answers: 11)

"TRAVELLER CAMPAIGN" Conference 82.2644 FORD AND ZAPHOD, organizer, about "LETS GET TO IT!!!" (answers: 2)

"CHARACTERS" Conference 82.2645 FORD AND ZAPHOD, organizer, (answers: 2)

"TV ADS" Conference 82.2826 RUSS MCFATTER, organizer, about "ONES YOU'VE ALREADY SEEN" (answers: 25)

"EXPORTS" Conference 82.2910 INC-EXPORTS, organizer, about "SMALL BUSINESS OPPORTUNITIES IN THE EXPORT MARKETS" (answers: 1)

"LETTERS ON EXPORTS" Conference 82.2914 INC-EXPORTS, organizer, about "PLACE FOR LETTERS TO THE EDITOR" (answers: 1)

"EMP. MOTIVATION" Conference 82.2915 INC-MOTIVATION, organizer, about "COMPENSATION, MANAGEMENT STYLES, AND OTHER MOTIVATIONAL TECHNIQUES" (answers: 0)

"IBM USERS GROUP" Conference 82.2998 MERLYN, organizer, about "IBM NATIONAL COMMUNICATION" (answers: 3)

"SUPPORT" Conference 82.3269 STC CUSTOMER SUPPORT, organizer, about "STC's CUSTOMER SUPPORT FACILITY" (answers: 0)

"U*U*U" Conference 82.3710 THE SOURCERER, organizer, about "U*U*U - THE UNITED UNDERGROUND USERS GROUP" (answers: 4)

• Step 2

Next, you should focus on the "PARTI" conference. This is the main trunk of PARTICIPATE. It is open to everyone and it contains many branches. At the action prompt, type PROFILE "PARTI" (the quotation marks are required) and the word CONTENTS. Then hit <ENTER>.

This will generate a list of most of the informal conferences currently taking place on the system (see Figure 10.3).

───── **Figure 10.3. Conferences Branching Off "PARTI."** ─────

"PARTI" is the main or "trunk" conference on PARTICIPATE. To see what sub conferences branch off "PARTI," you can type PROFILE at the action prompt and then select CONTENTS at the "Contents, Joiners, Addressees?" prompt. Or you can batch the commands and type PROFILE "PARTI" CONTENTS at the action prompt. Please keep in mind that this figure contains *just those conferences branching off of "PARTI."* Many of these sub conferences have branches of their own. And you generate a list of them in the same way (with the PRO-FILE command).

```
ACTION-> Read, Write, Other?
PROFILE "PARTI"

"PARTI" Conference 82.1 PARTICIPATION SYSTEMS, organizer, about "NEW CONFERENCE
OPENERS TARGETING THE BROADEST AUDIENCE: JOIN HERE FOR ANNOUNCEMENTS
ABOUT PUBLIC CONFERENCES" (answers: 358) FRI, 01/01 00:00 (0 characters)

Contents, Joiners, Addressees?
CONTENTS
  13 "SYSTEMS", 82.245 (60)
  14 "BUSINESS ON SOURCE", 82.263 (10)
  24 "VENIS", 82.421 (20)
  25 "USER-PUBLISHING", 82.526 (15)
  41 "CRT ERGONOMICS", 82.869 (14)
  45 "WORD PROCESSING", 82.987 (2)
  46 "EMPLOYEE/EMPLOYER", 82.989 (8)
  47 "YOU AND ME", 82.1008 (7)
  52 "POTPORI/SHALI", 82.1209 (104)
  62 "VENIS VERSION 2", 82.1399 (18)
  68 "INTRO", 82.1447 (3)
  70 "BULLETIN BOARD", 82.1471 (14)
  73 "JOKES", 82.1503 (81)
  74 "IBM PC", 82.1508 (24)
  78 "HELICOPTERS", 82.1537 (6)
```

Figure 10.3 continued

```
 83 "BOSTON", 82.1618 (4)
 85 "AI", 82.1629 (10)
 86 "KEYWORD: GOD/MAN", 82.1659 (38)
 88 "INFORMATION EXCHANGE", 82.1695 (16)
 89 "ARTS/HUMANITIES", 82.1723 (30)
 91 "PEACE", 82.1745 (28)
 96 "SUGGESTIONS", 82.1767 (176)
 98 "L-5 SPACE SETTLEMENT", 82.1854 (59)
 99 "COMMERCIALS", 82.1856 (1)
110 "DREAMS", 82.1960 (36)
111 "EIES", 82.2058 (17)
113 "UCSD", 82.2010 (11)
118 "ADVENTURE ON PARTI!", 82.2172 (16)
121 "GLIDE FORMATION", 82.2215 (22)
125 "TO MOTHERMIND", 82.2296 (5)
126 "SCIENCE FICTION", 82.2303 (42)
132 "AUSTRALIA, ET AL.", 82.2327 (4)
151 "BRIARPATCH", 82.2781 (29)
153 "MICRO ACCTG SYS???", 82.2793 (6)
154 "PORTABLES???", 82.2794 (15)
157 " PARTIPOST", 82.2835 (25)
158 "QUASAR HHC", 82.2851 (4)
160 "THE FORMATION-OPEN", 82.2865 (2)
162 "SOURCE SURVEY", 82.2948 (4)
165 "POCKET", 82.2968 (3)
174 "POST SOFTWARE", 82.3117 (9)
176 "GETTING HELP", 82.3210 (0)
178 "RELIGIONS", 82.3134 (31)
180 "PROJECT STARTS", 82.3178 (2)
182 "SOURCE SERVICES", 82.3202 (104)
185 "SLAVERY TODAY", 82.3223 (42)
189 "MANUAL UPDATES", 82.3262 (42)
193 "INQUIRIES", 82.3336 (28)
195 "PRINTERS", 82.3397 (15)
197 "EDUCATION OF ADULTS", 82.3438 (17)
199 "PEN NAMES", 82.3452 (9)
202 "UNIX", 82.3517 (130)
203 "KNOWLEDGE BASE", 82.3523 (7)
206 "PARTI PROCESS", 82.3622 (7)
210 "TRANSFORMATION", 82.3654 (19)
217 "U*U*U", 82.3710 (12)
221 "TELENET", 82.3839 (34)
222 "TYMNET", 82.3840 (28)
223 "TOFFLER", 82.3844 (5)
235 "CP/M USERS GROUP", 82.4045 (19)
241 "VIDEO/SATELLITE", 82.4065 (3)
242 "R&R/MOVIE GOSSIP", 82.4066 (13)
244 "APPLE II", 82.4099 (4)
```

247 "APPLE ///", 82.4122 (16)
249 "IXO TELECOMPUTER", 82.4136 (22)
259 "CHATTER", 82.4361 (95)
266 "NUCLEAR ARMS RACE", 82.4418 (40)
269 "R&B MUSIC", 82.4453 (1)
275 "SOFTWARE", 82.4483 (7)
277 "CUSTOMER SERVICE", 82.4544 (11)
278 "BIT OF THIS & THAT", 82.4552 (3)
282 "SCANNERS", 82.4574 (14)
288 "VIDEO DEMOCRACY", 82.4704 (18)
289 "HAMRADIO", 82.5073 (0)
290 "NEW VENTURES", 82.5083 (37)
292 "SEX SEX SEX", 82.5093 (12)
293 "PRACTICE", 82.5107 (89)
299 "CRACKING", 82.5282 (9)
301 "WORD FOG", 82.5295 (75)
304 "PHREAKING", 82.5353 (12)
307 "COMMUTE OR COMPUTE?", 82.5393 (42)
313 "HEALTH/SAFETY", 82.5452 (14)
328 "TRADING", 82.5779 (4)
330 "MOD VOTE", 82.5810 (5)
332 "BUG REPORTS", 82.5865 (17)
336 "EROS EXCHANGE", 82.5936 (10)
339 "RECIPE EXCHANGE", 82.5997 (4)
350 "HANDICAPPED PARTIERS", 82.6227 (1)
351 "ONLINE RETRIEVAL", 82.6275 (3)
352 "4X4S & OUTDOORS", 82.6279 (0)
356 "HOT PEOPLE ON PARTI", 82.6336 (0)
357 "MIND IN SPORTS", 82.6338 (0)
358 "RESPONSIBILITY&CRIME", 82.6339 (0)

- Step 3
  Many of the conferences branching off of "PARTI" contain branches of their own. To generate a list of these, type PROFILE "CONFER-ENCENAME" CONTENTS where "CONFERENCENAME" is the name of the conference you want to explore. Again, the quotation marks are required.

  Not all "PARTI" subconferences have branches. And there is no way to tell without entering a PROFILE command. Let your personal interests be your guide.

- Step 4
  At this point you will have quite an extensive list of conferences. The documentation available online will show you how to go directly to the

conferences that interest you, how to read comments, and how to JOIN to receive future replies.

Online Tip: Fluidity is one of the main advantages PARTICI-PATE offers. There are no rules on when a conference can begin or end. Each is viewed as having its own lifespan. However, once a conference has run its course and people are no longer adding comments on a regular basis, the conference transcript may still be available. This is a very important feature. It means, for example, that if a discussion has been held on tips for using a particular brand of computer, all of the information contributed may still be available to you—even though the conference is no longer active. This amounts to a tremendous online "library" of valuable information.

Interestingly, the decision on whether a file is maintained or not is up to PARTICIPATE users. The system has a built-in purging mechanism that will erase a file if it is not accessed a certain number of times over a certain period. This keeps computer storage costs down. But as long as enough users "vote" to maintain the file by accessing its information, it will continue to be available.

Costs and Sign-up Procedures

PARTICIPATE

As mentioned previously, any subscriber to The Source is free to use PARTICIPATE at any time at no additional charge. The sign-up procedure is also covered above.

EIES

An independent system operated by the Computerized Conference and Communications Center of the New Jersey Institute of Technology, EIES describes itself as a "fixed-capacity resource" dedicated to exploring, developing, and testing the concept of computerized conferencing. Consequently, membership is subject to approval, and preference is given to groups or individuals interested in that field.

Two types of membership are offered. Class One is designed primarily for businesses and other organizations. The cost is a flat $75 per month, plus Telenet or Uninet communications costs. Class One memberships include the option of establishing a closed conference for individuals using the membership and storage space on the system equivalent to 5000 lines of text.

Class Two memberships are designed for individual users. The cost is $8.00 per hour, plus communications charges. And there is a minmum of $25 per month, exclusive of Telenet and Uninet charges. (If you don't use $25 worth of time during the month, you will still be charged $25.) Class Two members do not receive any personal storage space, but otherwise they have full access to all EIES features.

Communications charges are as follows:

• Telenet

6:00 AM to midnight EST, and all day Saturday and Sunday, $6.00 per hour (U.S. mainland fees).

All other times, $9.50 per hour (U.S. mainland fees).

$8.25 per hour for access from Hawaii and Canada.

$15.50 per hour from Alaska.

Access from Belgium, France, The Netherlands, Puerto Rico, U.K., West Germany, Switzerland, Spain, Hong Kong, Italy, and Japan. Contact EIES for subscription and Telenet rates.

• Uninet

$7.00 per hour (U.S. mainland only).

For more information, contact:
EIES
Computerized Conferencing and Communications Center
323 High Street
Newark, NJ 07102
(201) 645-5211

"Turnkey" Software and Other Systems

Although computer bulletin board systems offer some form of computerized conferencing (see Chapter 8), PARTICIPATE and EIES are the most appropriate dedicated systems for most individual personal computer owners. But computer conferencing has many applications for business. And if you are a businessperson, you'll be happy to know that both PARTICIPATE and EIES may be available to run on your in-house computer.

This amounts to a "turnkey" system—you have only to install the software, and your computerized conferencing system is ready to go. The EIES system currently runs on Perkin Elmer's INTERDATA line of minicomputers, but it is estimated that it could be transferred to other machines with about four person-years of computer programming work.

The software needed to create your own private PARTICIPATE conferencing system is available from Participation Systems, Inc. (PSI). The software can be configured to run on most minicomputers or mainframe "in-house" computers, and the package includes on-site user training. For more information, contact:

> Participation Systems, Inc.
> 43 Myrtle Terrace
> Winchester, MA 01890
> (617) 729-1976

Another turnkey system worthy of note is designed for businesses who own Digital Equipment Corporation (DEC) computers. The firm to contact is Cross Communications Company of Boulder, Colorado. Ask about "Matrix," the company's complete teleconferencing software package. Minimum hardware requirements are a DEC computer with BASIC-PLUS-2 software and a memory capacity of 16K. The package includes an electronic mail feature, a bulletin board, a system directory that can also be used as a corporate phone book, as well as a sophisticated computerized conferencing system. The address is:

> Cross Information Company
> 934 Pearl Street, Suite B
> Boulder, CO 80302
> (303) 499-8888

Customized systems are also available to businesses, as are systems offered by the two major packet-switching networks. Here are just a few of the firms you might want to contact as you explore this area:

Tymshare, Inc.	GTE Telenet	Dialcom
20705 Valley Green Drive	8229 Boone Boulevard	1009 Spring Street
Cupertino, CA 95014	Vienna, VA 22180	Silver Spring, MD
(408) 446-6236	(703) 827-9565	20910
		(301) 588-1572

Online Tip: If you would like to look into the possibility of starting your own conference system on your own computer, you might contact CommuniTree Group™. For $120 this firm will sell you a conferencing software package designed to run on an Apple II or Apple II+ computer with a Hayes MicroModem II.

For a *free demonstration,* dial (415) 928-0641 from your computer or terminal and hit <ENTER> twice once you are connected. You can contact CommuniTree Group at:

470 Castro Street, Suite 207-3002
San Francisco, CA 94114
(415) 474-0933 (voice phone)

Conclusion

Computerized conferencing has been called an enhanced form of electronic mail. But it is really far more than that. Unlike electronic mail, which is virtually always limited to one-to-one communication, computerized conferencing gives you the opportunity for many-to-many communication. It allows you to speak to and listen to many individuals *that you would never meet otherwise.* It allows you to seek and share information, advice, and opinions on any topic.

But most important of all, it makes you a part of a thriving electronic community—filled with ideas and personalities—that is probably unlike anything you have ever experienced before. For many people, computerized conferencing is one of the best reasons for buying a personal computer in the first place.

...11...

Telecommuting
Communicating to Work—
The Home/Office Interface

"It's easier to move information than it is to move people."
—Pat McKinnie, Alternate Work Sites Program
Control Data Corporation

"For anyone whose job involves handling information, there is definitely going to be a refocusing of work around a computer work station in the home. In time it will affect everyone."
—Dr. Vincent Guiliano, Senior Consultant
Arthur D. Little, Inc.

Ms. McKinnie and Dr. Guiliano should know. Both are intimately involved with what is one of the most logical applications of personal computer communications technology—"telecommuting," or as a 1982 seminar of The World Future Society put it, "communicating to work." It may not be time to pack up your desk and head for your home in the country just yet. But if your job involves the handling, manipulating, retrieval, or creation of information, working at home may be a distinct possibility for you in the very near future.

The concept and rationale are simplicity itself. If your job normally involves sitting at a terminal or word processor entering data or typing reports, what difference does it make where the terminal is? As long as the machine can communicate over the telephone, both it and you could be sitting in front of a roaring fire in a cabin in Vermont. When you have finished your quota for the day, you simply dial up your firm's computer and transmit the work to your former office.

Similarly, if you are an executive responsible for collecting and analyzing information, making decisions, issuing reports, and communicating with others, you may be able to perform all of these functions at home. Dr. Guiliano, for example, reports that he regularly arranges four-day working weekends at his island cottage.

With his personal computer he can communicate with clients via a national electronic mail system. He can create memos and reports, transmit them to his firm's central computer, and have them printed and distributed without ever going near the office. Using that same central computer, he can call up the information he needs from the firm's database and record it or print it out at home. The central computer also gives him access to a huge "electronic filing cabinet" containing a copy of everything he has ever written.

Proven Programs

Professional writers, entrepreneurs, computer programmers, independent business and investment consultants, and other individuals have been using personal computers and word processors to work at home for several years. They use their machines to create text, analyze information, perform online research, and—if the client has the proper equipment—to deliver finished products over the telephone. But this is not telecommuting.

The idea, and possibly even the work, is the same. The difference is that these people are self-employed. True telecommuters are people who would otherwise be traveling to and from their employer's office every day instead of doing their work at home with a communicating computer. The distinction is significant because more than 50 million employees—almost half the U.S. work force—work in occupations that lend themselves to telecommuting. This is where the revolution is and where the impact will be felt, not in the self-employed sector.

There are at least three organized, company-sponsored telecommuting programs underway already. The first was established in 1978 by Blue Cross/Blue Shield of South Carolina. Nicknamed the "Cottage Keyers," the program provides employees with personal computers to use to key-in medical claim form data at home. Employees are paid by the number of claims processed and can work whenever they like. When they have completed a batch, they phone the central office and transmit the work over the phone.

In the summer of 1981, Continental Illinois Bank began a similar program. After a one-week training program on a Wang word processor and another week familiarizing themselves with the bank's procedures, a number of employees were given the necessary equipment to do word processing at home. Recorded dictation comes in over the telephone; the employees transcribe it and record it on disk; then they dial up the bank's computer and transmit the finished copy.

Unlike the Cottage Keyers, the bank's employees are paid an hourly wage and work a 40-hour week. Each is required to be at the terminal from 9:00 AM to 11:30 AM and from 2:00 PM to 4:30 PM. The other three hours can be spent at any time—as long as the work is transmitted to the main office by 8:00 AM the next day.

The third company is Control Data Corporation (CDC). The firm started a program called Homework in 1978 to offer handicapped individuals the opportunity for meaningful employment. Individuals are trained in computer programming, provided with a Texas Instruments Silent 700 terminal, and permitted to work at home and transmit their programming to a central computer.

Homework was an immediate success, prompting CDC to establish the Alternate Worksites program a year later. Under this arrangement nearly 100 CDC employees—analysts, programmers, managers, educational courseware writers, and clerical workers—work either at home or at satellite offices the firm has opened in areas close to many employees' homes. This too has been quite successful, with some employees reporting that they have reduced their driving by 500 miles per month, for a savings of about $90 per month in gasoline costs alone.

Potential Benefits

Telecommuters and their companies benefit in many other ways as well:

- More time with friends and family and less time in traffic jams or crowded train cars.

- Opportunity to get off to a fresh start each morning without fighting your way through crowds or getting drenched in a sudden downpour.

- Reduced child-care costs.

- Reduced clothing costs. (You can work in your bathrobe and who's to know?)

- Increased motivation and productivity. CDC reports telecommuter self-ratings of 12 to 20 percent increases in productivity. The firm itself foresees 200 to 300 percent increases in the future.

- Opportunity to work at odd hours. Ideal for when that masterful idea hits you at three in the morning.

- Reduced cost for office space. A significant factor, particularly in areas where costs may be $50 or more per square foot.

• Reduced heating, cooling, and electrical costs to the firm.

Potential Drawbacks

Of course, there are drawbacks to telecommuting as there are with anything else. The most important one is what a sociologist might describe as the "reduced opportunity for social interaction made possible by the office environment." Or, to put it another way, when you work at home, you won't be swapping stories around the old water cooler. This is probably the most significant problem. Others include the need for self-discipline, keeping well-meaning but curious family members away from the system, and the potential expense of buying any equipment that your firm won't agree to supply. There is also the office political problem of "out of sight, out of mind."

How to Become a Telecommuter

It is important to remember that this whole field is just beginning to open up. It will be several years before the concept is widely accepted. And it will be several more years before "carefree communications equipment" eliminates the need to worry about hardware interfaces and protocols. But it's coming, and if you want to be a pioneer, this section will give you an idea of how to go about stocking your wagon.

Your biggest problem may be getting clearance from your supervisor. That is completely up to you, but you might point out the potential savings and the possible increases in productivity. You might also suggest that you try it one day a week for several months to "see how it goes." Remember, there's no reason why you have to be a telecommuter 100 percent of the time. You could even suggest that the experiment might be worthy of a coauthored trade journal article about how the XYZ Company is on the cutting edge of technology.

Assuming that you've gotten a go-ahead to at least study the plan, you will have three major things to consider: hardware, software, and company support.

Selecting Your Hardware

"Hardware" usually refers to just computer and communications equipment. But here it includes everything else you will need to set up an effective telecommuting home office. We'll look at the computer first.

The System Itself. Before you do anything, arrange to meet with your firm's data processing supervisor. There are no universal standards for interfacing a personal computer with a business computer over the telephone. The Source, CompuServe, and other databases *must* be able to talk to all personal computers, but business computers are under no such requirement.

That does not mean that they don't talk ASCII or that you can't effect *some* kind of communication. It means that different mini- and mainframe computers have different protocols that must be met for data to be transferred problem-free. One individual routinely uses his Apple computer to talk to the DEC PDP-11s and DEC System 10s at his office and laboratory. The "Cottage Keyers" mentioned earlier use Texas Instruments computers to talk to IBM 3033s.

The upshot is that it can be done, if you know what you're doing. If you don't, your data processing manager does. At the very least, he or she ought to be able to tell you what the company's system requires in the way of protocols. Unfortunately, you yourself may have to serve as a human interface between the DP manager's mainframe world and the personal computer-store salesperson's microworld.

Get the specs and then do a little research. It may be less difficult than it sounds. If you haven't bought a machine yet, you should definitely give strong consideration to a model using a 16-bit microprocessor instead of the 8-bit processor found in most "first-generation" machines. The software to fully tap the 16-bit potential may not exist when you buy your system, but it will before long and you will appreciate the power.

If you already have an 8-bit machine, you're not out of luck. It's just that 16-bit machines can be more easily adapted to *multiple* communications protocols. You may be able to purchase a card (plug-in circuit board) that will give your present machine 16-bit capabilities. (Availability depends upon the particular brand of computer, but most cost upwards of $600.) And, whether you have an 8-bit or a 16-bit machine, you may be able to find a card that will allow your system to "emulate" a terminal of your firm's mainframe. Such a card will automatically generate all of the protocols the mainframe needs to see.

Once you decide on the make and model of personal computer to buy, the next question will be how to equip it. Keep in mind that you don't have to buy all of the peripherals and memory cards at once. You can get by with a lesser system than the one described below. But for serious telecommuting you will need at least:

- The system itself (computer)
- 48K of RAM
- One floppy disk drive (a second drive is optional but desirable)
- A communications card
- Ability to generate an 80-column display

- A monochrome monitor (TV set as temporary solution)
- An inexpensive dot-matrix printer
- A modem

Total estimated cost: $3000 to $4000

The Modem. For all intents and purposes, you will need a 1200-baud direct-connect modem. At 300 baud, you would spend an inordinate amount of time sending and receiving data. And an acoustical modem can allow communication errors to creep into your data stream. Besides, there is little if any difference in price between a direct-connect modem and an acoustical modem. (See Chapter 2 for more information on selecting a modem.)

A "Surge Suppressor" or "Voltage Spike Eliminator." This little plug-in appliance is not widely known—yet. But it's a sine qua non for a business user. The electrical power coming into your home is not terribly "clean." It is subject to fluctuations in voltage that may not bother your Cuisinart or Mixmaster, but can play havoc with your computer. No one really cares if the system locks up in the middle of a game of Pac-Man™ or Defender™. But if the display and cursor suddenly freeze on you after you enter the last figure of a painstakingly researched quarterly report, well, you're likely to utter some words that will not enhance your work environment.

A surge suppressor or voltage spike eliminator smoothes out the flow of power to your machine. It consists of a little black box with a male plug on one side and a female receptacle on the other. You plug it into your electrical outlet and then plug your machine into it.

Surge suppressors come in two varieties: those that eliminate voltage spikes, and those that eliminate AC "noise." Buy the later of the two. A hair dryer, a refrigerator, a power drill in the hands of some handyman who shares the same electrical transformer in your neighborhood—all have the potential of generating the kind of noise that your machine won't like. The first type, without AC noise filtering, is about $90; the second type is about $110.

You may be able to find this equipment in computer stores, but if you can't, you might try one of the data processing catalog houses like IN-MAC (2465 Augustine Drive, Santa Clara, California 95051). As more and more personal computers are used for business purposes in the home, these devices will become more widely available.

A Second Telephone Line. A single telephone line will do—unless you have a "Call Waiting" feature. With "Call Waiting" the phone line clicks and beeps whenever your phone is in use and another call comes in. If you happen to be using your phone to send or receive data at the time, this interference can cause data distortions or even disconnect you from the computer at the other end. In addition, it can be convenient to be able to talk to associates while your system is uploading or downloading, something you can't do with only one line.

A Telephone Answering Machine. Suppose your supervisor calls with an urgent request. You may be working an average of 10 hours a day, but at that particular time you are not in your office. For political reasons, as well as for its true effectiveness, you will eventually have to have a telephone answering machine.

Optional and Miscellaneous Equipment. Printer paper, printer ribbons, several boxes of disks, a bulk eraser to erase a whole disk in a few seconds without turning on your machine, connecting cables, power strips with multiple plugs, filing cabinets, bookcases . . . you should consider the need for each of these miscellaneous items.

In the purely optional category, there are two items you might eventually want to add. The first is a digital clock that will enable you to send information to your firm's system automatically, regardless of where you are or the time of day. The Chronograph made by Hayes Miocrocomputer Products, Inc., is perhaps the best-known product in this area.

The second optional, but convenient, piece of equipment is a telephone headset, the "professional" type with one or two lightweight earphones and a microphone no bigger than a pencil eraser. Your need for such a device will be determined by how much time you spend on the phone. But if you're tired of cradling a telephone handset between your neck and shoulder, and if you would like to be able to walk around your office while continuing a conversation, a headset may be worth looking into. Prices start at about $125. Two companies you might contact are Anixter Communications, (800) 323-6645 and, in Illinois, (800) 942-1110; and Danavox in Eden Prairie, Minnesota, (800) 328-6297.

Software

Communications software can be vital to your success when using a personal computer. Here again, you should check with your firm's DP manager for specifics. But in general you should try to find a software package that offers "translation tables." These tables can be used to convert input and output from your machine into any of the ASCII characters. Most tables can also be used to generate "code" numbers beyond the 128 that ASCII provides. This can be important if your company's computer needs certain special codes to communicate effectively. For a fuller explanation of translation tables and their applications, see Chapter 12.

Chapter 2 provides more information on the features to look for when selecting communications software. But it should be emphasized here that for telecommuting purposes, one of the most important features is the ability to transfer files from your machine to your company's computer. For example, you would not want to send a 10-page report that looks fine on your machine but appears on your corporate computer with an extra space between every letter.

Since the possible combinations of microcomputers and mini- and mainframe computers is so great, there can be no universal guidelines. However, you might consider setting up a test of a particular personal computer/software combination. You might be able to persuade your computer dealer to phone your firm's computer and transmit a file to see how it comes across. If you will be buying equipment from the dealer, this should not require too much persuasion.

In addition to communications software, you will also need a *word-processing* package. Without it you will have great difficulty creating reports, memos, and other textual material. In addition, you might also consider a database management program and one of the "spreadsheet" programs like VisiCalc™ or SuperCalc™. Obviously, a personal computer can do much more than communicate, and you will ultimately want to take advantage of its other powers.

Online Tip: Who's going to pay for all of this? Well, that depends. Some companies will eventually develop policies regarding what is "covered" and supplied for free, and what you must buy on your own. But until that happens, you may be forced to use all of your persuasive powers to get the company to foot as much of the bill as possible. You should also talk to a tax advisor about the possibility of deducting and depreciating the equipment you buy. The field is too new for major IRS rulings, but your office may qualify. And you may be entitled to a number of tax breaks. Again, check with your advisor.

Company Support

Naturally it's important to have a supervisor who's "in your corner." But you may need more than that. You may need someone in the office you can count on to make sure that your reports get printed and distributed and to look into any problems you may encounter.

You may also need to get your firm to agree to provide you with some kind of office space. This could be a desk shared by one or more other telecommuters, for example. You'll need a place to meet clients, customers, and others—a conference room, a satellite office, or some other arrangement. Finally, you will probably have to work out some kind of agreement for paying the telephone bill. The company ought to pay for the calls you would have made at the office, and it should reimburse you for telephone charges associated with going online in the service of the firm. This may require an additional bookkeeping step on your part— you will have to keep track of things or go through the bill each month identifying personal and business charges. But it is definitely something you should consider and get "nailed down" before you become a pioneer telecommuter.

...12...

Getting Technical
Bits, Bytes, and Other Telecommunications Basics

T here is absolutely nothing wrong with "cookbook communications." There is no reason why you can't set your baud rate, parity, word length, stop bits, and other communications parameters by simply following the "recipe" set forth by the information utilities, databases, and CBBSs you want to access. You don't have to know what these settings mean to use your equipment effectively.

The technical side of computer communications is not difficult to understand, however. It's just detailed. The fact that the subject is usually explained by technicians and engineers with a habit of saying, "From this equation it is obvious that . . ." doesn't help matters, because most of the time "it" is not obvious at all.

In this chapter we'll look at two major areas: how information gets transmitted between computers, and how to directly connect two computers to transfer information back and forth. We will assume that you have already read Chapter 2 and are aware of the difference between "parallel" and "serial" data communications. We'll pick things up at the point where "bits" are marching out of your machine single-file. Finally, for the time being, we're going to pretend that the modem isn't there. It is essential in actual practice, of course, but it's not essential in the explanation that follows.

The Basics of Computer Communications

Everything in computer communications is based upon two fundamental questions:

1. How can we send information as a series of computer bits?

2. How can we make sure that the information is accurately received?

What Is a Bit?

To answer question number one, the first thing you must do is take a look at what you've got to work with. The "rules of the game" state that you must transmit information, but you can only use *two* signals to do so. You've got your 1 bit and you've got your 0 bit, and that's it. The *physical* difference between the two is a matter of voltage. The rules of the game state that a 1 bit consists of negative voltage (-3 down to -25 volts), and a 0 bit consists of positive voltage ($+3$ up to $+25$ volts).

How can you use just two signals to send information? That's the same question Samuel F. B. Morse faced when he invented the telegraph. He could only use a "dot" and a "dash." So before he could get to the "What hath God wrought!" stage, he had to invent some sort of a code composed of various combinations of those two elements.

Before he could do *that*, Morse had to ask himself, "How many individual pieces of information do I have to be able to send?" The answer: all 26 letters of the alphabet, all digits from 0 to 9, a period, a comma, a quotation mark, and a number of other punctuation symbols. If he limited himself to just two signals per piece of information, he would have only four possible combinations of dots and dashes: (dot, dot); (dash, dash); (dot, dash); and (dash, dot). Clearly he needed a code that would provide enough different combinations to represent each piece of information. And that's what he created.

It is important to point out that Morse could use as many dots and dashes per character as he pleased. The code was whatever he said it was, with no limitations or restrictions. Consequently, an "A" in Morse code consists of two signals—a dot and a dash. But a "B" consists of four signals—a dash followed by three dots. A zero is five dashes.

The same logic Morse applied to his dots and dashes applies when dealing with the 1 bits and 0 bits used in computer communications, with at least one major exception. There is no question about the need for some sort of code made up of ones and zeroes. But computers will not tolerate the kind of variety found in Morse code. Whether the bits come in one at a time or all at once, computers always communicate in eight-bit segments. That means that any code we create can have a maximum of eight bits per information unit.

It also means that if the code has *fewer* than eight bits per information unit, all units had better have the same number of bits. For example, if a seven-bit code is used, an "A," a "B," and a zero must all be represented by some combination of seven bits.

How Many Bits Do We Need?

At this point, let's take it as a given that computers can communicate using some sort of code made up of 1 and 0 bits and that we can use any number of 1 and 0 bits to represent information units in the code. The only stipulation is that all information units must contain the same number of bits. We could thus have a five-bit code, or a six-bit, seven-bit, or eight-bit code.

Now the question becomes how many bits do we need to use to create a code that will have enough different combinations to accommodate all of the information we want to send? To answer that question, we should first look at the information itself.

Morse could send only capital letters, but we want to be able to send both upper- and lowercase. So we'll need two alphabets, for a total of 52 different characters. In addition to the 10 digits from 0 to 9 and all of the same punctuation symbols Morse could send, we also want to add things like a dollar sign, a pound sign (#), and mathematical symbols ($+$, $-$, $=$, $>$, $<$, %, and so on). Yet even these aren't enough. We also have to be able to send a signal to tell a printer to feed in one more line of paper, and a signal for a "backspace," and where would any of us be if we couldn't send a "break" signal to stop an on-screen printout?

Remembering that we can build a code based on any combination of bits from two to eight, which one should we choose? A code using our two possible signals (1 or 0) in units of six signals each would give us a maximum of 64 possible combinations ($2 \times 2 \times 2 \times 2 \times 2 \times 2$ or $2^6 = 64$). That's not enough. We would run out of possible combinations shortly after the upper- and lowercase alphabet.

The next possibility is a seven-bit code. That would raise the potential combinations by another power of 2, for a total of 128. And that is exactly what has been done. There are always exceptions, but for now it's safe to say that microcomputers normally communicate with the outside world using a code in which each unit consists of some combination of *seven* 1s and 0s.

As explained in Chapter 2, these combinations are called "words" or "characters." And this is what is meant by "word length" or "character length." When The Source of CompuServe tell you to set your communication parameters to a word length of seven, they mean that their computers will be expecting you to send them characters that consist of some combination of seven 1 and 0 bits.

The ASCII Code Set

There *are* other codes, most notably IBM's EBCDIC, but as mentioned in Chapter 2, the code all microcomputers use is called ASCII ("as-key"), for "American Standard Code for Information Interchange." Created by the American National Standards Institute, Inc., (1430 Broadway, New York, New York 10018), this code assigns a number to every upper- and lowercase character, every punctuation mark, and every digit. There are also numbers for such "device control" functions as a linefeed and a form feed. There is even a code that can be used to ring a bell or sound a buzzer on the receiving machine.

All together, there are 128 codes or code numbers that virtually everyone has agreed upon. There are some variations in the way different systems interpret certain codes, but everyone agrees on the upper- and lowercase alphabet, the 10 digits, and the standard punctuation marks. Thus, any system that can "talk ASCII" can communicate with any other system with the same ability.

How the Code Is Set Up

In moving from Samuel Morse and his telegraph to today's personal computers, we have leaped over an entire era of communications devices like Teletypes and other *electromechanical* machines. But the ASCII code was originally developed for use with these machines, and the vestiges of that era are still apparent in the code set (see Appendix G for the complete ASCII code set).

For example, the ASCII code 25 is identified as the code signaling "end of medium." This is the code that one Teletype would send to another when it ran out of the prepunched paper tape that contained the message to be sent.

Other code numbers are used only for *synchronous* computer-to-computer communications, a subject that need not concern us here. But some codes originally designed for Teletypes, like an ASCII 10 or "line feed," *are* useful for personal computer communications. The "line" that's being "fed" may be a line space on your screen, but both the concept and the need are the same.

The codes we have spoken of so far are often called "low codes" because they run from 0 to 32 in a code set that totals 128 numbers. The ASCII code numbers used to represent characters that people, as opposed to machines, can understand beginning at 33 with the exclamation point (!). Quotation marks, the pound sign (#), dollar sign, percent sign, and other punctuation marks come next. Then, with an ASCII 48 or 0, the digits begin. There are some other punctuation marks, followed by the uppercase alphabet, followed by more punctuation marks, followed by the lowercase alphabet, followed by some miscellaneous characters.

Control Characters

If you count them, you'll find that you have perhaps 50 different keys on your personal computer that can be used to send or type characters. If you hold the <SHIFT> key down, you can probably generate 50 more characters, including all of the uppercase alphabet and such "shift-activated" characters as the dollar sign and the colon. Many microcomputers have considerably fewer keys, but let's assume that you can generate about 100 different characters either by hitting the keys singly or by hitting them while holding the <SHIFT> key down.

The question is, how do you generate the remaining 28 ASCII characters? How do you send an ASCII 7 to ring a bell or sound a buzzer on the receiving machine when you don't have a key labeled "BELL"? The answer lies with the <CONTROL> key (or your machine's equivalent). The <CONTROL> key acts exactly like the <SHIFT> key in giving you the ability to generate characters that are not on your keyboard.

For example, you may not have a <BELL> key, but if you know that the combination of the <CONTROL> key and the <G> key will generate an ASCII 7, you *can* ring the other system's "bell" (if it has a speaker that will generate a tone, of course). In fact, assuming that the particular software package you are using will support this feature, you can generate *any* of the "low codes" from 1 to 26 by holding down your <CONTROL> key and hitting one of the letters from A to Z. (See Figure 12.1.)

———————— **Figure 12.1. ASCII Control Codes.** ————————

Note: The numbers here are ASCII code numbers. The <CTRL> followed by a letter means that you must hold your <CONTROL> key down while pressing the letter key to send the appropriate ASCII code. The phrases refer to the generally accepted meaning for each ASCII code. Only a few of them are relevant to personal computer communications, and they are self-evident.

```
 0 Null Code—No character; filler

 1 <CTRL>-A—Start of Heading
 2 <CTRL>-B—Start of Text
 3 <CTRL>-C—End of Text
 4 <CTRL>-D—End of Transmission
 5 <CTRL>-E—Enquiry
 6 <CTRL>-F—Acknowledge
 7 <CTRL>-G—Bell
 8 <CTRL>-H—Backspace
 9 <CTRL>-I—Horizontal Tab
10 <CTRL>-J—Line Feed
11 <CTRL>-K—Vertical Tab
12 <CTRL>-L—Form Feed
13 <CTRL>-M—Carriage Return, or <ENTER>
14 <CTRL>-N—Shift Out
15 <CTRL>-O—Shift In
16 <CTRL>-P—Data Link Escape
17 <CTRL>-Q—Device Control 1
18 <CTRL>-R—Device Control 2
19 <CTRL>-S—Device Control 3
```

Figure 12.1 continued

```
20 <CTRL>-T—Device Control 4
21 <CTRL>-U—Negative Acknowledge
22 <CTRL>-V—Synchronous Idle
23 <CTRL>-W—End of Transmission Block
24 <CTRL>-X—Cancel
25 <CTRL>-Y—End of Medium
26 <CTRL>-Z—Substitute
```

> **Online Tip:** If you refer to chapters describing the commands to be used to control the on-screen printout of information coming in from a database or information utility, you will find that many of them ask you to send a [<CONTROL><S>] to freeze the screen and a [<CONTROL><Q>] to get it started again. A Control-Q sends an ASCII 17 and a Control-S sends an ASCII 19. These are "device control" codes known as X-Off and X-On, respectively. And they are used to turn the on-screen scroll off and on.

The 26 "control" codes do not always mean something, and many of them may be ignored by the receiving system. It all depends upon that system's requirements. But if you've got a <CONTROL> key, you can probably generate them. Some other ASCII characters can only be generated by communications software.

Translation Tables

Let's suppose that you have a TRS-80 Model III computer. If you do, you well know that there is no key on the keyboard that will generate square brackets ("[" and "]"). But there are ASCII code numbers for square brackets: an ASCII 91 for the left one and an ASCII 93 for the right. If you could somehow figure a way to generate those two ASCII codes, you could *send* square brackets to another machine. Your own screen would display a strange Radio Shack graphic character, because that is the way the Model III is set up. But assuming that the machine you were talking to could receive and display those characters, it wouldn't care what *your* screen looked like.

This is not an insignificant problem. There are some private corporate systems that need to "see" precisely those square brackets to execute important functions. And there are executives with TRS-80s and other machines that are effectively barred from accessing their firms' computers with their own microcomputers because their keyboards cannot generate the necessary characters.

But it doesn't have to be this way. In fact, *there is no reason why most personal computers can't generate the full range of the ASCII code.* The secret, as with so many things about the microcomputer world, is in the software. Or more specifically, it is in the access to "translation" tables that some communications software provides.

This feature is not found in all software, and it certainly isn't necessary for 98 percent of personal computer owners 98 percent of the time. But if you need to be able to generate "special" characters like square brackets, translation tables are the way to do it. There are two caveats, however. First, a software package that includes a translation table feature may not yet be available for your machine or the machine you are considering. And second, if the feature *is* offered, it will almost certainly be available only on the more expensive ($150 and up) packages.

Here's how it works. You may not be able to "get at it" to make changes, but almost all communications software uses a set of translation tables to tell the system what ASCII code numbers to send and how to interpret those that it receives. Part of such a table might look like this:

```
RS-232-C Output Conversion Table
1. Convert (0) to (0)
2. Convert (0) to (0)
3. Convert (0) to (0)
4. Convert (0) to (0)
5. Convert (0) to (0)
Do you wish to convert any of these (Y/N)? Y
Which one (1-5)? 1
Convert (0-128)? 64
. . . to (0-128)? 91
```

Before anything could be entered here, it was necessary to look up the appropriate ASCII code number on the ASCII code table. Reading down the table we saw that the ASCII code for an "at sign" is the number 64, and that the ASCII code for a left square bracket is the number 91. So in this example we have told the system that every time we hit the "at sign" (@) we do not want it to send the standard ASCII number of 64. Instead, whenever we generate a 64 by hitting the @ key, we want it to send an ASCII 91—the code number for a left square bracket ([). When the final question has been answered, the table disappears and then reforms itself as below:

```
RS-232-C Output Conversable Table
1. Convert (64) to (91)
2. Convert (0) to (0)
3. Convert (0) to (0)
4. Convert (0) to (0)
5. Convert (0) to (0)
Do you wish to convert any of these (Y/N)? Y
Which one (1-5)? 2
Convert (0-128)?
```

Notice that the table now displays the conversion we have made, and that we have begun the process to make another change by answering the prompts once again. This example is adapted from a TRS-80 Model III program called Intelliterm™ sold by MicroCorp of Philadelphia, but other software takes the same approach.

If your own communications software offers this feature, the manual will describe the commands you must enter to use it. However, there are a few general points you should be aware of. First, a table of the sort illustrated above is almost always given a name and then permanently recorded on a floppy disk. When you want to take advantage of the conversions you have ordered, you just put the proper disk in one of your disk drives and "load" the table. From then on, every time you hit the @ key, your system will send out the ASCII code for a left square bracket. And that's what the system you are communicating with will receive. Obviously, you may have as many "conversion" or translation tables as you have space for on a floppy disk. You can load one table for one purpose and load another for another.

Second, just as the output translation table filters and changes the signals you "send out the door," a companion "input" translation table can be created to change the codes of the characters you receive. As a quick example, you could create an "input" table that would convert a capital "A" sent to you by another system to a capital "Z." The phrase "Apples Are Above Average" sent from the other system would then appear on your screen as "Zpples Zre Zbove Zverage."

Finally, when using translation tables you may have to "give up" one or more of your regular keys. If the output table described above had been loaded into your system, you would no longer be able to use the "at sign" key to send an at sign. As long as the table was in effect, every time you hit the @ key, your system would send the code for a left square bracket. *However*, some software packages include a feature that will allow you to "program" certain keys. That is, they offer a special table that will let you arrange to send a square bracket code each time you hold down a key like the <CONTROL> key and strike a number. Since there is no such thing a "Control-1," this can eliminate the need to sacrifice one of the keys you might normally use.

Going Binary

The last step in answering that very first question about how we can send information as a series of computer bits is relatively easy to take. All that is required is to convert the decimal numbers of the ASCII code into the binary numbers that a computer can understand. This is briefly described in Chapter 2, and it is explained in much more detail in computer manuals. For our purposes here, the question is, what is physically sent when we tap a key and thus tell the computer to send a particular character over the communications line?

It goes without saying that all ASCII decimal numbers can be represented in binary form as a series of some combination of seven 1 and 0 bits. A capital "T," for example, has been assigned the ASCII decimal number 84. In binary form that is represented by the following combination of 1 and 0 bits: 1010100. Binary numbers go "out the door" from right to left. So, remembering that a 0 bit is represented by one electrical voltage level and that a 1 bit is represented by another, that means that a capital letter "T" is physically transmitted as two 0 bit voltage levels, followed by a 1 bit voltage level, followed by a 0 bit, followed by a 1 bit, and so on.

"Bit Times"—The Final Component

If all binary numbers consisted of alternating patterns of 1 and 0 bits, the question of "bit times" might not come up. But as we have just seen, to transmit the ASCII number for a capital "T" in binary form (1010100), we read from right to left and then must deal with two 0 bits in a row right off the bat. The question is, how can the receiving system tell where the first 0 bit ends and the second 0 bit begins?

The answer is "by watching the clock." For example, at a transmission rate of 300 baud, the voltage associated with a single bit exists for 3.33 milliseconds. If the receiving system notices that the 0 bit voltage has been coming through for 6.66 milliseconds, it knows that it has received not one, but two 0 bits. We're cutting some corners here, but this is the basic idea of how it works. The same principle applies, of course, to the voltage associated with a 1 bit.

What happens if we want to send information at a rate of 1200 baud? Well, if the information is going out four times faster, then each bit time must be much shorter. And it is. At 1200 baud, the voltage associated with a single bit exists only one fourth as long as at 300 baud. The actual figure is 3.33 milliseconds divided by four, or 833 *micro*seconds.

Here are the bit times for the most common baud rates used by personal computers:

	Bit Times
1200 Baud	833 microseconds
600 Baud	1667 microseconds
300 Baud	3.33 milliseconds
150 Baud	6.67 milliseconds
110 Baud	9.09 milliseconds

To complete the picture, just remember that the bits leave your computer as different voltage levels and head into your modem. The modem converts the bits to a form that can be transmitted over the telephone line. These modem signals are taken in by the receiving modem and converted *back* to the proper voltage levels. Then they are fed to the receiving computer.

Next: A Question of Accuracy

If you read about data communications, you will eventually come across a statement to the effect that two computers cannot be connected if they are more than 50 feet apart. The reason for this prohibition is potential voltage loss. You might say that after traveling through a wire 50 feet long, the voltage levels that represent the bits "run out of gas." In actual practice, you can probably get away with connecting two computers that are much farther apart—as long as you are careful to keep the cable away from electric motors and other sources of electrical noise. But the point is well taken.

Voltage loss, electrical "noise," and similar kinds of interference can be serious problems in data communications, whether you are communicating computer-to-computer or over the telephone lines. They can cause changes in the signals that make the receiving computer misunderstand what has been sent.

Because of this, a number of techniques have been developed to reduce the chances of transmission and reception errors. Of these, the one that is most important to personal computer owners is "parity checking."

First we will look at the mechanics of *how* parity checking works, and then we will see *why* it works.

Parity: Odd, Even, or None

The concept of parity checking is not difficult to understand if you recall two things. First, remember that the ASCII code uses characters of seven bits. And second, remember that computers have an eighth bit to "play with." The subject of parity centers around that eighth bit.

There are three types of parity: odd, even, and none. Since even parity is the type you will use most often, we will focus on it here. The same explanation, though, applies to odd parity (we'll deal with "no parity" in a moment). The key point concerns whether the seven 1 and 0 bits in each character add up to an even or an odd number. It is very important to understand that the binary numbering system has *nothing* to do with this. It is a strictly first-grade arithmetic problem of adding one plus zero plus one, and so on.

As an example, consider the binary representation of the ASCII code number for a capital "T" again. If you add up all of the 1 bits, you find that the total is 3, an *odd* number:

$$1+0+1+0+1+0+0 = 3$$

Now here's what happens when two systems have agreed to use even parity and one of them is getting ready to transmit the number for a capital "T." The transmitting system looks at the 1 and 0 bits and adds them up just as we did. It notices that the sum is an odd number. But because it has agreed to communicate at even parity, it knows that it can only send out characters whose sum is even. The solution is simple: the transmitting system adds an eighth bit to make the total come out even. In this case, it must add a 1 bit to bring the total up to four.

If the character were a capital "K," represented as 1001011, the 1 bits would add up to an even number (4). But the transmitting system must still add something. The receiving system is expecting it. So, to avoid upsetting the applecart, the transmitting system adds a 0 as its eighth bit. That still makes for a total of eight bits, but it doesn't affect the evenness of the character.

Those are the mechanics of the process. Now here's how it helps improve the accuracy of computer communications. When even parity is in effect, the receiving machine checks each incoming character to make sure that the 1 bits add up to an even number. Since both machines have "agreed" beforehand to use even parity, the receiving machine knows that it can count on the sender to transmit only even characters. Therefore, if it receives an odd character, it knows that something is wrong.

Any of a number of types of interference can transform a 1 bit into a 0 bit, or vice versa, as it moves on down the line. Changing just a single bit can result in a completely different, but perfectly intelligible, character being received by a computer. Since the computer can't read, it has no way of knowing that what you really meant to send was "The" instead of "khe." But if the transformed character comes in odd when the receiver is expecting all even characters, it knows that all is not as it should be.

At that point, it may transmit a signal to the other machine saying "Hey, we've got some noise on the line. You'd better send that character again." Or it may ignore the error. It depends on the software. In any case, once the parity bit has served its function, the receiving machine "strips" it off and throws it away.

Parity checking is based upon the probability that one of the bits in a character may get transformed, but that the odds are much greater against *two* bits being changed. If two bits were changed, the resulting character could be incorrect and still add up to an even number. If that happens, there is no way for the receiving system to catch it. Thus, parity checking is not foolproof. But it is a relatively simple thing for both systems to do, and it does reduce the chances of errors going by undetected.

Pieces of the Frame

There is one more piece of information you must have to complete the portrait of a computer character all suited up to go out into the world. And that is the matter of "start" and "stop" bits. In asynchronous communication, no character gets out of the machine alive without having a "start" bit tacked onto its front end and a "stop" bit pinned to its tail.

These so-called "framing" bits do exactly what you think they do. The start bit is always a 0 bit. It hits the receiving machine first and in effect shouts "Incoming!" That lets the receiver know that the next bit out of the chute is going to be an "information bit"—one of the seven needed to make up a complete character. The stop bit is always a 1 bit and it says "That's all, folks." This way the receiving machine knows that it has received all of the bits that make up a character.

Here, then, is the complete representation of all of the bits that get transmitted when you send a letter or other character from your computer. There are 10 of them, as you can see:

Stop Bit	*Parity Bit*	*ASCII Character*	*Start Bit*
1	1	1010100	0

$$\longrightarrow$$

This Way to the Modem and the Outside World

Online Tip: It is not likely that you will ever be communicating directly with an electromechanical machine like a Teletype. But if you do, you will have to use a baud rate of 50 or 110, and you will have to tell your system to add *two* stop bits. The slower speed and the additional stop bit are necessary to give the print head of the receiving machine time to "return" before it has to print another line.

Eight Bits/No Parity

A seven-bit code made up of 128 possible combinations, including 0000000 or the "null code," is not the only possibility. You could create a code that used all eight bits generated by a microcomputer. That would *double* the number of possible combinations to 256 (2×128 or 2^8). You could still use the numbers from 0 to 127 to "talk ASCII," but you would have a whole range of numbers beyond 127 to use for other purposes.

These numbers are often called "high codes," and the eighth bit that makes them possible is often called "the high bit." High codes are used to transmit special characters that are not a part of the ASCII code set.

These include characters like the copyright symbol (©), the trademark sign (™), foreign language symbols, and others.

The only way for a microcomputer to generate these codes is through a software-based translation table of the type described earlier. It is difficult to imagine a situation in which most personal computer users would ever need this capability. But to users of dedicated word processors, whose work involves text creation, these special symbols can be essential.

Consequently, most dedicated word processors have been designed to generate such characters from their keyboards when used as word processors. And most can transmit them as well when they go online. The problem is that *there is no standardization of the high codes.* Each word processor manufacturer is free to assign any high-code number to any special character. This works quite well when both communicating machines are made by the same company. The two will even be able to transmit and receive underlined characters, thanks to the software created by the manufacturer. But things become a bit complex when the machines are made by different companies, each with its own high-code set.

Online Tip: Why can't personal computers transmit an underline? You *can* transmit a plain horizontal line (ASCII 95). But under most circumstances you will not be able to underline characters when you are online. The reason is that an underlined character actually consists of *three* signals: the character, a backspace, and the underline. The problem is that the backspace wipes out the original character on the screens of most systems, leaving you with just the horizontal line. Consequently, most people use *beginning and ending* asterisks to signify an underlined word when online.

Online Tip: There is no way to make an underlined character appear on most personal computer screens. And there is no way to transmit underlined characters, per se. However, if you are using a word-processing program like WordStar to create text, you will find that special control character "escape" codes are used to signal the beginning and the end of underlined text. These codes are meant for your printer, but since they are part of the ASCII code set, they can be transmitted and received. The upshot is that you *can* send WordStar and similar text files containing underline escape codes. The escape codes will appear on your correspondent's

Online Tip continued
screen as some kind of graphic character. But when your friend "looks at the file" using WordStar, the codes will appear just as if you had sat there and entered them yourself. Your friend can then print the file and watch the underlining appear on the final copy. Obviously, you must both either use the same word-processing program or work out a translation table to make the necessary conversions.

It *is* possible to send and receive special characters when using two different brands of word processors, but only if you can get at the input and output translation tables each uses. If this can be done, the next step is to find out what code numbers each machine uses for the special symbols you want to use. Then create the translation tables necessary for direct communication.

Online Tip: Personal computer software often will permit you to use settings of eight for "word length" and to specify "no parity." These two settings are a matched pair. If the eighth bit is being used to send high codes, it obviously can't be used as a parity bit as well.

Online Tip: Let us suppose that you have used a translation table to enable your computer to send the "high code" 196. And let's suppose that you expect the receiving computer to look at that 196 and produce some special graphic character on the screen. Instead, every time you send a 196, your correspondent's screen displays a capital "D." What's wrong?

The answer is that the receiving machine is "throwing away the high bit." To send a 196, you must use an eight-bit word length. In the binary system, that eighth and last bit represents the number 128. If the receiving system ignores it or throws it away, it will read just seven bits. This has the effect of reducing 196 by 128, leaving 68—the ASCII code number for a capital "D." You may not be able to do anything about it, but it is helpful to know what is happening.

Online Tip: If you aren't a computerist, you may not be aware that your machine can probably save files two ways when it records information on disk. It can store information in a binary format, or it can store it in ASCII. Computers normally like to use the binary format because it is compressed and thus saves space. So unless you tell your machine not to, it will probably store your files in binary form.

This is fine for most purposes, but it's not good for communications. If you have created a text file, for example, and you want to upload it to a computerized conference or a CBBS, you must first "save it in ASCII." It's a simple—but essential—procedure. See your manual for specific instructions.

How to Connect Two Computers

You can use the same cable that you normally plug into a modem to directly connect your machine to another machine nearby. And there are a number of reasons why you might want to do so. If you use a portable microcomputer, for example, you might want to be able to take the machine into the office and download information stored in your company's word processor or microcomputer. Or you might want to upload material created at home or elsewhere. Similarly, you might want to connect your machine to a friend's to swap programs that you have written.

Whatever your goal, you will find that direct connection has at least two advantages. The first is speed. When you take the phone lines out of the communications picture and eliminate the modem, you can communicate at much higher speeds. With a direct connection, for example, you may be able to send and receive data at rates as high as 9600 baud. Second, short of sending data over the phone, a direct connection of this sort is usually the only way to transfer data between two different (and therefore incompatable) brands of computer.

What we will describe here is the basic outline of the hardware connection. But you must always remember that the communications software the two machines are running can be vital to your success.

The key to connecting two computers is the RS-232-C interface. As you know by now, this is a standard that specifies what communications signals will be sent and received on each of some 25 pins or plugs. Look at the plug on the end of the ribbon cable that connects your serial card to your modem. You should see 25 neatly arranged "pins." Then look at Figure 12.2 to get an idea of what each pin means.

————— **Figure 12.2. The RS-232-C: Pins with a Purpose.** —————

1. Protective Ground
2. Transmit Data
3. Receive Data
4. Request to Send
5. Clear to Send
6. Data Set Ready
7. Signal Ground
8. Carrier Detect
9. Not Connected
10. Not Connected
11. Not Used
12. Secondary Carrier On
13. Secondary Clear to Send
14. Secondary Transmit Data
15. Transmission Signal Timing
16. Secondary Received Data
17. Receiver Signal Timing
18. Not Used
19. Secondary Request to Send
20. Data Terminal Ready
21. Signal Quality Detector
22. Ring Indicate
23. Data Rate Select
24. Transmission Signal Timing
25. Not Used

A first look at the RS-232-C standard can be rather dismaying—until you realize that of the 25 pins, personal computer owners need only be concerned with six or seven when preparing for direct connection. Here are the main pins you may have to deal with:

1. Protective Ground
2. Transmit Data
3. Receive Data
4. Request to Send
5. Clear to Send
6. Data Set Ready
8. Carrier Detect
20. Data Terminal Ready

Of these, the ones responsible for sending and receiving data are the most important. The others may or may not be necessary. The protective ground is just that, a connection to protect your equipment. Signals 2 and 3 are self-explanatory. All of the other signals are normally used as part of a dialog between your computer and your modem to make sure that everything is ready before any data is transmitted.

The "Request to Send" signal is sent from your computer to the modem, and it has the effect of saying "Okay, modem, let's go online." The modem performs whatever tasks are necessary to get ready, and when it has completed them, it turns on the "Clear to Send" circuit to tell the computer that it is ready. This signal can mean slightly different things with different modems. It can mean that the modem is ready, for example, or it can mean that the modem is ready and a carrier has been detected. The same might be said of the other signals.

Fooling the System

The important thing to remember is not what each signal does, but that both the RS-232-C interface and the signals were designed for use with a modem. In addition, most computer software "expects" to be talking through a modem. If the computer does not get the "modem" signals it needs to assure it that everything is ready, it may refuse to send any data. When you connect two computers with an RS-232-C interface, it is thus necessary to "fool" the system into thinking that it is really talking to a modem.

> **Online Tip:** The voltage levels you will be working with in this area are very low. Generally the worst that can happen is that you will make a wrong connection and cause your system to lock up. If that happens, you have only to reboot your program. It is not likely that you will damage your computer in any way, but if you feel uncertain about what you are doing, by all means consult a technical expert before proceeding.

You can do this by connecting the "Request to Send" pin from one machine to the "Clear to Send" pin from the other machine. Similarly, since each system is set up to transmit data on pin 2 and receive data on pin 3, you can mate the transmit pin of one machine to the receive pin of the other, and vice versa.

This is normally done with a "null modem" or "crossover" cable. The cable has the proper sex RS-232-C plug on each end, but the pins have been rewired as described above. This is the basic concept of computer-to-computer connections. Your computer dealer should be able to make up such a cable for you. But if this is not possible, you can find the necessary plugs and cable at your local Radio Shack store. The plug to ask for is:

D-Subminiature Flat Cable 25-pin Connector
Catalog Number: 276-1565 (female)
                           276-1559 (male)
Cost: $5.00 each

You might also consider contacting a catalog supply house like Inmac (2465 Augustine Drive, Santa Clara, California 95051) for the cable you need.

"Crossing over" the "Transmit/Receive Data" and "Request/Clear to Send" pins *may* be all you will have to do. But each system is different, and you may have to fiddle with some of the other pins. The first thing to do if you are having trouble is to get the "pin-out" (the list of what signals are on which pins) for your particular machine. The ones described so far are standard, but some equipment requires additional signals. Then, in addition to the crossover already described, you may want to try one or more of the following connections:

System A		*System B*
Pin 1	*to*	*Pin 1*
Pin 6 *and/or* *Pin 8*	*to*	*Pin 20*
Pin 20	*to*	*Pin 6* *and/or* *Pin 8*
Pin 7	*to*	*Pin 7*

Conclusion

There are two things that are well worth remembering about the technical side of data communications. First, as a consultant in the field once said, "Telecommunications is still something of a 'black art.'" This is partially due to its complexity and partially due to the general lack of good explanatory material.

The second point to remember is that with very few exceptions, you can get any piece of equipment to "talk" to any other piece of equipment. The only question is, is it worth the effort to figure out what must be done? Is it worth the money you may have to spend on special interface boards, software, and custom cables?

For example, connecting one personal computer to another is relatively easy and inexpensive. But connecting a computer to a printer not designed for it can be extremely difficult, even when both machines talk ASCII. In such cases, it is often cheaper to buy a new printer than to attempt a connection.

If you decide to become more involved in this field, one of your first steps should be to visit either a technical bookstore or a college library. These are the only places you will be able to find the books and magazines you need. You might also consider writing to a number of computer and data communications equipment manufacturers to ask about the availability of any *internal* training manuals and texts. The larger companies have entire libraries of information on telecommunications, and you may be able to persuade them to make certain publications available to you.

Finally, as mentioned elsewhere, you should also try to find one or more experts in the field, people who know what they are talking about and are willing to answer your questions. Technical specialists employed by various computer firms are your best bet, but you may be able to find the expertise you need in the service department of a local computer store.

With these resources to draw upon, you will be well equipped to sally forth into the technicalities of telecommunications. If you're willing to spend the time and effort, there's no reason why you can't develop the necessary expertise.

Appendix A
The "GIGO" Eliminator[*]

GIGO ("guy-go") is an old term that stands for "garbage in/garbage out," and while it doesn't apply precisely to data communications, there may be times when you will see "garbage" on your screen. There may also be times when incoming data do not appear in the desired format, and there may be times when two machines coupled by a crossover or "null modem" cable will apparently refuse to communicate. The GIGO Eliminator is designed to help you quickly identify and correct any of these problems.

Most of the time your communication with databases and online services will be problem-free, as long as you are careful to set your system to the baud rate, parity, word length, and other protocols a given system requires. If you do experience problems, the chances are that they are the fault of either the database's computers or of the packet-switching network you are using. In either case, there is nothing you can do about them.

Problems are much more likely to occur when you are trying to communicate with a friend or associate's computer, either over the telephone or through a direct connection. There are so many systems and so many software packages that it isn't possible to cover all of the variables. But it is possible to present the major ones and the "garbage" they generate.

Online Tip: If you find that the sentences you receive from a database or online service are wrapping around and being split up because they are too long for your screen width; or if you find that information is coming into your system in chunks containing more lines than your screen can accommodate, the problem may lie with

---

[*]*Note:* Before using this troubleshooting guide, you should read Chapter 12 for an overview of the topics cited here.

the terminal specifications "on file" under your name with the particular service.

CompuServe, Dow Jones, and the PARTI section of The Source, for example, all allow you to specify how many characters per line your screen can accommodate and how many lines per "page." You may have set these parameters long ago and forgotten about them, or you may never have set them in the first place. Check your manuals and call Customer Service to ask about this point.

If you are having problems communicating with another system, the first rule is: *Don't overlook the obvious.* Is your modem turned on? Is it even plugged in? Is your printer out of paper? Any of these obvious oversights can prevent your system from working properly. And each is much easier to solve than some of the more exquisitely complex possibilities.

So before you automatically assume that you have a real problem, run down the following checklist.

Troubleshooting Checklist

1. Are all cables securely inserted? In your system? In your modem? What about the cable from your modem to the phone jack?
2. Is one modem set to "Originate" and the other set to "Answer"?
3. Is the modem turned on?
4. Is the printer cable properly inserted? Is the printer physically on and in its "online" mode? Does it have enough paper?
5. Have you loaded a particular translation table and forgotten that it is in the system?
6. If you are directly connecting two systems, did you remember to use a crossover or "null modem" cable? Does the pinout of the other system match that of your own system? Are you sure that each system is receiving a "Clear to Send" and a "Data Set Ready" signal? If not, you may have to do a little rewiring of the cable.

If you can answer "yes" to each of these questions and you still have a problem, go on to the next part of this section and see if you can find an example of what you are seeing on your screen. It's important to be aware, however, that if you do not proceed methodically, you will end up in a labyrinth of communications parameters. This is why we suggest following a few simple rules.

The Rules of the Game

1. Write down the communications parameters both you and your correspondent are currently using.
2. Leave plenty of room on the paper for notes on "what happens when," as "when at even parity, this happens. . . ."
3. Hold one system constant. If possible, talk to the person on the phone and try to get both systems set to the same parameters.
4. Be methodical. Try one setting and make a note of what happens. Then try the next setting, and make a note; and so on.
5. Be patient. There is no substitute for this ancient virtue when trying to beat two systems into perfect communication. When you feel yourself getting frustrated, take a break.

Online Tip: To make a thorough test of the settings you should use when talking to another system, prepare and record a file containing the following:

THE QUICK RED FOX JUMPS OVER THE LAZY
     BROWN DOG.
the quick red fox jumps over the lazy brown dog.
1 2 3 4 5 6 7 8 9 0

Add any other characters you can generate from your keyboard. This file will thus contain every visible character you can generate. Use it as a test file, sending it to your correspondent after each change you make. When all the characters are received correctly, you will know that you've solved the problem.

Possible Communications Problems and Their Solutions

In each of the following units, we will assume that the same test sentence is being used either by you or by your correspondent. That sentence is the classic example that includes every letter of the alphabet:

THE QUICK RED FOX JUMPS OVER THE LAZY BROWN DOG.

Problem 1
Your correspondent sends you the test sentence and it appears on your screen like this:

X*XX@<XXXX'XXXX

Your system is probably set at 1200 baud and the sending system is set at 300. Make the change and have him retransmit.

Generally, anytime either of you are getting "garbage characters" like this, it is because the two baud rates do not match. This is true regardless of what specific rates are involved.

Problem 2
You send or receive the test sentence and either of you sees some of the correct characters intermingled with garbage characters, like this:

TH**)QUIC@## K $?RED

The problem probably lies with the parity setting. Make sure that you are both using odd, even, or no parity. If you use no parity, be sure to set your word length to eight instead of seven.

Problem 3
Your correspondent sends you the test sentence and any of the following happen:

• Your screen goes blank except for the blinking cursor.

• Question marks separated by spaces appear randomly like this:

?   ?

?   ?
?

• A few of the letters appear but are widely separated on several lines all across the screen and intermingled with block graphic characters. (In the example below, # stands for an undefined graphic character):

H   #   U ##   K#
D#   #   S#

This is probably a word length or "character length" problem. Have your correspondent verify his word length setting (seven or eight bits) and make sure that the two systems match.

Problem 4
If you are having difficulty communicating at 1200 baud, try the following settings or various combinations thereof:

Baud: 1200
Parity: no parity

Word length: 8
Stop bits: 1 or 2

Different software and systems have different requirements. So in some cases, simply setting your system to 1200 baud and using the standard settings for the other parameters may work quite well. In other cases you may have to fiddle a bit. Sending and receiving files directly from disk at 1200 baud can also cause problems if you don't make some adjustments. The problem has to do with each computer's internal "clock speed," but the technicalities need not concern us here. The point to remember is that a given computer may not be fast enough to send *and* display data at 1200 baud. If you can, you should try to toggle off the video display or disable the echo setting—anything to keep the information from being displayed on a screen while it is being sent or received. If you don't do this, you may find that you are losing data during transmission.

Problem 5—Linefeed (LF) Related Problems
If each line you send overwrites the previous line on your correspondent's screen and/or printer, one of two things must happen. Either he must set his system to generate an internal linefeed after receiving each carriage return ("ENTER") from you, or you must send him a linefeed on each carriage return.

This is a function of the software, and most better programs automatically send a linefeed each time they send a carriage return code. If your software does not include this feature, and if you can't add a programming patch yourself, you will have to get new software.

Too many linefeeds can also cause problems. For example, if your system is adding a linefeed each time it sees a carriage return, and if at the same time your correspondent is sending a linefeed on carriage return, you are going to have too many blank lines on your screen. The only solution is for one of you to stop sending an automatic linefeed on carriage return. And again, this is a function of the software. Check your manual to see how to disable this feature.

Conclusion

There is no getting around the fact that computer-to-computer communication is complex. But if you go at it methodically and are careful to take notes at each step, it is probably fair to say that any two computer or computer-like machines can be made to communicate successfully.

Appendix B
Secrets of Using
Telenet and Tymnet

GTE's Telenet and Tymshare's Tymnet are the two main services that make it possible for you to dial a local number that will connect your personal computer to hundreds of databases, information utilities, and other computer-based systems all over the world. Technically, they are called "packet-switching networks," a reference to the fact that they work their magic by dividing computer data into discrete "packets" before routing them through their respective systems.

Each packet contains a set number of computer bits, and whenever the information you are sending or receiving is too small to fill a whole packet, fillers or "padding" signals are added to round things out. Each packet is electronically stamped with an address code that tells the system its destination. Then, like a telephone call, each packet is sent along the best available route through the system's many computers to the "host" system you are accessing.

The process is complex, but it is "transparent" to the user. Most personal computer owners are aware that there is a nearby Telenet or Tymnet number that will serve as a gateway to the electronic universe. After the connection with the host system has been made, it is as if Telenet and Tymnet weren't there at all.

But they are *always* there. Indeed, when you "talk" to The Source or CompuServe or Dow Jones, you are actually "talking" to Telenet or Tymnet. You talk to them, and they talk to the host system. Then they listen to the host's response and relay it to your terminal.

Most of the time the transparent presence of Telenet or Tymnet will make no difference to you at all, but there are at least three ways you can take advantage of these systems to communicate more effectively. These include: free telephone numbers and other information, stop/start "flow control," and more effective and accurate file uploading. In each case, all you need to know are the correct commands to enter.

Free Phone Numbers and Tymnet Online Newsletter
   Both Telenet and Tymnet offer extensive, constantly updated online lists of their access phone numbers—for free. Tymnet even offers a 14-item menu of "features" including American and Canadian (DataPac) phone numbers, log-on instructions, system announcements, and a newsletter, all for free.
   In both cases, all you need is a local phone number and your "terminal identifier" code, both of which you can obtain by dialing Customer Service and asking them for the 300-baud or 1200-baud number nearest you. Here are the toll-free numbers to dial:

Telenet	*Tymnet*
(800) 336-0437	(800) 336-0149 in the East
(800) 572-0408 in Virginia	(800) 323-7389 in the West

Note: Either Tymnet number will work, regardless of your location. The two numbers reflect Tymnet's internal policy of dividing the workload.

Free Phone Numbers from Telenet

   When you dial the number you have obtained from Telenet Customer Service, the first thing you will see on your screen is the word CONNECT. At that point, hit your <ENTER> key *twice*. The word TELENET will then appear, and underneath it some numbers identifying the particular "node" you are accessing.
   Type in the terminal identifier code you have gotten from Customer Service. The code for most microcomputers is D1, but be sure to check. The Telenet "at" sign (@) prompt will then appear. At that prompt, type in the word MAIL. When you see the phrase "User name?" type the word PHONES, and when you see the "Password?" prompt, type PHONES again. (This time the word will not appear on your screen as you type it. Note: if you want international Telenet access numbers, type INTL/ASSOCIATES at the "User name?" prompt.
   From this point on, the Telenet system will tell you what to do to obtain the information you want. Part of this process is displayed below.

```
CONNECT

TELENET
609 17A

TERMINAL=D1
```

@MAIL

User name?   PHONES
Password?

Welcome to TELEMAIL!
Your last access was Thursday, MMM DD, YYYY   3:49 PM

CHECK these bulletin boards: TELEMAIL

WELCOME TO THE TCO ACCESS LISTING.
THERE ARE SEVERAL WAYS YOU CAN GET INFORMATION ON OUR
TCO'S. PLEASE SPECIFY WHETHER YOU WANT INFORMATION ON
A 'STATE', 'AREA.CODE', 'ALL' OR 'SALES.OFFICE'
LOCATIONS BY TYPING THE WORD THAT IS IN DELIMITERS.

LAST UPDATE: MM/DD/YY

★ NEW TELENET CENTRAL OFFICE
NEW 1200 BAUD ACCESS AVAILABLE
& NEW TELENET CENTRAL OFFICE ADDED CURRENT MONTH
$ NEW 1200 BAUD ACCESS AVAILABLE ADDED CURRENT MONTH
% NEW LEAD NUMBER/NUMBER CHANGED

GTE/TELENET PROVIDES LOCAL NETWORK ACCESS IN THESE U.S.
CITIES OF 50,000 POPULATION OR MORE. IN-WATS ACCESS IS
AVAILABLE IN OTHER LOCATIONS. 1200 BPS ACCESS NUMBERS
REQUIRE THE USE OF BELL 212- OR VADIC 3405- COMPATIBLE
MODEMS, AS NOTED. (B)=BELL 212, (V)=VADIC 3405,
(B/V)=EITHER BELL 212 OR VADIC 3405.

< > INDICATES THE ACTUAL LOCATION OF TELENET
FACILITIES. IN SOME CASES, LOCAL ACCESS MAY REQUIRE
EXTENDED METRO TELEPHONE SERVICE OR INVOLVE MESSAGE
UNIT CHARGES.

TELENET CUSTOMER SERVICE:
   CONTINENTAL USA—   800/336-0437
   IN VIRGINIA—   800/572-0408
OUTSIDE CONTINENTAL USA—   703/442-2200

TELEMAIL CUSTOMER SERVICE: 703/442-1900

PLEASE ENTER
'STATE', 'AREA.CODE', 'ALL', OR 'SALES.OFFICE'.
(NOTE: ENTER (.) BETWEEN AREA.CODE AND SALES.OFFICE)

STATE,AREA.CODE,ALL,SALES.OFFICE: state

DO YOU WANT INWATS OR A STATE BEGINNING WITH A-TO-L?
<YES OR NO>
no

Tymnet Free Phone Numbers and Other Online Features

The same general procedure applies to Tymnet. Call Customer Service and ask for your terminal identifier and the 300- or 1200-baud Tymnet phone number nearest you.

Call the number and hit your <ENTER> key twice after you see the word CONNECT. Do not be disturbed if you see "garbage" on your screen. Tymnet has installed a number of nodes that can handle both 300 and 1200 baud by sensing what rate you are using. The garbage lasts only until the system locks onto your rate. It may type over your terminal identifier when you type it in. Most microcomputers have been assigned the code A, but check.

At the "Please log in:" prompt, type the word INFORMATION, followed by *two* semicolons. If you make a mistake, you will probably see the prompt "User name:". In that case, type the same word and semicolons again. If you see a prompt calling for "Project code:," just hit your <ENTER> key.

You will then see a rather confusing prompt asking for an item number or a question mark (?). Enter the question mark to generate the 14-item menu. From this point, the system will guide you through the steps to obtain the information you want. The only points that are not completely clear are these:

• DataPac is Tymnet's Canadian subsidiary

• The "BLUEBOOK" is Tymnet's directory of all of the firms and databases accessible via the Tymnet network. You can order a copy by contacting Customer Service.

• THUGS is the Tymnet users group.

• ONTYME II is Tymnet's electronic mail service.

Here is part of what you will see on your screen as you follow this procedure.

CONNECT
x| | x° | xxx<°xx°se type your terminal identifier
-1703-103-
please log in: INFORMATION;;

Tymnet Information System

ENTER ITEM NUMBER OR A ? :.?
Choose the information you would like from the following menu. Enter 'STOP' to abort an unwanted listing or 'QUIT' to get out of the system. All input must be in CAPITAL letters.

ITEM	FILE NAME	DESCRIPTION
1	@STATE	TYMNET domestic access numbers by state
2	@TYMSAT	TYMNET public Tymsats sorted by node #
3	@CITY	TYMNET domestic access numbers by city
4	@NEWPHONES	New and recently changed access no#s
5	@INTLPRTCOM	Info on TYMNET international access
6	@CONFIG	Configuration of TYMNET internationally. Includes speeds supported and network names.
7	@DPACACCESS	DATAPAC access numbers
8	@HOWTOUSETYMNET	Basic How to use TYMNET manual
9	@BLUSEARCHCOM	Computer and Data Services Available Through TYMNET (The BLUEBOOK)
10	@BLUEINDEX	Key word index to the Computer and Data Services available in manual.
11	@THUGSNEWS	Quarterly TYMNET Newsletter.
12	@DATAPACTYMNET	Logging in from DATAPAC to TYMNET
13	@TYMNETDATAPAC	Logging in from TYMNET to DATAPAC
14	@ONTYMEII	How to use ONTYME II

ENTER ITEM NUMBER OR A ? :

"Flow Control" Commands

The term "flow control" refers to your ability to tell the host system to stop sending for a moment so that you can read what is on the screen. The process involves X-ON/X-OFF communications protocols. When you want to stop an on-screen scroll, you may be able to send the host an X-OFF (Control-S) to tell it to wait. When you want to resume, you may be able to send an X-ON (Control-Q).

Usually it is the host system that permits you to use flow control. But sometimes, as is the case with the Dow Jones News/Retrieval Service (DJNS), the host system does not support it. Even so, you may be able to actuate the feature by entering a command to your transparent friends, Telenet and Tymnet. Here's what to do.

Telenet Flow-Control-Enabling Commands

There is a Telenet booklet that describes all flow control and other commands available to anyone using the network. The booklet is called *How to Use Telenet*, and it is free for the asking. Just call Customer Service.

The two flow control commands you will be most interested in are ENAB FLOW and DISA FLOW. These stand for "Enable Flow Control," and "Disable Flow Control." Since the flow control feature has no effect unless you enter a Control-Q or Control-S, there is little reason for a personal computer user to disable it once it has been enabled. In fact, you may not need the command at all. Be sure to check the manual for the particular host system you want to access to see if it supports flow control. Or call the host's Customer Service number.

If you find that you do need Telenet flow control, you may enter the above commands whenever you see the Telenet "Network Command Mode" prompt—the "at" sign (@). That means you can enter the command after the very first "at" sign on sign-on, instead of the Telenet code for the host you want to access. This is usually the best thing to do if the commands are necessary. A second @ sign will then appear, and you may enter the host code number (or another Telenet command) at that point.

You can return to Telenet "Network Command Mode" at any time during a session with The Source or other database. Just hit <ENTER>, followed by an @ sign, followed by <ENTER>. This will cause the Telenet @ sign to appear, and you will be free to enter your command. After you enter your Telenet command, you will automatically be returned to The Source or whatever host you are accessing. (*Note:* The Source supports X-ON/X-OFF, so you will not need to use these commands when accessing that database.)

Tymnet Flow Control

If you are using Tymnet, you must enter all Tymnet commands immediately after you have typed in your terminal identifier and before you have entered the name of the host you want to access. If you want to enable flow control (Control-Q and Control-S), hold your <CONTROL> key down and hit the <R> key once. This sends your local Tymnet node computer a Control-R, telling it to enable flow control. Note that nothing will appear on your screen when you enter this command. And note that you must enter this command every time you want to access a database that does not support flow control.

Special Commands for File Uploading

When you are typing commands (or even straight text) at the keyboard of your computer, you will usually have no trouble entering information into your online files at CompuServe or The Source. The reason is that by data-communications standards, even the fastest typist is incredibly slow.

Uploading, or sending previously recorded files directly from your disk or internal buffer, however, is a different matter. Here you've got one computer talking to another—at computer speeds. And that can sometimes cause problems.

For example, you may have a beautifully prepared file recorded on disk. And you may want to upload the information into your filing cabinet on The Source with the intention of sending it to an electronic mail correspondent. (The Source has a command to let you do this when you are writing a letter. You merely type .LOAD followed by the filename of your file.)

Let's suppose that you open the filing cabinet by typing the word ENTER at The Source Command Level, followed by the filename. You hit whatever keys your computer and communications software require to initiate the upload. When the transmission has been completed, you hit your <ENTER> key twice to close the file. Then you type in TY (for "type"), followed by the filename.

Mercy heavens, what a mess! The sentences have been arbitrarily lopped off. Individual characters and entire words are missing. It's a disaster. You can never send the file to your correspondent looking the way it does. What to do?

Here's the problem and the solution. It is important to be aware that the information you send must travel a long and arduous route to reach your host. It must pass through many different phone lines, many of them rated at different speeds, and it must go through super-fast packet-switching "memory shufflers" before it arrives at its destination. In short, the particular "packets" that contain your information are constantly being speeded up or slowed down.

If the data are entered at human keyboard speeds, there is enough slack to prevent most problems. The Telenet or Tymnet systems can adjust. But if the information is being sent directly from a floppy disk—in a continuous, relentless stream—data loss and other problems may begin to crop up.

The solution is often to activate the buffers offered by the Telenet and Tymnet packet-switching networks. Without going into a lot of technical detail, the proper commands alert the networks that you are about to upload a file, causing them to activate certain buffers designed to smooth out the data flow.

Telenet Upload Commands

The thing to remember about Telenet is that it has two modes: the Network Command Mode and the Data Transfer Mode. When you first access Telenet and see the "at" sign, you are in the Telenet Network Command Mode. You enter the code number of the host you want to access and Telenet makes the connection. At that point it switches to its completely transparent Data Transfer Mode.

To alert Telenet that you are about to upload a file from disk or from your computer's internal buffer, you must "escape" from the Data Transfer Mode into the Network Command Mode. Then you must enter your command. Whenever you are using Telenet, you can escape to Network Command Mode by hitting the following sequence of keys [<ENTER> <@> <ENTER>]. This will cause the Telenet @ sign to appear on your screen, indicating that the network is awaiting your command.

With that as background, here is how to use Telenet's buffer when uploading files to The Source—if you find that you cannot do so successfully otherwise. The same general procedure applies to any other database accessible via Telenet, though you may want to experiment for best results.

1. Make sure that you are at The Source Command Level (–>).
2. Type the following keystrokes: [<ENTER> <@> <ENTER>]. This will put you into the Telenet Network Command Mode and cause the Telenet @ sign to appear.
3. Type in *either* DTAPE or TAPE immediately following the @ sign. These commands activate the Telenet upload buffer. File uploading is more reliable at half duplex, so the system goes to that setting when these commands are entered. Unfortunately, this makes you "blind." From this point on, until they are deactivated, you will not be able to see what you type on the screen.
4. Type the word ENTER, followed by the filename you have chosen. Wait for a moment until The Source comes back with "Enter text."
5. When you see that prompt, initiate your upload.
6. Your own system should tell you when the transmission has been completed. At that point, hit <BREAK> or your machine's equivalent. This will allow you to escape from the Network Command and upload mode to the regular Data Transfer Mode.
7. Hit your <ENTER> key twice to close the file. Then go in and look at it by typing TY followed by the filename at The Source Command Level.

Tymnet Upload Commands

Tymnet's equivalent is a Control-X. If you plan to do any uploading to a database you are accessing through Tymnet, this is the command to use. You must enter a Control-X [<CTRL> <X>] immediately after you have typed your terminal identifier, but before you have entered the host's name. Nothing will appear on your screen, but the command will enable the upload buffer.

Conclusion

You may or may not need the flow control and upload commands. It all depends on your particular machine and software, and on the particular database or online service you are accessing. However, you will benefit from the free online information provided by both services. Indeed, if you have a communicating personal computer, communications software, and a modem, these services offer an excellent way to introduce yourself to data communications at no cost.

Appendix C
Telex, TWX, FAX, Mail, Mailgrams™, and More

There are over 140,000 TWX and Telex machines in North America, and another 1.3 million machines in 152 countries around the world. There are innumerable facsimile or "fax" machines in business offices as well. And there are hundreds of companies with electronic mail addresses that have nothing to do with the information utilities.

You can talk to all of these machines, regardless of their locations, from your personal computer or communicating word processor.

How to Send a Telex or TWX

Using a service offered by Graphnet, a subsidiary of Graphic Scanning Corporation, you can send messages to any Telex or TWX machine anywhere in the world. The monthly account charge is about $5.00, and the costs per message are between 30 and 40 percent lower than the rates offered by Western Union, the owner of the Telex and TWX networks.

This is a truly remarkable breakthrough, both in terms of price and in terms of technology. But to fully appreciate it, it's important to understand the traditional operations of the Telex and TWX networks. Both are direct descendants of the old-fashioned telegraph. The word "Telex" is short for "telegraph exchange." ("TWX," pronounced "twix," stands for "teletype exchange.") There are many differences between and among Telex and TWX machines, but the primary distinction is one of speed. The Telex machine was invented in the 1930s and is capable of sending and receiving messages at a top speed of about 50 baud. The TWX machine—sometimes called a "Telex II"—is a late 1940s development, and its top speed is 110 baud.

Both devices are electromechanical. That is, they operate by converting electrical impulses into the mechanical motions of printing elements, paper feeders, and other typewriter-like functions. In fact, you might think of them as nothing more than printers with an ability to automatically answer the telephone and print out any information received. Telex and TWX machines, in effect, serve as hard-copy telephone answering machines.

Like a telephone, each Telex or TWX machine is connected to its own line with its own special phone-number-like address. When one Telex subscriber wants to send a message to another, the message is usually prepared beforehand and recorded on punched paper tape. Then the originator dials the correspondent's machine, makes a connection, presses a button, and runs the paper tape through the machine. The receiving machine chatters to life and prints out a hard copy of the message. Communication takes place in "real time"—the message is printed as it is received. And, as with a telephone, if the receiver's machine is busy printing another message, the sender must keep trying the number until it is free.

Because Telex and TWX machines are incompatible, two networks were established. Only recenty has it become possible to communicate in real time between the two. The telephone lines belong to the phone company, but the networks themselves are owned, operated, and maintained in North America by Western Union.

Telex and TWX subscription costs vary with geographical location. The cost for running a dedicated line to an office in a major metropolitan area will obviously be less than installing one at a more remote site. The "city" cost might be $25 a month, for example, while the "country" cost might be as much as $100 a month. There are also charges for sending each message. And, of course, you must either buy or rent an appropriate machine.

Enter the Personal Computer

Communication between personal computers and word processors and Telex and TWX machines is not impossible. But it is difficult, to say the least. As electromechanical devices, Telex and TWX machines are terribly slow, and both demand special codes and communications formats. In many ways their only advantage is that so many of them have been installed over the years and that each is linked to an extensive worldwide network.

The question is, can personal computer owners take advantage of this network to communicate with Telex and TWX subscribers, and can they do it in a way that is both easy and cost effective? The answer is yes, thanks to Graphnet.

Graphnet offers two basic services: The Graphnet Freedom Network, for real time communication between computers and Telex, TWX, or facsimile machines; and a "store-and-forward" service. All you need for either service is a communicating personal computer or word processor and modem, a Graphnet account number, and a telephone.

You can communicate with Graphnet at any speed you like, though 300 or 1200 baud are most common. You dial up the firm's computers, sign on, and then enter the Telex or TWX address of the firm you wish to contact. Graphnet will dial the appropriate number and make the connection. You then transmit your message. Graphnet takes care of all of the interface problems and communications protocols needed to communicate with your correspondent. Usually this will mean slowing down your 300- or 1200-baud transmission to 50 or 110 baud and adding the special codes that Telex and TWX machines need to see.

If your correspondent is also a Graphnet subscriber, the message will cost about 20 percent less than it would if you were using a Telex machine yourself and communicating through Western Union. If your correspondent is not a Graphnet subscriber, the system will access Western Union for you and transmit the message. The cost in this case will be identical to what Western Union charges. This is possible because of relatively new communications regulations providing for certain discounts to message providers. Western Union receives identical discounts when it provides a message to another network.

This real-time communication can take place domestically or internationally. The only requirement is that the recipient have a device that is accessible 24 hours a day by telephone line. That means that it is also possible to use a personal computer as a Telex or TWX machine replacement. For example, you might purchase an inexpensive computer, an auto-answer modem, and appropriate software. And you might arrange for an extra phone line to be used exclusively by your machine.

The machine would be up and running round the clock, ready to accept messages from all over the world—even from Telex and TWX machines—via Graphnet. You have only to notify Graphnet of your machine's communications requirements and telephone number. They will do the rest.

If you would rather not install a dedicated phone line and devote a computer to full-time communications chores, there is an electronic mailbox feature under Graphnet's store-and-forward service. This works exactly the way electronic mail services work: you sign on at your convenience and check your mailbox for any messages.

As its name implies, however, the principal use of this particular Graphnet service is the storing and forwarding of messages. Instead of waiting for a particular Telex, TWX, or other line to be free, you can call Graphnet at your convenience, key in your correspondent's address, and transmit your message to Graphnet's computers. The computers will take over, dialing the appropriate number repeatedly until a connection has been made. They will then transmit your message to the recipient's machine.

If you like, you can store any number of "mailing lists" on the system and send the same message to each addressee by entering only one or two words. And the system features "English-language mnemonics." This is a fancy way of saying that if you want to send a message to Ed at the ABC company in New York, you have only to key in "ED-ABC" instead of a long, complex series of letters and numbers when specifying the address. The system is programmed to automatically look up the correct phone number, protocols, and parameters for Ed's machine.

The fixed cost for a Graphnet subscription is $5.00 per month. There are some exceptions, but messages are normally billed on the basis of how many words they contain and delivery speed. For example, the cost of sending a Telex (50-baud delivery speed) anywhere in the United States is about 28¢ per 66 words. The cost of sending a TWX (110-baud delivery speed) is about 30¢ per 100 words. The same rate applies for sending 100 words to a computer at 300 baud.

Although other companies will undoubtedly follow suit, Graphnet is the first firm to offer services of this kind to owners of personal computers and word processors. For more information contact:

Graphnet, Inc.
329 Alfred Avenue
Teaneck, NJ 07666
(800) 631-1581
(800) 932-0848 in New Jersey

Graphnet, Inc.
Telemarketing Department
8230 Boone Boulevard, Suite 330
Vienna, VA 22180
(800) 336-3729
(703) 556-9397 in Virginia

For information on a similar service, you might contact:
SpeediTelex International
3400 Peachtree Road NE
Atlanta, GA 30320
(800) 241-1913

Two Other Alternatives

There are at least two other ways to use your personal computer to send Telex and TWX messages. One of them is hardware-based, the other is software-based. Chat Communications of Mountain View, California, offers a unit it calls The Chat II. Based on an 8085 microprocessor, the Chat II is a "smart box" with two communications ports and slots for three additional communications port cards. You connect the unit to your Telex/TWX telephone line and plug your computer into the proper interface. Then you dial the number of the Telex or TWX machine you want to talk to. The machine's internal intelligence enables it to perform all of the character, speed, and protocol conversions needed to let the two machines communicate.

The system retails for about $1650 and comes with 16K of RAM (expandable to 48K). It can store messages for later transmission and serve as an electronic mailbox for a local network. You can also add a floppy disk drive and a printer if you like. For more information, contact:

> Chat Corporation
> 2560 Wyandotte Street
> Mountain View, CA 94043
> (415) 962-9670
> TELEX 172385

When you use Graphnet, you rely upon the firm's computers to make the changes and adjustments necessary to allow you to talk to Telex and TWX machines. However, if you are willing to purchase special software, your own machine can make those adjustments for you. One of the most popular programs in this area is MICRO/Telegram™ ($250). This software is one of two main products published by Microcom, Inc., of Norwood, Massachusetts. The other is MICRO/Courier™, a program that is capable of transmitting charts, graphs, and VisiCalc™ files, as well as more standard information from one machine to another.

MICRO/Telegram was originally designed to run on the Apple II, though it will ultimately be available for the Apple III, the IBM/PC, and the Radio Shack TRS-80 Model III as well. The program offers a menu-driven format, a simple text editor, an auto-dial directory of frequently called numbers, a distribution list feature, and "clock and calendar" scheduling that lets the machine transmit messages whenever you tell it to without the need for human intervention.

Most important of all, the software automatically makes the adjustments necessary for you to talk directly to a Telex or TWX machine, and it gives you access to the entire Western Union network (send flowers, wire money, or check Western Union Infomaster® service for news, stock quotes, and weather information).

For more information, see your nearest Apple dealer, or contact:

> Microcom, Inc.
> 1400A Providence Highway
> Norwood, MA 02062
> (617) 762-9310

You might also want to send for information on the MicroTLX™ software package produced by Advanced Micro Techniques. Designed for computers runing the CP/M® operating system, MicroTLX will also allow you to access the Western Union network to send Telex, TWX, Mailgrams, and the like. The software supports most major modems and provides features like automatic dialing, automatic answer, unattended operation, and automatic retry of unanswered calls. The cost is $150.00. For more information, contact:

> Advanced Micro Techniques
> 1291 E. Hillside Blvd. Suite 209
> Foster City, CA 94404
> (415) 349-9336

Mailgrams™

A Mailgram™ is a Western Union product consisting of a hard copy printout of your message that is delivered to the recipient by the mail service. To send one, you must normally call Western Union and read your message or access the firm through a Telex or TWX machine. In either case, your message is sent electronically to a printing facility near your correspondent. The message is then printed and mailed. In many cases, the Mailgram will be delivered the next day.

Mailgrams can be sent using either the Chat II hardware interface or the software packages described above. Graphnet also offers a version of the service it calls Faxgram™. However, there is yet another alternative—The Source. If you type in MGRAM at The Source Command Level prompt (->), the following menu and information will appear on your screen:

MAILGRAM MESSAGE SERVICE

MGRAM
1 OVERVIEW
2 INSTRUCTIONS
3 RATES
4 SERVICES
5 SEND MAILGRAM

Enter item number or HELP 1

DON'T PICK UP THE PHONE TO SEND YOUR NEXT MAILGRAM MESSAGE!

You can use THE SOURCE's Mailgram* Service (MGRAM from Command Level) to send as many messages as you like, exactly the way you want them. If you send your SOURCE Mailgram message before 4 p.m. EST, on a business day, it's virtually guaranteed next business day delivery anywhere in the U.S., including Alaska and Hawaii.

You can maintain multiple address lists on THE SOURCE for frequent mass mailings and use MGRAM's file loading features, or you can use the text editor, which enables you to make changes with minimum effort.

The cost of sending Mailgram messages through THE SOURCE is competitive with other methods. You pay by the word, but the more addresses you send your message to, the less each one will cost. All messages you send will be strictly confidential. No one will read your message other than the recipient. MGRAM offers a host of Special Services like confirmation copies, mailing list entry and storage. Try the Special Services option from the lead menu.

*Mailgram service is a registered trademark of the Western Union Telegraph Company.

Here are the rates for sending one or more Mailgrams on The Source:

MAILGRAM MESSAGE RATES

# OF MGRAMS	1-100 WORDS	101-200 WORDS	201-300 WORDS
1	$5.15	$6.15	$7.15
2-25	4.25 ea.	5.25 ea.	6.25 ea.
26-100	3.50 ea.	4.50 ea.	5.50 ea.
101-200	3.00 ea.	4.00 ea.	5.00 ea.

You are not limited in the number of messages you may send. Just add $1.00 for each 100 words (or portion thereof) over 300 words.

Send SOURCE mail to STMGRM for a price quote on sending more than 200 Mailgram messages.

Quantity discounts apply only for the SAME message sent to multiple addresses.

CONFIRMATION COPIES

For Confirmation Copies of Your Message:
Up to 100 Words . . . . $2.00 ea. copy
101 - 200 Words . . . . $3.00 ea. copy
201 - 300 Words . . . . $4.00 ea. copy

Add $1.00 for each additional 100 words.

Electronic Mail Services

In addition to the electronic mail services offered by The Source and CompuServe, there are also a number of business-oriented mail systems available to personal computer and word processor users. The buzzword for these services is "Computer-Based Message System," or CBMS.

Aside from the fact that one of these systems (GTE's Telemail™) will allow you to upload and store files containing the control characters needed to transmit graphics, WordStar, and other files, there is little difference between them and the information utility-based services. They do offer some advanced features, but their main advantage is their growing subscriber base.

A business might not be interested in a subscription to an information utility. But businesses are definitely interested in systems that will allow communication between their various offices and between other firms. And that is what the CBMS services are designed to provide. The only problem is that if you are a Telemail subscriber, you cannot normally send messages to a firm that happens to subscribe instead to Tymshare's OnTyme II service. A number of other firms, notably Dialcom, are beginning to offer transfer services to make this possible.

CBMS services are priced for business use and so are likely to be of little interest to the individual or small business computer user. GTE Telenet's Telemail service, for example, charges subscribers $140 per month. After the first three months, subscribers are charged an additional $500 minimum for service, whether they use that much or not. Connect charges through Telenet are $14 per hour during business hours, $7.00 per hour from 6:00 PM until 9:00 PM, and $4.00 per hour from then until seven the next morning.

Comet, a service of the Computer Corporation of America, charges $100 per customer organization per month, plus $60 for each mailbox on the system. These fees entitle the user to up to nine hours of connect time and include storage space for up to 500 messages. Additional connect time is billed at $7.00 per hour, regardless of time of day. Telenet, Tymnet, and other common carrier charges are extra.

Clearly, CBMS services are not intended for the casual user. However, if you are interested in such services, here are the addresses to contact for more information:

> Comet
> Computer Corporation of America
> 675 Massachusetts Avenue
> Cambridge, MA 02139
> (617) 492-8860
>
> Dialcom
> 1109 Spring Street, Suite 410
> Silver Springs, MD 20910
> (301) 588-1572
> (Offers a variety of business communications
> services; a newly acquired division of ITT.)

Telemail
GTE Telenet
8229 Boone Blvd.
Vienna, VA 22180
(703) 442-1000

OnTyme II
Tymnet, Inc.
20665 Valley Green Drive
Cupertino, CA 95014
(408) 446-7000

These are not the only services available in this burgeoning field, but collecting and comparing the information supplied by each firm is an excellent way to start your investigation of CBMS services and whether they make sense for you.

Appendix D
How to Turn Your Personal Computer into a Typesetter

A properly equipped personal computer can not only communicate with mainframes, minis, and other microcomputers, it can also send information directly to a computerized typesetting machine. The technology is still developing, but a growing number of businesses are already taking advantage of this opportunity and saving up to 40 percent on their typesetting costs in the process.

To appreciate the difference that a communicating personal computer or dedicated word processor can make, it's important to have a broad overview of the traditional typesetting procedure. You as the customer type up your material and hand it to the typesetter. The typesetter sits at a typesetting machine and *retypes* the entire document. In the process, certain typesetting codes are embedded in the text. These codes tell the machine what size type to use, whether to print a particular word in bold or italics, how to handle indentations, and so forth.

Modern machines record the typesetter's copy on magnetic tape or floppy disks. Then, when the operator enters the equivalent of a personal computer user's "Print" command, the machine generates a photostat of the now typeset text. Photostats containing blocks of text are cut into pieces, and pasted down in their proper positions. The process is called "paste-up," and the end product is a "mechanical." Mechanicals are the master image from which the actual printing elements are made.

Now let's suppose that the typesetting machine is computerized. It has a keyboard, a display screen, a floppy disk drive, software, *and* a serial card with an RS-232-C interface plug. In that case, you could create your text on your personal computer or word processor, dial the phone, and send your entire text directly to the typesetting machine. No one would have to sit down and laboriously *retype* everything you had written (and no one will introduce errors and "typos" into your copy). "Capturing the keystrokes" in this way saves time and money for both you and the typesetting firm. Your copy can be typeset instantly, and the resulting photostats can be on their way to you the same day via overnight courier.

Striving Toward the Ideal

That at least is the ideal. But while this goal can be achieved right now, it must be said that bringing things to the point where. you can effortlessly transmit information and receive typeset copy in a packet the next day can take more than a little effort. The reason is lack of standardization of word-processing and typesetting control codes.

The software used by personal computers and dedicated word processors is designed to "talk" to your printout device, not to a typesetter. It allows you to place certain non-printing symbols in the text you type to tell the printout device what to do. These symbols are often called "escape codes," because they allow the printer to "escape" from one printing mode to another and back again.

For example, MicroPro's popular WordStar™ word-processing program allows you to place a " Control-B" symbol in the text to signal the beginning and ending of bold printing. If you want a sentence to be printed in bold, you hold your <CONTROL> key down and hit <B>. This causes your computer screen to display a circumflex-like symbol followed by the letter "B." This symbol will not print, but it has the effect of saying to your printer, "Okay, printer, escape from your normal printing mode and make everything that follows me bold." A second "Control-B" is entered at the end of the bold text to tell the printer to stop bold printing and escape back to its normal mode.

If all personal computer word processing software, all dedicated word processors, and all computerized typesetters used the same "Control-B" to signify the beginning and end of bold print, there would be few problems. The "Control-B" symbol is transmitted as an ASCII 2, and it can be sent and received as easily as any other character in the ASCII code set. (See Chapter 12 for more information on ASCII and control characters.)

The problem, of course, is that each brand of typesetter and each word processor or word-processing program uses *different* codes, not only for bold print, but also for underlining, for superscripts and subscripts, for tabulation, and for all of the other printing options. In addition, these machines and their programming may also insert other codes that can further confuse things. A dedicated word processor, for example, will probably have both "hard" and "soft" hyphens. Both may look the same on the screen, but the soft hyphen is entered and removed by the machine as necessary for word division whenever text is adjusted. The hard hyphen is user-entered, and remains in the text regardless of any adjustments.

The point is that all of these codes may exist in the text you create at your machine. All of them are certainly essential when using your computer and printer to generate hard copy. But they can cause complications when you are sending text to a typesetter. It's important to realize that there is an ASCII code number for each of these special symbols—either in the standard ASCII code set or in the nonstandard "high" codes that range from 128 through 255—and if they are in the text, they *will* be transmitted to the typesetting machine.

Now for the Tricky Bit

As in so many other parts of the microcomputer world, what we have here is a failure to interface. Generally speaking, plain text flows smoothly from microcomputer to typesetter, whether through a "null modem" or crossover cable connecting the two, or over the telephone. It is the special codes that cause the problems. The typesetting machine *must be told what to do* with each and every one of the special codes you transmit. There are two basic choices: the machine can either convert the code to its own equivalent, or it can ignore the code completely.

For example, suppose that part of your text includes a pair of "Control-B" codes designed to tell your printer to begin and end bold printing, and suppose that the typesetting machine's code for bold printing is a "Control-Z." Ideally, the typesetter would automatically change each of your incoming "Control-Bs" into "Control-Zs." But suppose your machine also sends some kind of margin line made up of a series of high ASCII codes that mean nothing to the typesetter. In this case, the typesetter must be told to ignore these incoming numbers.

Translation Tables

There are two ways to solve this problem. Both depend upon translation tables, and they are not mutually exclusive. (For more information on translation tables, see Chapter 12.) First, given the proper communications software, the typesetting machine can be equipped with a translation table that will automatically convert *your* control codes into *its* control codes. Second, again given the proper software, you can create a translation table that will perform many of the same conversions.

The first solution is called "converting on input," and the second, "converting on output." The ultimate solution may involve a combination of both of these techniques. It depends on your word-processing software, your communications software, and the requirements of the particular typesetting machine you want to "talk" to. In addition, many typesetting firms use their own microcomputer to download text from your machine and later transmit the copy from the micro to their typesetter. This can add yet another degree of complexity to the process.

Creating the Tables

Because there are so many variables to consider, creating the translation table or tables and working out a definitive procedure for transmitting and typesetting text usually requires a good deal of work. You have to identify all of the control codes and special codes used by both computer and typesetter, and you have to decide how each one should be handled. You may or may not receive the help you need from your equipment manufacturer. And even if the manufacturer is willing, you may have difficulty locating employees who know enough to be of any help.

Your best bet is to contact a typesetting firm with experience in this new field, preferably one that has worked with your brand of computer and has already prepared the necessary translation table. As more and more firms gain this experience, and as more tables are created, typesetting via personal computer will become increasingly easy. However, you should be aware that it may never be possible to eliminate the need for at least some keyboard "massaging" of your text by the typesetter. There may be codes, for example, that only the typesetting machine can enter. Consequently, although industry sources estimate total potential savings of approximately 40 percent, your actual savings will probably be less. Even a savings of half that amount, however, would be well worth the time and effort required, particularly if you or your firm do a lot of typesetting. In fact, after all parties have the procedure down pat, it is conceivable that you will find yourself typesetting reports and presentations that would otherwise never have seen the inside of a print shop.

What You Need to Get Started

It is impossible to specify the exact equipment and software needed in every case. However, there are some general guidelines to keep in mind.

Obviously, you'll need a modem and a personal computer or dedicated word processor equipped for communications. Since any document that is a candidate for typesetting is likely to be at least several pages long, you should give strong consideration to buying a high-speed (1200-baud) modem. As a rule of thumb, you can assume that six double-spaced typewritten pages (1000 to 1500 words) will require from three to four minutes to transmit at a rate of 300 baud. The same amount of material can be sent four times faster at 1200 baud (three quarters of a minute to a minute).

You might also consider the possibility of eliminating the phone connection altogether and simply carrying your personal computer to the typesetter. With a null-modem or crossover cable, you will be able to connect your computer directly to the typesetter. And, since there are no phone lines to worry about, you may be able to transmit at a rate of 9600 baud or higher.

If you are using a personal computer, you will need a word-processing software package. However, if you have not yet purchased a machine and you plan to do a great deal of text preparation, you should look into buying a dedicated word processor instead of a microcomputer. Computers are designed to compute, and word processors are designed to process words. Both can be made to perform both functions, but each is significantly better at its given task. There are many fine personal computer–word-processing packages on the market, but for all of their power, none can hold a candle to a dedicated word processor when it comes to ease of text creation.

You will also need communications software. And here you will want to be particularly careful in making your selection. You want more than a simple terminal package. You will need one that permits you to create translation tables and, most important, one that "supports" X-ON/ X-OFF communications protocols. These signals are necessary any time you transmit large quantities of text, as opposed to entering commands or typing at your keyboard.

For example, suppose you are sending copy from your personal computer to a typesetting machine, and that the typesetter has been programmed to wait until its internal buffer (holding tank) has been filled and then write the contents to disk. You send your material and the typesetter's buffer begins to fill. When the buffer has reached its capacity, the typesetter sends your machine an X-OFF signal (Control-S) saying, "Hold up for a minute while I record all of this information." Your software must know it should stop sending information when it receives that signal. Once the typesetter has taken care of business, it sends an X-ON (Control-Q) to tell your machine to begin sending again. Without this protocol, your machine would continue to send information regardless of whether the receiving machine was ready or not.

You should also try to find a software package that is capable of sending (and receiving) all 256 ASCII codes. Many packages are limited to just the codes from 0 through 127—the standard ASCII code set. This is fine for most purposes, but it may not provide the flexibility you need, or the convenience you would like, when talking to a typesetter.

> **Online Tip:** You may be able to learn which software packages are appropriate from a computer-store salesperson, but you will be much better off if you contact one of the typesetting firms specializing in this area. (See the list at the end of this appendix.) These firms will be able to tell you which packages experience has shown to be most effective.

Finally, you will need a typesetting firm with experience in this field, or a firm willing to work with you to develop a procedure. In the latter case there are two points to keep in mind. First, if the firm's machine has a display screen, there is a good chance that the machine can be equipped with a communications card and the necessary software. This can cost the firm well over $1000, so the owner is most likely to be interested only if you can guarantee a certain amount of business. Second, once the procedure has been developed, it represents a product or service that the typesetter can offer to other customers. Consequently, considering the essential services you are helping to create, you should be able to negotiate some kind of price concession on your first few jobs.

Here is a list of firms you might want to contact.

Typesetting Houses

Amnet
1015 Gayley, Suite 288
Los Angeles, CA 90024
(213) 907-5015

Buckland Printing Comany
P.O. Box 1157
99 Willie Street
Lowell, MA 01853
(617) 452-0111/458-2522

Duarte Company
  Phototypesetting
P.O. Box 2025
1035 Lisbon Street
Lewiston, ME 04240
(207) 782-5246
Source Mail: TCU554

Expertel
300 Park Avenue South
New York, NY 10010
(212) 420-0990
Source Mail: TCU479

Cimarron Graphics
Box 12593
Dallas, TX 75225
(214) 691-5092
CIS: 70130,161

Letterform Graphics, Inc.
8200 Greensboro Drive,
  Suite 403
McLean, VA 22101
(703) 893-1313
Source Mail: ST1902

Pacesetting Services
200J North Crescent Way
Anaheim, CA 92801
(714) 956-0860

The Letter Space
13 East 16th Street
New York, NY 10003
(212) 255-7115
Source Mail: TCU772

Tate Publishing
Box 906
North Clemsford, MA 01863
(617) 692-8395
Source Mail: TCD 671

Bye & Bye, Inc.
110 South Main
Holstein, IA 51025
(712) 368-4353

Related Products

Cybertext Corporation
P.O. Box 860
Arcata, CA 95521
(707) 822-7079
Sells interfaces to drive MicroComposer typesetting equipment. For direct connection of all TRS-80 models, S-100 systems, and CP/M-based systems

Small Business Systems Group
6 Carlisle Road
Westford, MA 01886
(617) 692-3800
TELESET-80™ typesetting communications package for TRS-80 Scripsit™ files.

Computer Graphics World
P.O. Box 122
Tulsa, OK 74101
(918) 835-3161
Magazine. One year: $30. Source of teletypesetting information, firms, software, and more.

Online Tip: With some firms, you will be able to upload all of the text destined for typesetting to your filing cabinet on The Source, CompuServe, or the Telemail electronic mail service offered by Telenet. You can upload at your convenience, and the firm can access the file on the system at its convenience. These services can thus serve as a common meeting place.

There are at least three points to keep in mind. First, you will

Online Tip continued

have to consult your manuals to find out how to lower the protection level of your file on the system. This is necessary to allow the
typesetting firm access to it. Second, you should read Appendix B
regarding the special commands you may want to enter when uploading a text file to a mainframe served by Telenet or Tymnet
(TAPE and DTAPE, for example). And third, the two utilities will
not accept and store control codes in the filing cabinets they offer.
Telenet's Telemail, however, does offer this feature. Any typesetting firm offering this service should be able to provide you with
all necessary instructions.

Appendix E
Electronic Mail Directory

The following directory contains The Source or CompServe Information Service (CIS) electronic mailbox addresses of a number of publications, firms, and professionals. Derived from published sources, it makes no claim to being comprehensive. But it is a beginning, and you may find it useful.

Consultants and Communicators

Beal Systems Group
Tracks IBM/PC news and developments.
Source: BSG001

Scott Burns (Boston, MA)
Syndicated investment columnist
Source: TCX200

Cross Communications (Boulder, CO)
Teleconferencing and software to support it.
Source: TCA246

CZ Ware (Conti, CA)
Specializes in design of data acquisition systems for instrumentation and control. Medical applications.
CIS: 70110,254

Frank Derfler
Telecommunications columnist, *Microcomputing Magazine*.
Source: TCB967
CIS: 70003,455

G. Elman (Philadelphia, PA)
Attorney specializing in biotechnology law.
Source: TCM524

EMCO Systems (Van Nuys, CA)
Energy management.
Source: TCT910

Environs Design Group
Home design.
Source: TCK369

Future Enterprises, Inc. (Washington, DC)
Office automation; seminars in CP/M.
Source: TCX567
CIS: 70675,144

S. Garber (San Francisco, CA)
Time-sharing and database construction.
Source: CLO512

Alfred Glossbrenner
FireCrystal Communications
Comments and suggestions about this book are welcome.
Source: TCS772
CIS: 70065,745
EIES: # 377

R. Halloran (San Francisco, CA)
Construction industry microcomputer applications.
CIS: 70110,114

W. Heid (Pittsburgh, PA)
Custom business, investment, and graphics software—Apples.
Source: TCX671

Bryon Kirkwood (Dallas, TX)
Consultant on microcomputer marketing.
CIS: 70315,1313

Lindbergh Systems (Holden, MA)
Telecommunications; Omniterm.
Source: TCA818
CIS: 70310,267

Participation Systems, Inc. (PSI) (Boston, MA)
Electronic mail and conferencing software and consulting.
Source: PS0001

Red Bank Information Service
High-tech information search service.
Source: TCD621

Bob Rice, "The Computer Tutor"
Specializing in IBM/PC.
Source: TCT335

B. Starr (San Francisco, CA)
Attorney specializing in networking and legal protection for artists and
inventors.
CIS: 70003,240

Clubs and User Groups

Battle Creek Micro Club (Battle Creek, MI)
Mainly TRS-80.
CIS: 7150,416

Central Alabama Micro Society (Montgomery, AL)
Source: TCG794
CIS: 71545,1261

Chicago Atari Users Group (Clarendon Hills, IL)
CIS: 70545,513

ET-3400 Users Group (El Monte, CA)
Heath ET-3400 computers.
CIS: 70250,463

Health Users Group (Spokane, WA)
CIS: 70235,313

Surrey Microcomputer Users Group (Surrey, British Columbia)
CIS: 70525,735.

Education

Antioch School of Law
Courses in law for non-lawyers.
Source: CL2542

Colorado Technical College (Colorado Springs, CO)
Professor David Hughes
Source: TCE054

Computer Social Impact Research Institute (San Jose, CA)
Nonprofit organization; research on impact of computers on society and
similar subjects.
Source: CLI951

Memphis State University (Memphis, TN)
Computer literacy.
Source: TCX616

Thomas Throop
Computer bridge (cards) expert.
Source: TCA122

University of South Alabama
College of Education
Source: ST2256

Miscellaneous

Commodore Computer Dealers
Source: TCE803

The Exploratorium (Mill Valley, CA)
Sound and light experience.
CIS: 70110,426

General Videotex (Cambridge, MA)
Delphi (information utility under construction).
Source: TCI050
CIS: 71715,1356

Legal Users Group
Source: TCW543

National School Public Relations Association
Source: TCA-NSPRA

Random Electronics (Plainsboro, NJ)
Apple and TRS-80 chips.
Source: TCH563

Williams Radio and TV, Inc. (Jacksonville, FL)
Back issues of most computer magazines.
Source: TCE230

Xerox Store (Great Neck, NY)
Source: TCG451

Publications

Americàn Association for Medical Systems and Informatics Newsletter
on computer applications for medical cáre.
Source: TCP230

Apple City
Source: TCD912

Creative Computing
Will Fastie, IBM columnist.
Source: TCP394

HamSource (HAM radio)
Source: TCU366

IBM PC Gazette
Source: TCA257

"IPCO Info" (International Personal Computer Owners)
Newsletter for IBM/PC owners.
CIS: 71545,467

New York Zoetrope, Inc.
Publisher; primarily film-related books.
Source: TCN121
CIS: 71715,727

PC Magazine
The Independent Guide to IBM Personal Computers
Source: STO948
CIS: 70370,532

Popular Computing
Source: TCG847
CIS: 70045,1320

"The Recruiting Search Report"
For professional personnel recruiters.
Source: CSI036

"SATGUIDE"
Guide to TV programs available via backyard dish antenna.
Source: TCE618

Services

Automated Information Resultants, Ltd. (Jackson Hts., NY)
Local area networking using The Source.
Custom document printing using material uploaded to Source.
Source: TCT593

Computer Multiple Listing Service
Organizes exchanges of hardware.
Source: CML001

Find Your Ancestors
Source: TCI342

National Institute of Relocation Services, Inc. (Conyers, GA)
Professional real estate service.
Source: TCU955

The Ride Exchange (RIDEXCHANGE)
"Going My Way?"
Source: STO926

Travel Automation
Shares travel information among brokers.
Source: TCX405

Software

Advanced Investment Strategies, Inc. (Washington, DC)
Tax calculation/projection models (software).
Source: TCN024

Astrology Software (Tucson, AZ)
CIS: 70030,257

Custom Computing Services (Leawood, KS)
Source: CLO200

Front Range Computing (Boulder, CO)
Custom programming.
Source: TCA246

Halpurr Software (Los Gatos, CA)
Sorce: TCF468

MicroCorp (Philadelphia, PA)
TRS-80 and IBM/PC.
Source: TCM033
CIS: 70335,1027

Microtronics (Northridge, CA)
CIS: 70305,1264

Mr. Software's Catalog
Source: TCE523

"Photographer's Delight"
Apple software to make film development easier.
Source: TCV533

The Program Store (Washington, DC)
Source: TCC358

Robert Rosen Associates
Source: TCA943

Software Sorcery, Inc. (McLean, VA)
Craig Vaughn, President
Source: TCA099

The Software Specialist (Washington, DC)
Source: TCU873

Southeastern Software (New Orleans, LA)
Source: TCV989

Superior Software, Inc. (Kenner, LA)
Source: TCY806

Syntax Corp. (Prairie Village, KS)
Source: TCA282

Visual Communications (Simi Valley, CA)
Source: TCV533

Zolatek Systems (Glastonbury, CT)
Source: CLI202

Appendix F
Database Directories and Publications

Directory of Online Databases
Cuadra Associates, Inc.
2001 Wilshire Blvd., Suite 305
Santa Monica, CA 90403
(213) 829-9972
Facts, figures, costs, and other information on over 1,350 individual databases. Updated constantly.
Quarterly: $60/year; $66 in Canada and Mexico; $72, elsewhere.
   Single copies available @ $29.95 from:
   New York Zoetrope, Inc.
   Suite 516
   80 East 11th Street
   New York, NY 10003
   (212) 420-0590
   Source: TCN 121
   CIS: 71715,727

Information Industry Market Place
R. R. Bowker and Company
1180 Sixth Avenue
New York, NY 10036
(212) 764-5100
Annual edition: $39.95

Encyclopedia of Information Systems and Services
Gale Research Company
Book Tower
Detroit, MI 48226
Cost: $190

Computer-Readable Databases: A Directory and Data Sourcebook
Knowlege Industry Publications, Inc.
701 Winchester Ave.
White Plains, NY 10604
(914) 328-9157

Datapro Directory of On-Line Services
Datapro Research Corporation
1805 Underwood Boulevard
Delran, NJ 08075
(609) 764-0100
Two-ring-binder volumes. Updated monthly.
Cost: $390 per year.

Online and *Database*
Online, Inc.
11 Tannery Lane
Weston, CT 06883
(203) 227-8466
Publications for professional researchers.
Online: $78/year; six issues.
Database: $56/year; four issues.

"VideoPrint"
International Resource Development, Inc.
30 High Street
Norwalk, CT 06851
(203) 866-6914
Twice monthly newsletter covering all aspects of the "Information Age."
Cost: $155/year; 24 issues.

"Electronic Mail & Message Systems" (EMMS)
International Resource Development, Inc.
30 High Street
Norwalk, CT 06851
(203) 866-6914
Twice monthly newsletter on electronic mail systems and developments.
Cost: $210/year; 24 issues.

Appendix G
The ASCII Code Set

ASCII is a seven-bit code. However, because each ASCII character is usually sent with an eighth or parity bit, it is sometimes referred to as an eight-bit code.

Many of the codes from 0 through 37 are used for synchronous communications and for communicating with teletype-like devices. They have special meanings in those situations, but those meanings are largely irrelevant to personal computer users.

With the exception of an <ESCAPE> key, there are no specific keys for the codes 0 through 31 on most machines. These codes can be sent, however, using the <CONTROL> key (or your machine's equivalent), a letter key, and in some cases the <SHIFT> key as well.

		Control Character Keystrokes
0	NUL (Blank or Null)	<CONTROL> <SHIFT> <P>
1	SOH (Start of Header)	<CONTROL> <A>
2	STX (Start of Text)	<CONTROL> <B>
3	ETX (End of Text)	<CONTROL> <C>
4	EOT (End of Transmission)	<CONTROL> <D>
5	ENQ (Enquiry)	<CONTROL> <E>
6	ACK (Acknowledge—Positive)	<CONTROL> <F>
7	BEL (Bell)	<CONTROL> <G>
8	BS (Backspace)	<CONTROL> <H>
9	HT (Horizontal Tabulation)	<CONTROL> <I>
10	LF (Line Feed)	<CONTROL> <J>
11	VT (Vertical Tabulation)	<CONTROL> <K>
12	FF (Form Feed)	<CONTROL> <L>
13	CR (Carriage Return or ENTER)	<CONTROL> <M>
14	SO (Shift Out)	<CONTROL> <N>
15	SI (Shift In)	<CONTROL> <O>
16	DLE (Data Link Escape)	<CONTROL> <P>

17	DC1 (Device Control 1)	\<CONTROL> \<Q> (X=ON)
18	DC2 (Device Control 2)	\<CONTROL> \<R>
19	DC3 (Device Control 3)	\<CONTROL> \<S> (X=OFF)
20	DC4 (Device Control 4)	\<CONTROL> \<T>
21	NAK (Negative Acknowledge)	\<CONTROL> \<U>
22	SYN (Synchronization)	\<CONTROL> \<V>
23	ETB (End of Text Block)	\<CONTROL> \<W>
24	CAN (Cancel)	\<CONTROL> \<X>
25	EM (End of Medium)	\<CONTROL> \<Y>
26	SUB (Substitute)	\<CONTROL> \<Z>
27	ESC (Escape)	\<CONTROL> \<SHIFT>\<K>
28	FS (File Separator)	\<CONTROL> \<SHIFT>\<L>
29	GS (Group Separator)	\<CONTROL> \<SHIFT>\<M>
30	RS (Record Separator)	\<CONTROL> \<SHIFT>\<N>
31	US (Unit Separator)	\<CONTROL> \<SHIFT>\<O>
32	SP (Blank Space)	\<SPACEBAR>
33	Exclamation point—!	
34	Quotation mark—"	
35	Pound sign—#	
36	Dollar sign—$	
37	Percent sign—%	
38	Ampersand—&	
39	Apostrophe or Closing Single Quote—'	
40	Left parenthesis—(	
41	Right parenthesis—)	
42	Asterisk—*	
43	Plus sign— +	
44	Comma—,	
45	Hypen—-	
46	Period—.	
47	Slash—/	
48	Zero—0	
49	One—1	
50	Two—2	
51	Three—3	
52	Four—4	
53	Five—5	
54	Six—6	
55	Seven—7	
56	Eight—8	
57	Nine—9	
58	Colon—:	
59	Semicolon—;	

60 Less than—<
61 Equals—=
62 Greater than—>
63 Question mark—?
64 At sign—@
65 A
66 B
67 C
68 D
69 E
70 F
71 G
72 H
73 I
74 J
75 K
76 L
77 M
78 N
79 O
80 P
81 Q
82 R
83 S
84 T
85 U
86 V
87 W
88 X
89 Y
90 Z
91 Left bracket—[
92 Reverse Slant—\
93 Right bracket—]
94 Circumflex accent— ^
95 Underline—__
96 Opening single quote— '
97 a
98 b
99 c
100 d
101 e
102 f

103 g
104 h
105 i
106 j
107 k
108 l
109 m
110 n
111 o
112 p
113 q
114 r
115 s
116 t
117 u
118 v
119 w
120 x
121 y
122 z
123 Left brace—{
124 Vertical line—|
125 Right brace—}
126 Tilde mark—˜
127 DEL (Delete or Rubout)

This is the end of the standard ASCII Code Set. The so-called "high codes" begin at 128 and continue through 255. These are nonstandard and their meanings vary with the software or the computer.

Appendix H
Information Utility
Quick Command Reference

Nothing is more frustrating than to be online and be unable to make an information utility computer do what you want it to do because you can't remember the correct command to enter. Usually your only alternative is to page madly through the manual looking for the right spell to cast. And all the while, the meter is running. This appendix won't solve the problem completely, but by presenting the most important commands for each of the three information utilities in one place, it might save you a bit of money.

The Source

Address
The Source
1616 Anderson Road
McLean, VA 22102

Hours of Operation
24 hours a day
(Down once or twice a week for maintenance. Usually Wednesdays and Thursdays between 4:00 AM and 5:00 AM.)

Customer Support
(800) 336-3300
(703) 734-7540 in Virginia; Canadian callers may call collect
Hours: 24 hours a day.

Action	*Command*
To sign off	Enter: OFF at the Command Level Prompt (–>)
To get out of a program and return to Command Level	Enter: <BREAK> Enter at any time. Causes program to stop and present program prompt. Enter: QUIT or STOP Returns you to Command Level (–>)
To stop a scroll	Enter: [<CONTROL><S>]
To restart a scroll	Enter: [<CONTROL><Q>]
To scroll without pause	Enter: NO CRT Enter command at first -MORE-prompt. (Only applicable for programs in the Genindex format, the ones using paragraph numbers.)
To move within a program	Enter: P Enter at a -MORE- pause in the scroll. Will return you to the previous prompt. If entered at a menu prompt, will return you to previous menu.

To go to Main Menu   Enter: MENU or M

                                       Enter at Command Level.
                                       Or at most prompts and -MORE-
                                       pauses.

To generate a list of available   Enter: DATA SYSCOM
commands

                                       Enter at Command Level.

Add Your Own Quick Commands Here:

CompuServe

Address
CompuServe Information Service
5000 Arlington Centre Blvd.
P.O. Box 20212
Columbus, OH 43220

Hours of Operation
Weekdays 6:00 PM to 5:00 AM (your local time)
All day weekends and holidays.

Customer Service
(800) 848-8990 from anywhere in the U.S. and contiguous countries
(614) 457-8650 when calling within Ohio
Hours: 8:00 AM to midnight, EST. Monday–Friday.
2:00 PM to midnight, EST. Weekends.

Action	*Command*
To sign off	Enter: OFF or BYE at the Display Prompt (= !)
To get out of a program and return to Display Prompt	Enter: [<CONTROL><C>] Acts like <BREAK>. May have to enter several times before scroll stops.
To stop a scroll	Enter: [<CONTROL><S>]
To restart a scroll	Enter: [<CONTROL><Q>]
To scroll without pause	Enter: S at the prompt reading "Key S or <Enter> to Continue = !"

To move within a program	The following commands may be entered whenever you see the Display Prompt (= !):
	   B (for Backward)——Will display the *previous* page.
	   R (for Resend)——Will cause the system to send you the current page *again*.

F (for Forward)——Will display the *next* page.

M (for Menu)——Will take you to the menu you used most *recently*.

To go to the CompuServe TOP or "Main Menu"

Enter: T

Will immediately take you to CompuServe's TOP menu (CIS-1).

To get a list of commands

Enter: H

Will generate a list of all available commands and short explanation of each.

Add Your Own Quick Commands Here:

Dow Jones News/Retrieval Service

Address
Dow Jones News/Retrieval Service
P.O. Box 300
Princeton, NJ 08540

Hours of Operation
6:00 AM to 4:00 AM, EST. Seven days a week.

Customer Support
(800) 257-5114
(609) 452-1511 in New Jersey
Hours: 9:00 AM to 11:00 PM, EST. Monday–Friday.
          9:00 AM to 5:00 PM, EST. Saturday.

The DJNS Main Menu

//ENCYC	ACADEMIC AMERICAN ENCYCLOPEDIA
//FTS	FREE TEXT SEARCH OF DOW JONES NEWS
//MEDGEN	MEDIA GENERAL
//MMS	MONEY MARKET SERVICES
//MOVIES	CINEMAN MOVIE REVIEWS
//SPORTS	SPORTS
//WTHR	WEATHER
//WSW	WALL $TREET WEEK

Flow Control
    When accessing through Tymnet, you must type [<CONTROL> <R>] at the PLEASE LOG IN prompt to enable flow control commands. No special command need with Telenet.

Action	*Command*
To stop a scroll	Enter: [<CONTROL><Q>]
To restart a scroll	Enter: [<CONTROL><S>]
To scroll without pause	Hit <ENTER> once for each page of the story you are reading.
To move within a program	Whenever the scroll stops, you may enter:

<ENTER> to go on to the next
page

<R> to return to the previous
page

<T> to go to the TOP or Main
Menu

<M> to go to the *previous* menu

<P> <page number> to go to a
specific page

To get help   Enter: //(database) HELP

To sign off   Enter: DISC (for "disconnect"; no
                               slashes).

Glossary

Note: The definitions contained in this glossary generally pertain to the field of telecommunications only.

acoustic coupler: A type of modem designed to transmit and receive data through a telephone handset. The handset is placed in a cradle consisting of two rubber cups, one for the earpiece and one for the mouthpiece. Sometimes called a "data set."

ASCII: Acronym for American Standard Code for Information Interchange. Pronounced "as-key." Used in virtually all personal computer data communications, the ASCII code set consists of 128 numbers ranging from 0 to 127, each of which has been assigned a particular meaning. ASCII is a seven-bit code (seven binary bits are required to represent each number). However, because each character is usually transmitted with a parity bit, it is sometimes referred to as an eight-bit code.

asynchronous communication: Data communication of the start-stop variety. Each character is transmitted as a discrete unit with its own start bit and one or more stop bits.

auto-dial/auto-answer: A feature offered by more expensive modems. The auto-dial feature allows you to dial your telephone by typing the numbers from the keyboard. This feature also lets you use communications software to record phone numbers on disk and dial each by pressing a single button.

baud: A unit for measuring the speed of data transmission. Technically baud rates refer to the number of times the communications line changes states each second. Strictly speaking, baud and bits per second are not identical measurements, but most non-technical people use the terms interchangably.

Baudot code: The five-bit code used when communicating with Telex, TWX, and other telegraphy-based machines.

Bell-compatible: A term used to describe modems. The term means that the audio tones issued by the modem meet Bell Telephone standards. Variants of the term include Bell 103-compatible (standard for 300-baud modems) and Bell 212A-compatible (standard for full duplex, 1200-baud modems).

bibliograhic database: A database that provides information in the form of bibliographic citations that include the name of the printed work, the author, the publisher, and other information to enable you to locate the work. Short summaries of the work or abstracts are usually available as well. See Chapter 6.

bit: Acronym for "*bi*nary digi*t*." The smallest unit of information in the computer world. Eight bits together are called a "byte," and four bits are called a "nibble."

buffer: A "holding tank" inside your machine. A buffer actually consists of a number of memory chips that have been designated as such by your communications software. In communications, buffers are most often used to capture incoming data. Buffers can be opened and closed from the keyboard. Buffers can be emptied to make room for more information. But if you want to save their contents, you must dump (record) the buffer to disk or to the printer. Otherwise, the buffer and all of its contents disappear when the power is shut off.

carrier signal: A signal whose characteristics can be altered to carry data. This is the signal a modem looks for before it will begin to send data.

CBBS: Computer Bulletin Board System. The name of what is generally acknowledged to be the first bulletin board program (written by Ward Christensen and Randy Suess), CBBS is raidly becoming a generic term for all computer bulletin board systems, regardless of the particular software they run.

character: Any alphabetic letter, number, punctuation mark, or special symbol transmitted in data communications. Same as "word."

character length: A communications setting referring to the number of data bits in each character transmitted. Since seven data bits are required to transmit each character in the standard ASCII code set, the character length under these circumstances is seven. To transmit characters represented by numbers above 127, eight binary bits are required. In such cases, the character length is said to be eight.

communicating word processor: A word processor that has been equipped with a communications board and communications software.

communications board: The circuit board that enables your machine to communicate. See "serial interface."

communications settings: The settings that establish an agreement between two computers on how they will communicate. Settings are controlled by the software and normally include baud, duplex, parity, character length, and number of stop bits.

communications software: The computer program containing the instructions your machine needs to communicate. Like all software products, communications software is available in both bare-bones versions and full-featured versions.

connect time: The time you spend online with a database. Connect time, measured in fractions of an hour, is the usual basis of database billing.

control character: A non-printing character designed to send a special signal (like a carriage return or linefeed) to a remote device. Control characters are generated by holding down the <CONTROL> key, or your machine's equivalent, and pressing one of the letter keys. Like the other characters in the ASCII code set, control characters have standard meanings in most systems.

controlled vocabulary search: This technique is used when the abstracts or other units of information in a database include an index or subject line. When those items are physically typed into the database, someone must decide which words to include on the index line. The words are selected from a large, but limited list of "controlled vocabulary" words. To search such a database, you must use only words on that list as your keyword or keywords. The lists are published in the thesaurus supplied to each user.

crossover cable: Cable designed to connect the serial ports of two computers. See "null modem cable."

CUSIP: Commission on Uniform Securities Identification Procedures. A stock's CUSIP symbol is the abbreviation used to refer to it on the stock exchange. Relevant for stock quote information for various databases.

data bits: Also known as "information bits." These are the seven or eight bits that signify a character in asynchronous communications. The data bits of each character are always "framed" by a start bit, a parity bit (usually), and one or two stop bits.

data set: A modem. Usually an acoustical modem.

DDD: Direct Distance Dialing. The technique most personal computer owners use to access databases, computer bulletin boards, and other online services. The term is most significant in the data communications industry, where DDD is but one form of computer access.

download: To capture the information sent to your computer by another computer, as opposed to letting it disappear as it scrolls off the screen.

FAX: Short for "facsimile machine." A FAX machine is designed to send and receive hard copy or printed matter over the telephone. No disks or tapes are involved. The actual piece of paper whose image you want to send is placed in a scanning device designed to convert the information to digital signals for telephone transmission. The receiving machine reverses the process to create a hard-copy image of the original. These machines are relevant to personal computer users because many of them can be used to communicate with computers. See Appendix C regarding Graphnet, a firm offering this service.

flow control: Controlling the on-screen scroll by using the X-ON/X-OFF commands, [<CONTROL><Q>] and [<CONTROL><S>], respectively.

framing bits: The start, parity, and stop bits that "frame" the data or information bits in each character transmitted during asynchronous communication.

free text search: A search in which the database computer scans the entire text of documents in its files looking for a match with the keyword or keywords you have specified. This is as opposed to a "controlled vocabulary search" (q.v.).

full-duplex: A communiations setting that enables you to send and receive information simultaneously the way you do when talking on the telephone.

half-duplex: A communications setting in which data can travel in only one direction at a time. A special signal, equivalent to saying "over" when using a CB radio, must be sent at the end of each transmission to tell the receiving machine that it is free to transmit.

handshaking: The little ritual of exchanged signals two computers go through before communications can begin.

hard-wired modem: A modem that plugs directly into a telephone jack. Also called a "direct-connect modem."

Hertz: A measure of frequency. Same as cycles per second.

high codes: ASCII code numbers above 127. High codes are nonstandard and are used to represent a wide variety of characters.

IEEE-448 interface: A standard created by the Institute of Electrical and Electronics Engineers to define the signals used for a parallel interface. One might say that this is the parallel equivalent of the "RS-232-C" (q.v.). Commodore VIC, PET, and CBM computers use this interface instead of an RS-232 serial card. The firm sells adapters to convert the IEEE-448 to an RS-232, but as long as you buy a Commodore modem, this will not be necessary.

iteration: See "loop."

keyword and keyword search: A single word you feel is likely to be included in any database file on a particular subject. A keyword is usually a word that comes as close as possible to describing the topic or piece of information you are looking for. In a keyword search, the database computer scans its files looking for a match between the keyword and the words in the file. Matches are often called "hits." In more refined searches, more than one keyword may be used.

loop: See "iteration."

mainframe: The largest of the three broad classes of computers. The other two, in descending order, are minicomputers and microcomputers, often called minis and micros. Personal computers are microcomputers.

modem: An acronym for "*mo*dulator/*dem*odulator." This is the device that translates the signals coming from your computer into a form that can be transmitted over standard telephone lines. A modem also translates incoming signals into a form that your computer can understand. Two modems, one for each computer, are needed for any data communications over telephone lines.

null modem cable: A cable designed to connect two computers via the serial ports that are ordinarily connected to a modem. A null modem cable "fools" each system into thinking that it is actually talking to a modem instead of another computer.

originate/answer: The two modes of operation for a modem. In any communications arrangement, one modem must be set to "originate" and the other must be set to "answer."

packet-switching networks: The electronic networks that enable you to access a remote database by dialing a local phone number. Information going to and from your computer is segmented into "packets" and given an address. The packets are then sent through the network to their destination much as a letter travels through the postal system, only infinitely faster. The three major networks are Telenet, Tymnet, and Uninet.

parity: A form of error checking used to increase the chances that each character has been received correctly. Systems can be set to odd, even, or no parity. When odd parity is used, the system adds up the 1s and 0s of the seven bits used to transmit a character and then adds an eighth bit. If the sum of the bits in the character is even, the system will add a 1 bit to make it odd. If the sum is odd to begin with, the system will add a 0 bit to leave it unchanged. Even parity works the same way. When no parity is used to transmit characters in the standard ASCII code set, the eighth bit is still transmitted, but it is ignored by both systems.

polling: The technique database computers use to make sure that everybody is served in turn. The mainframe computer repeatedly cycles through the entire list of online users asking each if they have anything to send. If they do, the mainframe deals with that particular

request and moves on. Often you won't notice any delay in the mainframe's response time. However, if a large number of other users are
online with the same system at the same time, each polling cycle will
take longer, and you may experience some delays.

protocols: Another name for "communications settings" (q.v.).

RCPM: Remote CP/M system. Accessible by telephone, such systems
serve as repositories for a vast array of public domain CP/M software. Anyone with a CP/M system running MODEM 7 or MODEM 4
software can dial up an RCPM system and download software at no
charge.

ring-back: Technique used by some CBBS SYSOPS to avoid installing a
separate telephone line for their computer. To use a CBBS with a
ring-back specification, dial the number, let it ring once, hang up,
then redial with your computer ready to communicate.

RS-232-C: A standard developed by The Electronics Industry Association (EIA) specifying what signals and voltages will be used to transmit data from a computer to a modem. The full standard covers some
25 pins on the RS-232-C plug interface found on a serial card, but
most personal computers make use of only a handful of these. The "C"
is often dropped when using this term.

scroll: Refers to the movement of incoming text and other information
on your computer screen. Information appears at the bottom of the
screen first and moves upward as new information arrives. Used as a
verb or as a noun.

SDI or "Selective Dissemination of Information": Information industry
jargon used to describe "current awareness" services offered by
databases like DIALOG, BRS, and NewsNet. Allows you to enter an
interest "profile" listing one or more topics. Every time new material
is added to the database, the system automatically searches through
it for references to your interests. The next time you sign on, you will
be automatically notified of any matches that have been found. Service is usually offered at an additional cost.

search strategy: The sequence of keywords one enters to search a database for desired information. Some databases will allow you to store
search strategies in electronic filing cabinets for repeated use. May
also be called "search argument."

serial interface or serial card: A circuit board installed in a computer or
word processor designed to convert the machine's internal parallel
(eight-bits-at-a-time) communications into serial communications (one-
bit-at-a-time). The card includes an RS-232-C interface plug to accept
the cable that connects your machine with your modem.

start bits/stop bits: In asynchronous communications, a start bit is
transmitted at the beginning of each character to notify the receiving

system that the next seven or eight bits will contain information. One
or two stop bits are transmitted at the end of each character to tell
the receiving system that the whole character has been sent and to
prepare it for the next start bit. These bits are often called framing
bits because they frame the data bits carrying the information.

synchronous communication: Data communications technique in which
bits are transmitted and received at a fixed rate. Used to transmit
large blocks of data over special communications lines. Much more
complex than asynchronous communication, this technique has little
application for most personal computer users.

sysop: Pronounced "sis-op." The system operator. The individual who
operates and maintains a computer bulletin board system.

Telex: Short for "*telegrah ex*change." Telex machines are special printers that serve as hard copy answering machines. Each machine has an
address similar to a telephone number, and each machine requires a
dedicated telephone line. Machines can also be used to transmit messages, of course. Telex machines communicate in Baudot code. Top
speed is 50 baud. They are accessible to personal computer users
through Graphnet, a subsidiary of Graphic Scanning Corporation. See
Appendix C for more information.

terminal mode: When communicating with a large computer, your machine must appear to the mainframe as merely one of its own terminals. Communications software creates this illusion or "emulation."
Any time you are communicating, you are in terminal mode.

terminal program: See "communications software."

TWX: Short for "teletypewriter exchange." Like a Telex machine, only
faster (110 baud). Many units can communicate in both Baudot and
ASCII. See Appendix C for more information.

UART: Acronym for "Universal Asynchronous Receiver/Transmitter."
Pronounced "you-art." This is the microchip responsible for converting parallel signals into serial signals and vice versa. It is the heart of
a serial interface card.

upload: To send information over the telephone lines to another computer directly from your floppy disk or cassette tape player, as opposed to typing at your keyboard.

word: See "character."

user-friendly: The computer industry's equivalent of EPA miles per
gallon ratings for automobiles. Your experience may vary, but generally the term is applied to anything not requiring graduate work in
advanced computer science to use with reasonable ease.

X-ON/X-OFF: These are start/stop signals issued by two communicating computers to make sure that each is ready to send or receive at

the proper time. This protocol is usually built into the communications software, and in most cases you will not be aware that the signals are being sent and received. However, you can generate each signal yourself to stop or start an on-screen scroll when accessing most databases. X-ON is generated by entering a Control-Q, and X-OFF by entering a Control-S.

ABI/INFORM, 145, 149, 152, 158
Academic American Encyclopedia,
    130–133, 139, 150–151
acoustic couplers, 28–29
ADTRACK, 153
AGRICOLA, 158, 162–163
AIRSCHED, 55
America: History and Life, 153
AMI (Advertising/Market Intel-
    ligence), 168–169
Antiope, 43
Artbibliographies Modern, 153
ASCII (American Standard Code for
    Information Exchange), 3,
    25–26, 239–245
  binary form of, 244–245
  control codes for, 241–242
  full code set for, 297–300
  translation tables and, 242–244
asynchronous communication, syn-
    chronous vs., 26
Atari, "firmware" cartridges of, 4, 24
Augment, 211
auto-answer/auto-dial modems, 33,
    34, 35
auto log-in feature, 38–39

banking, electronic, 3, 14, 10, 95–96,
    200–203

barter, electronic, 9, 14, 55, 196,
    203–206
Barter Worldwide, see Tradenet
Baudot, J. M. E., 29
baud rates, 29–31
  downloading and, 30
  without telephone lines, 43, 251
  uploading and, 30–31
BBSs, see computer bulletin board
    systems
Bell 103 standard, 22
Bell 113 standard, 22
Bell 202 standard, 23
Bell 212A standard, 23
Bibliographic Retrieval Services, see
    BRS
BI/DATA TIME SERIES, 152–153
Biography Master Index, 152
Biosis Previews, 153
bits, 18, 20–21, 237–239
  for asynchronous communication,
    248
  for electromechanical machines, 248
  for parity, 246–247
BIW (Business Information Wire),
    93
Book Review Index, 152
Books in Print, 151
bps (bits per second), baud rate vs.,
    30

317

BRS (Bibliographic Retrieval Services), 3, 10, 11, 128, 159–161
  bulletin board feature of, 160
  cost of, 160–161
  Dow Jones News/Retrieval Services vs., 160
  electronic mail feature of, 160
  full text format of, 147
  history of, 159
  scope of, 159–160
  subscribing to, 160–161
  see also individual databases
buffer auto-dump, 40
buffers, 36, 86
buffer status report, 40
BULLET, 92, 110–111
bulletin boards, *see* computer bulletin board systems
bus, 19
bytes, 18–19

cables:
  between computers, 43, 253–254
  crossover, 3, 43, 253
  between modem and computer, 23
  null-modem, 43, 253
  ribbon, 23
  sexes of, 23
Career Network, The, 54
Career Placement Registry, 152
carrier detect LEDs, 33
CA Search, 153
cassette tape records, software stored on, 4, 24
CATAFAX, 151
CBMS (Computer-Based Message System) services, 277–278
CC, *see* conferencing, computerized
CEEFAX, 43
central processing unit (CPU), 18, 19
CHAT, 50, 81–82
CHEMDEX, 162
Chronograph (Hayes), 34, 86, 234
Chronolog Newsletter, 157
C__ID files, 84–85
CIS (CompuServe Information Service), *see* CompuServe

CIS (Congressional Information Service, Inc.), 154
CIS Personal Computing Guide, 95, 102, 108, 118
CITY CON, 55
CLAIMS, 154
CNS (Commodities News Service), 51, 93
Collegecash, 54
Comet, 277
ComLink, 99–100, 113
command files, 40
Command Output (CO) files, 70
comm programs, 34–35
  see also communications software
communications cards, 17, 19–21, 27–28
  with built-in modems, 29
communications software, 24–25
  auto log-in feature in, 38–39
  "default" values of, 37
  long-distance telephone services and, 39
  parameter settings and, 35, 37–38
  upload/download abilities of, 35
  for word processing, 45
Compendex, 154
Comprehensive Dissertation Index, 155
Comp-U-Card of America, Inc., 14, 55, 96, 196–200
CompuServe, 3, 9, 16, 90–123
  access to, 99
  aircraft flight information via, 97
  Associated Press Newswire via, 93
  availability of, 99
  banking via, 95–96, 196, 200–203
  bill payment through, 196, 201, 202
  bulletin board of, 92, 110–111
  business and financial information through, 93–94
  CB simulator feature of, 92, 111–113, 116
  Command Level of, 107
  commands within display area of, 106–108

commodity news via, 93
computerized conferencing through, 96
cost of, 88, 99–100, 122–123
customer service for, 92, 95, 102, 103, 122
display area of, 90–91, 103–104, 105–108
downloading software with, 120–122
electronic mail system of, 92, 95, 108–109
games on, 96, 104, 117
history of, 90–91
introductory sessions with, 113–118
mail sent via, 92, 95, 108–109
manuals ordered through, 92, 95, 102, 115, 116
menu selection with, 104–106
MicroNET service of, 90–91, 94, 103–104, 108
Mini Editor of, 108–109
newsletters for users of, 94–95
newspapers transmitted by, 93
online documentation for, 91
pages in display area of, 105
passwords used with, 115
Prime Service of, 100
quick command reference for, 304–305
shopping with, 93, 96
signing off, 107
SIGs (Special Interest Groups) within, 92
software available through, 95
The Source vs., 88–89
subscribing to, 100–102
terminal default changes with, 104, 118–119
terminal types used with, 115, 118–120
time-sharing service of, 90
Tymnet and, 99, 113
user directory of, 92, 109–110, 117–118
User's Guide to, 91, 102, 108
Videotex area of, 90–91

word-processing with, 95, 109
World Book Encyclopedia on, 97–98
CompuServe Games Guide, 102
CompuServe Personal Computing Guide, The, 95, 102, 108, 118
Comp-U-Store, 55, 96, 126, 196–200
auction service of, 198
merchandising guarantees with, 199
subscribing to, 198–199
computer bulletin board systems (CBBSs), 3, 5, 7, 13–14, 184–195
of CompuServe, 92, 191
directory of, 191
equipment necessary for, 186–187
setting up, 194–195
signing on to, 188–190
software for, 188–189, 194–195
of The Source, 48, 49–50, 77, 80–81, 191
for special interests, 192–193
Computer Market Observer, 11
computer-to-computer connections, 251–254
conferencing, computerized, 3, 7, 14–15, 208–227
branching in, 218, 221–223
controlled access in, 210
public vs. closed, 213
software for, 225–227
turnkey systems for, 225–226
see also EIES; PARTICIPATE
control characters, 26
CPU (central processing unit), 18, 19
crossover cables, 3, 43, 253
CRT displays, 24

databases:
directories of, 295–296
locations of, 16
logging in procedures for, 38–39
logging off procedures for, 42–43
protocols of, 35
variety of, 7, 8–9
DataPac, 16, 99, 113, 135

DataSpeak O/A-300, 32
DB connectors, 23
DCE (Data Communications Equipment) wiring, 23–24
Deadline Data on World Affairs, 169–170
defaults, terminal, 118–119
delivery mechanism, 8
DELPHI, 10
Dialcom, 277–278
DIALOG, 3, 10, 11, 16
  access to, 155
  cost of, 156–157
  customer service for, 157
  history of, 155–156
  search commands for, 156, 157
  training programs for, 157
digital information vs. sound, 21
direct-connect modems, 28–29
  FCC certification of, 32
Disclosure II, 127, 133, 135, 140, 170
DISEARCH, 48, 76–77, 81, 82–83
DJNS (Dow Jones News/Retrieval Service), 9, 16, 124–142
  Academic American Encyclopedia on, 130–133, 139
  access to, 124, 134, 135, 136, 137–138, 140, 141–142
  Apple and, 124, 132
  Blue Chip Membership subscriptions to, 133, 134
  "breaking" with, 137–138
  command approach to, 136–137
  cost of, 128–130, 132–134
  customer service of, 135–136, 140
  DataPac and, 135
  Dow Jones News Service on, 125–126
  Executive Membership subscriptions to, 133, 134
  financial information on, 126–128
  free subscription to, 2
  Free Text Search feature of, 126, 128–130, 133, 139
  history of, 124–125
  introductory sessions with, 139
  marketing of, 125
  menu selection with, 136
  movie reviews on, 8, 126
  online encyclopedia of, 3
  program access to, 40
  scrolling control with, 137–139
  shopping with, 126
  The Source vs., 88–89
  specialized software for, 139–140
  sports reports on, 125, 126
  subscribing to, 133, 135
  UPI World Report on, 126
  Wall Street Journal Highlights Outline on, 126
  weather reports on, 126
Dowline, 140
downloading, 30, 35, 36–37, 120–122
DTE (Data Terminal Equipment) wiring, 23–24

EBDIC, 239
EIES (Electronic Information Exchange System), 15, 208, 211
  conference topics of, 214–215
  cost of, 224–225
  features of, 213–214
  membership in, 224–225
  PARTICIPATE vs., 216
  turnkey system for, 225–226
  see also conferencing, computerized
electronic banking, 3, 10, 14, 95–96, 200–203
electronic mail, 7, 10, 48, 50, 83, 92, 95, 108–109, 277–278, 287–294
electronic shopping, 9, 10, 14, 55, 93, 96
"Electronic Yellow Pages," 11–12, 150
EMAIL, 92, 95, 108–109
EMI flight plans, 97
EMISARI (Emergency Conferencing System and Reference Index), 208–209
encyclopedic databases, 3, 9, 10–11, 143–164
  abstract format of, 145, 146–147
  bibliographic citation format of, 145–146
  comparison of, 144

cost of, 149–150
information data bases vs., 143
keyword searches in, 148
ordering full text from, 147
research procedure for, 147–148
royalties and, 11
scope of, 150–155
Engineering Literature Index, 158
ERIC, 155, 156, 158, 161
Excerpta Medica, 153
expansion slots, 27
experts, need for, 42, 255

Fact Finder (DJNS), 135, 137
Federal Index, 154–155
FEEDBACK, 92, 95, 102, 115, 116
FINTOL, 94
floppy disk drive, 4
floppy disks, software stored on, 24,
86
Fluegelman, Andrew, 35
Free Text Search Manual, 130, 135,
139
full-duplex communication, 23, 31–32

General Videotex Corporation, 10
Genindex format programs, 71, 73
GIGO eliminator, 3, 256–260
Globe Data, 170
GPO Monthly Catalog, 154
GPO Publications Reference File, 158
GRANTS, 155
Graphnet, 270–273
Guide to DIALOG Searching, 156
Guiliano, Vincent, 228–229

half-duplex communication, 23, 31–32
Hayes Microcomputer Products, 29
Hayes Stack 300-baud Smartmodem,
34
"Health Tex," 93
high codes, 248–250
Hiltz, Starr Roxanne, 209

IBM, 1
IEEE-448 interface card, 19–20
Index of Services and Subjects (CIS),
102
Infomart, 10
Information Bank, The, 165
controlled vocabulary vs. keyword
search in, 166–167
cost of, 172–173
publications list of, 167–168
sample abstracts from, 170–172
information providers (IPs), 10–11,
143
information utilities, 3, 7, 9–10
encyclopedic databases vs., 143
European versions of, 43–44
*see also individual information
utility databases*
INFOX, 52
INSPEC, 154, 158
International Software Directory, 151
INTRO, 130
IOD (Information on Demand), 58–59
IXO Telecomputer, 7

keyboarding, 15
keys, programmable, 40
keystrokes, nonstandardized, 4
keyword search, 11–12, 148
KNOWLEDGE INDEX, 156,
157–159

linefeeds, 189, 260
line turnaround, 31
logging in procedures, 38–39
logging off procedures, 42–43
loop-timing value, 38

McKinnie, Pat, 228
Magazine Index, 151
mainframes, 7
male-female compatibility, 23
Management Contents, 152
MARC, 152
MATHFILE, 154

Matrix, 211, 226
Media General DataBank, 9, 127
MEDLINE, 153, 158
memory expansion cards, 26–27
message exchange systems, 7
   see also computer bulletin board
    systems
Micro Advisor, The, 95
Microcomputer Index, 151
Microcomputer Index, 41
MicroNET, 90–91, 94, 103–104
MicroQuote, 94
MM-103 communications card, 29
modem-on-a-card, 2
modems, 1, 2, 17–18, 21–23, 245–246
   acoustic couplers vs. direct-con-
    nect, 28–29
   auto-answer/auto-dial features of,
    33, 34
   basic recommended features of, 32
   baud rates of, 29–31
   cables connected to, 23
   DCE vs. DTE wiring in, 23–24
   with full- vs. half-duplex ca-
    pabilities, 23, 31–32
   originate only vs. originate/answer
   power source for, 32
   self-testing feature of, 33
   for telecommuting, 233
   "whistles and bells" features of,
    32–33
modes, originate vs. answer, 22
modular jacks, 28
modulator/demodulators, *see* modems
Morse, Samuel F. B., 238, 239

National Newspaper Index, 158
*Network Nation: Human Communi-
   cation via Computer, The*
   (Turoff and Starr), 209
news and specialized business information databases, 9, 11–12
NEWSEARCH, 151
Newsletter on Newsletters, 11
NewsNet, 3, 8, 11, 165, 175–183
   access to, 178
   commands of, 178–180

cost of, 181–183
customer service for, 183
equipment rental from, 183
Newsflash feature of, 182
newsletters available on, 177–178
sample output of, 178–179, 180–181
UPI and, 182
New York Times Information Service
   (NYTIS), 3, 11, 165–175, 183
cost of, 172–173
customer service for, 174–175
databases within, 166
hard copy available from, 174
offices of, 175
special school programs of, 174
stored searches of, 174
training programs for, 175
   see also Information Bank, The
Novation, Inc., 5, 29, 161
null code, 248
null-modem cables, 43, 253
NYTIS Thesaurus, 166–167

offline data preparation, 36
*On-Line Computer Telephone Direc-
   tory, The*, 191
online conferencing, *see* conferencing,
   computerized
OnTyme, 277–278
optional line feed control, 39
ORBIT, 3, 10, 11
   customer service of, 163
   history of, 162
   scope of, 162
   subscribing to, 162
   training programs for, 163
   see also individual databases
Osborne 1 computers, wiring of,
   23–24
Other Networks Newsletter, 185, 193

packet switching networks, 16, 42,
   261–269
   see also DataPac; Telenet; Tymnet
PAR (Political Action Report), 51
parity, 3, 37, 246–247, 248–251

PARTICIPATE (PARTI), 15, 50, 77, 83, 191, 208, 211, 216–226
  branching in, 218, 221–223
  cost of, 224
  EIES vs., 216
  features of, 213–214
  instructions for, 217
  PRACTICE conference of, 217
  turnkey system for, 225–226
  see also conferencing, computerized
"PC-Talk," 35
peripherals, 2, 17
Pocket Guide (DIALOG), 157
polling, 42
ports, 19, 20, 23, 25, 27, 34
POST, 48, 49–50, 77, 80–81
Prestel, 43–44
printers, 4
  serial vs. parallel, 20
PRINTWIZ, 58
Private Sector, 48
programmable keys, 40
programming/storage devices, 4
PSYCINFO, 158
PUBLIC, 78, 83, 84

Quadboard, 28
Quadram Corporation, memory expansion cards of, 27
QuickQuote, 94

Racal-Vadic standard, 23
Reader's Guide to Periodic Literature, 41, 151
RECON, 156
REMARC, 152
remote data processing (RDP) services, 7–8
ribbon cables, 23
RS-232-C interface, 20, 251–253
RS-232 ports, 23, 25, 27, 34

SCAN line specs, 216

SDI (selective dissemination of information) services:
  of NewsNet, 176
  of NYTIS, 174
Seattle Computer Company, memory expansion cards of, 27
serial cards, 1, 2, 19
  see also communications cards
shopping, electronic, 9, 10, 14, 55, 93, 96, 126, 196–200
SID files, 84–85
sign-on procedures, variety of, 16
SMAIL, 48, 83
Source, The, 46–89
  airline schedules through, 55
  "automatic execute" files in, 84–85
  background of, 46–47
  bartering through, 196, 203–206
  bulletin board of, 48, 49–50, 77, 80–81
  Command Level of, 67–69
  command strings with, 69
  commodities news on, 51
  CompuServe vs., 88–89
  computerized conferencing through, 15, 50, 77, 83
  computer manuals ordered from, 50, 53
  computer programming with, 53
  control characters for, 26
  cost of, 59–60, 87–88
  customer support for, 65
  demonstrations of, 62–64
  DJNS vs., 88–89
  electronic mail system of, 48, 83
  financial services accessible through, 51–52
  games on, 56–58
  Genidex format programs and, 71
  introductory sessions with, 79–83
  job searches through, 54
  magazine abstracts accessible through, 51
  Mailgram service with, 275–276
  mail sent via, 48, 83
  manual for, 64–65
  menu selection number strings and, 66–67

Source, The *(cont.)*
  menu selection with, 66, 68
  movie reviews in, 56
  newsletters accessible through,
    50–51
  online conversations with, 50
  PARTICIPATE and, 216
  personal filing cabinets in, 51, 53,
    84–85
  private databases in, 52–53
  quick command reference for,
    302–303
  restaurant information in, 55–56
  shopping with, 55
  signing off, 80
  signing on, 79
  stock market quotations from, 51
  subscribing to, 61–62
  suggestion box of, 48
  Texas Instruments computers and,
    62
  travel reservations through, 56
  UPI Newswire through, 51
  uploading to, 86–87
  user directory of, 48, 76–77, 81,
    82–83
  User Publishing program of, 78,
    83, 84
  Western Union Mailgrams via, 50
  word-processing with, 53–54, 84
Source Digest, 66
Source Editor, 53–54, 84
SourceMail, 48
SOURCE*PLUS services, 60
Sourceworld, 59, 66
Southam, Inc., 10
STC (Source Telecomputing Corpora-
    tion), *see* Source, The
Stevens, Chandler Harrison, 211
STOCKVUE, 51
stop bits, 3, 37, 248
strings, 67
SUGBOX, 48
SUMM, 169
surge suppressors, 233
synchronous communication,
    asynchronous vs., 26

tax deductions, online charges as, 44
Tax Notes Today, 11
Telecommunications Corporation of
    America, 46
telecommunications software pack-
    ages, 1–2
telecommuting, 3, 15, 228–236
  benefits of, 230–231
  "Call Waiting" and, 233–234
  drawbacks of, 231
  hardware for, 231–234
  initial cost of, 232–233
  modem for, 233
  software for, 234–235
  translation tables for, 234–235
teleconferencing, *see* conferencing,
    computerized
"Teleguide to Ontario," 10
Telemail, 277–278
Telenet, 3, 15, 16, 42, 63–64, 124,
    134, 135, 149, 178, 181, 225
telephone answering machines, 234
telephone interface box, *see* modems
Telex, 3, 7, 270–275
TEXNET, 62
time sharing, 8, 90
Today, 103, 115
TOLLFREE, 59
Torstar Corporation, 10
Tradenet, 196, 203–206
Transend, 41
translation tables, 3, 40, 234–235,
    242–244, 249, 250, 281–282
TRS-80 Model III, control characters
    of, 26
turnkey systems, 225–226
Turoff, Murray, 208–209, 211
TWX, 3, 7, 270–275
Tymnet, 3, 16, 42, 63–64, 99, 113,
    124, 134, 135, 140, 149, 178, 181
typesetting by computer, 279–286

UART (universal asynchronous
    receiver/transmitter), 19
UDS (Universal Data Systems), 32
Uninet, 16, 181, 225

Update, 103
uploading, 30–31, 35–36
  to The Source, 86–87

Value Line Database II, 94
VICODEM, 2
VisiCalc, 40–41, 211
Vislink, 40–41
voltage spike eliminators, 233

Washington Metro Restaurant Guide, 56
Wilkins, Jeffrey M., 122
word-processing:
  with CompuServe, 95, 109
  manufacturers of, 1
  software package for, 45
  with The Source, 53–54
words, computer, 18–19, 239
World Book Encyclopedia, 97–98